Please return/renew this item by the last date shown.

To renew this item, call **0845 0020777** (automated)
or visit **www.librarieswest.org.uk**

Borrower number and PIN required.

Adrian Mitchell (1932-2008) was a prolific poet, playwright and children's writer. Born in London, he worked as a journalist from 1955 to 1966, when he became a full-time writer, publishing three novels with Cape, *If You See Me Comin'* (1961), *The Bodyguard* (1970) and *Wartime* (1973). He gave many hundreds of readings throughout the world in theatres, colleges, pubs, prisons, streets, public transport, cellars, clubs and schools of all kinds. Many of his plays and stage adaptations were performed at the National Theatre as well as by the Royal Shakespeare Company and other theatre companies. In 2002, the socialist magazine *Red Pepper* dubbed him Shadow Poet Laureate and asked him to write regular republican poems for their columns. In a National Poetry Day poll in 2005, his poem 'Human Beings' was voted the poem that most people would like to see launched into space.

After four collections with Cape – *Poems* (1964), *Out Loud* (1968), *Ride the Nightmare* (1971) and *The Apeman Cometh* (1975), Allison & Busby published *For Beauty Douglas: Collected Poems 1953-1979* (1982), *On the Beach at Cambridge* (1984) and *Love Songs of World War Three* (1989). His later poetry titles were all published by Bloodaxe: *Adrian Mitchell's Greatest Hits: His 40 Golden Greats* (1991), *Blue Coffee: Poems 1985-1996* (1996), *Heart on the Left: Poems 1953-1984* (1997), *All Shook Up: Poems 1997-2000* (2000), *The Shadow Knows: Poems 2000-2004* (2004), the posthumously published *Tell Me Lies: Poems 2005-2008* (2009), and his retrospective *Come On Everybody: Poems 1953-2008* (2012).

His collected poems for children, *Umpteen Pockets* (Orchard Books), and *Shapeshifters*, his versions of Ovid's Metamorphoses, illustrated by Alan Lee (Frances Lincoln), were both published in 2009. *Just Adrian*, a collection of his theatre writings, edited by Celia Mitchell and Daniel Cohen, was published by Oberon Books in 2011; his adaptation of Pushkin's *Boris Godunov* is published by Oberon in 2012.

Adrian Mitchell's website: www.adrianmitchell.co.uk

COME ON
EVERYBODY
POEMS 1953-2008

BLOODAXE BOOKS

ISBN: 978 1 85224 946 5

First published in 2012 by
Bloodaxe Books Ltd,
Highgreen,
Tarset,
Northumberland NE48 1RP,

www.bloodaxebooks.com
For further information about Bloodaxe titles
please visit our website or write to
the above address for a catalogue.

Supported using public funding by
**ARTS COUNCIL
ENGLAND**

Cover design: Neil Astley & Pamela Robertson-Pearce.

Printed in Great Britain by
Bell & Bain Limited, Glasgow, Scotland.

Most people ignore most poetry
because
most poetry ignores most people

ACKNOWLEDGEMENTS

Come On Everybody is a retrospective of Adrian Mitchell's poetry drawn from these books, all published by Bloodaxe Books: *Heart on the Left: Poems 1953-1984* (1997), *Blue Coffee: Poems 1985-1996* (1996), *All Shook Up: Poems 1997-2000* (2000), *The Shadow Knows: Poems 2000-2004* (2004), and the posthumously published *Tell Me Lies: Poems 2005-2008* (2009). *Heart on the Left* was itself a retrospective drawn from *Poems* (1964), *Out Loud* (1968), *Ride the Nightmare* (1971) and *The Apeman Cometh* (1975), published by Cape, and *For Beauty Douglas: Collected Poems 1953-1979* (1982), *On the Beach at Cambridge* (1984) and *Love Songs of World War Three* (1989), published by Allison & Busby. The final poem, 'My Literary Career So Far', is previously unpublished. The poems are arranged in thematic sections which follow Adrian Mitchell's own groupings in the original collections; the selection was made by Neil Astley with Celia Mitchell.

EDUCATIONAL HEALTH AND SAFETY WARNING

None of the work in this or any other of my books or plays is to be used in connection with any examination or test whatsoever. If you like a poem of mine, learn it, recite it, sing it or dance it – wherever you happen to be. But don't force anyone to study it or vivisect it or write a well-planned and tedious essay about it. This is the first step in The Shadow Poet Laureate's scheme to destroy the examination systems of the world, which have made true education almost impossible. Free the teachers and the children!

The Shadow reminds all students who are not happy that no law compels them to attend school – so long as it can be proved that they are being educated satisfactorily. (Contact Education Otherwise for information and help.) It is very hard for teachers and children to be happy in overcrowded schools. The Shadow would ask you to consider the ideal size for a school class. Most teachers agree with me that it would be about twelve. Even Jesus couldn't manage thirteen.

ADRIAN MITCHELL

CONTENTS

SONGS FROM SOME OF THE SHOWS

OUR BLUE PLANET

from **BLUE COFFEE:** *Poems 1985-1996*

from

HEART ON THE LEFT

POEMS 1953-1984

MY FAVOURITE ARCHIPELAGO

To You

One: we were swaddled, ugly-beautiful and drunk on milk.
Two: cuddled in arms always covered by laundered sleeves.
Three: we got sand and water to exercise our imaginative faculties.
Four: we were hit. Suddenly hit.

Five: we were fed to the educational system limited.
Six: worried by the strange creatures in our heads, we strangled some of them.
Seven: we graduated in shame.
Eight: World War Two and we hated the Germans as much as our secret
     bodies, loved the Americans as much as the Russians, hated killing, loved
     killing, depending on the language in the Bible in the breast pocket of
     the dead soldier, we were crazy-thirsty for Winston Superman, for Jesus
     with his infinite tommy-gun and the holy Spitfires, while the Japanese
     hacked through the undergrowth of our nightmares – there were pits full
     of people-meat – and the real bombs came, but they didn't hit us, my
     love, they didn't hit us exactly.
My love, they are trying to drive us mad.

So we got to numbers eight, nine, ten, and eleven,
Growing scales over every part of our bodies,
Especially our eyes,
Because scales were being worn, because scales were armour.
And now we stand, past thirty, together, madder than ever,
We make a few diamonds and lose them.
We sell our crap by the ton.
My love, they are trying to drive us mad.

Make love. We must make love
Instead of making money.
You know about rejection? Hit. Suddenly hit.
Want to spend my life building poems in which untamed
People and animals walk around freely, lie down freely
Make love freely
In the deep loving carpets, stars circulating in their ceilings,
Poems like honeymoon planetariums.
But our time is burning.
My love, they are trying to drive us mad.

Peace was all I ever wanted.
It was too expensive.
My love, they are trying to drive us mad.

Half the people I love are shrinking.
My love, they are trying to drive us mad.
Half the people I love are exploding.
My love, they are trying to drive us mad.

I am afraid of going mad.

Icarus Schmicarus

If you never spend your money
you know you'll always have some cash.
If you stay cool and never burn
you'll never turn to ash.
If you lick the boots that kick you
then you'll never feel the lash
and if you crawl along the ground
at least you'll never crash.
So why why why –
WHAT MADE YOU THINK YOU COULD FLY?

C'mon Everybody

There's a grand old dance that's rockin the nation
Shake your money and shut your mouth
Taking the place of copulation
S'called The Bourgeois.

See that girl with the diamond thing?
Shake your money and shut your mouth
Didn't get that by picketing
She done The Bourgeois.

Do-gooder, do-gooder where you been?
Shake your money and shut your mouth
Done myself good, got a medal from the Queen
For The Bourgeois.

   Is it a singer? No.
   Is it a lover? No.

Is it a bourgeois? Yeaaah!
Wave your missile around the vault
Shake your money and shut your mouth
Somebody suffers well it ain't your fault
That you're Bourgeois.

I play golf so I exist
Shake your money and shut your mouth
Eye on the ball and hand over fist
I do The Bourgeois.

Five days a week on the nine-eleven
Shake your money and shut your mouth
When we die we'll go to Bournemouth
Cos we're Bourgeois.

To Nye Bevan Despite His Change of Heart

Because I loved him
I believe that somebody dropped blood-freezing powder
Into the water-jug of vodka Nye Bevan swigged
Before he asked us:
Do you want Britain to go naked to the conference table?

A difficult question.
Whoever saw Britain naked?
Britain bathes behind locked doors
Where even the loofah is subject to the Official Secrets Act.
But surely Britain strips for love-making?
Not necessarily.
An analysis of British sexual response
Proves that most of the United Kingdom's acts of love
Have been undertaken unilaterally.
There have been persistently malicious rumours
From Africa and Asia
That Britain's a habitual rapist
But none of the accusers have alleged
That Britain wore anything less than full dress uniform
With a jangle of medals, bash, bash,
During the alleged violations.

So do you want Britain to go naked to the conference table?
Britain the mixed infant,
Its mouth sullen as it enters its second millennium
Of pot-training.
Britain driven mad by puberty,
Still wearing the uniform of Lord Baden-Powell
(Who was honoured for his services to sexual mania).
Britain laying muffins at the Cenotaph.
Britain, my native archipelago
Entirely constructed of rice pudding.

So do you want Britain to go naked to the conference table?
Yes. Yes Nye, without any clothes at all.
For underneath the welded Carnaby
Spike-studded dog-collar groincrusher boots,
Blood-coloured combinations
And the golfing socks which stink of Suez,
Underneath the Rolls Royce heart
Worn on a sleeve encrusted with royal snot,
Underneath the military straitjacket
From the Dead Meat Boutique –
      Lives
      A body
Of incredibly green beauty.

I Tried, I Really Tried

Mesh-faced loudspeakers outshouted Fleet Street,
Their echoes overlapping down Shoe Lane
And Bouverie Street, pronouncing:
WASH YOURSELF POET.
Blurred black police cars from the BBC
Circled me blaring: WASH YOURSELF POET
AND DON'T FORGET YOUR NAVEL.
My ears were clogged with savoury gold wax
And so I failed WASH to hear at first WASH.
WASH WASH YOURSELF
Since I was naked and they wore
Chrome-armoured cars and under the cars man-made fibre suits and under
    the suits Y-front pants and under the pants official groin protectors and
    under the groin protectors automatics,
I obediently ran to the city's pride,

The Thames, that Lord Mayor's Procession of mercury,
And jumped from Westminster Bridge.
Among half-human mud I bathed
Using a dead cat for a loofah,
Detergent foam for gargle.
I dived, heard the power station's rumble and the moan of sewers.
The bubbles of my breath exploded along the waterskin.
Helmeted in dead newspapers, I sprang
Into the petrol-flavoured air
And Big Ben, like a speak-your-weight machine
Intoned WATCH YOURSELF POET.
Clothed in the muck of London, I yelled back:
I HAVE BEEN WASHED IN THE BLOOD OF THE THAMES,
BIG BROTHER, AND FROM NOW ON I SHALL USE NO OTHER.

Nostalgia – Now Threepence Off

Where are they now, the heroes of furry-paged books and comics brighter than life which packed my ink-lined desk in days when BOP meant *Boys' Own Paper*, where are they anyway?

Where is Percy F. Westerman? Where are H.L. Gee and Arthur Mee? Why is Edgar Rice (*The Warlord of Mars*) Burroughs, the *Bumper Fun Book* and the *Wag's Handbook*? Where is the *Wonder Book of Reptiles*? Where the hell is *The Boy's Book of Bacteriological Warfare*?

Where are the *Beacon Readers*? Did Rover, that tireless hound, devour his mon-o-syll-ab-ic-all-y correct family? Did Little Black Sambo and Epaminondas shout for Black Power?

Did Peter Rabbit get his when myxomatosis came around the second time, did the Flopsy Bunnies stiffen to a standstill, grow bug-eyed, fly-covered and then disintegrate?

Where is G.A. Henty and his historical lads – Wolfgang the Hittite, Armpit the Young Viking, Cyril who lived in Sodom? Where are their uncorrupted bodies and Empire-building brains, England needs them, the *Sunday Times* says so.

There is news from the Strewelpeter mob. Johnny-Head-In-Air spends his days reporting flying saucers, the telephone receiver never cools from the heat of his hand. Little Harriet, who played with matches, still burns, but not with fire. The Scissor-man is everywhere.

Babar the Elephant turned the jungle into a garden city. But things went wrong. John and Susan, Titty and Roger, became unaccountably afraid of water, sold their dinghies, all married each other, live in a bombed-out cinema on surgical spirits and weeds of all kinds.

Snow White was in the *News of the World* – Virgin Lived With Seven Midgets, Court Told. And in the psychiatric ward an old woman dribbles as she mumbles about a family of human bears, they ate porridge, yes Miss Goldilocks of course they did.

Hans Brinker vainly whirled his silver skates round his head as the jackboots of Emil and the Detectives invaded his Resistance Cellar.

Some failed. Desperate Dan and Meddlesome Matty and Strang the Terrible and Korky the Cat killed themselves with free gifts in a back room at the Peter Pan Club because they were impotent, like us. Their audience, the senile Chums of Red Circle School, still wearing for reasons of loyalty and lust the tatters of their uniforms, voted that exhibition a super wheeze.

Some succeeded. Tom Sawyer's heart has cooled, his ingenuity flowers at Cape Kennedy.

But they are all trodden on, the old familiar faces, so at the rising of the sun and the going down of the ditto I remember I remember the house where I was taught to play up play up and play the game though nobody told me what the game was, but we know now, don't we, we know what the game is, but lives of great men all remind us we can make our lives sublime and departing leave behind us arseprints on the sands of time, but the tide's come up, the castles are washed down, where are they now, where are they, where are the deep shelters? There are no deep shelters. Biggles may drop it, Worrals of the Wraf may press the button. So Billy and Bessie Bunter, prepare for the last and cosmic Yarooh and throw away the Man-Tan. The sky will soon be full of suns.

So Don't Feed Your Dog Ordinary Meat,
Feed Him Pal, Pal Meat for Dogs,
P-A-L, Prolongs Active Life
(Enriched with Nourishing Marrowbone Jelly)

My bird had a grin like a water–melon,
My bird was a hopeless case.
She wanted to look like Elvis Presley
So she paid a man to wipe the smile off her face,

He was
My friend the plastic surgeon
Your friend the plastic surgeon
Your friendly neighbourhood plastic surgeon
(Enriched with nourishing marrowbone jelly).

My mate was a dirty little Fascist,
They shouted him down when he cursed the Jews,
And nobody recognised his patriotic motives
Till he hired a man to explain his views,

He got
My friend the public relations man
Your friend the PRO
Your friendly neighbourhood public relations man
(Enriched with nourishing marrowbone jelly).

My dad was a nervy sort of navvy
He insured his job and his life and me
Fire, flood, suicide and acts of God,
And then he insured his insurance policy,

He paid
My friend the man from the Prudential
Your friend the man from the Pru
Your friendly neighbourhood man from the Prudential
(Enriched with nourishing marrowbone jelly).

My mum spent her life watching telly
Till the Epilogue told her that her soul would burn.
Now she's got peace of mind and she still does nothing
For she pays one-tenth of all we earn

To
My friend the Anglican clergyman
Your friend the clergyman
Your friendly neighbourhood Anglican clergyman
(Enriched with nourishing marrowbone jelly).

The plastic surgeon and the public relations man,
The man from the Prudential and the man from God –
Pals, pals, every one a pal.
P-A-L,
Prolongs Active Life
(Enriched with nourishing marrowbone jelly).

Time and Motion Study

Slow down the film. You see that bit.
Seven days old and no work done.
Two hands clutching nothing but air.
Two legs kicking nothing but air.
That yell. There's wasted energy there.
No use to himself, no good for the firm.
Make a note of that.

New film. Now look, now he's fourteen.
Work out the energy required
To make him grow that tall.
It could have been used
It could have all been used
For the good of the firm and he could have stayed small.
Make a note of that.

Age thirty. And the waste continues.
Using his legs for walking. Tiring
His mouth with talking and eating. Twitching.
Slow it down. Reproducing? I see.
All, I suppose, for the good of the firm.
But he'd better change methods. Yes, he'd better.
Look at the waste of time and emotion,
Look at the waste. Look. Look.
And make a note of that.

Ode to Money

Man-eater, woman-eater, brighter than tigers,
Lover and killer in my pocket,
In your black sack I'm one of the vipers.
Golden-eyed mother of suicide,
Your photo's in my heart's gold locket.

You make me warm, you keep me cool,
You cure the terrifying dream.
Nature and art await your call.
Money, don't lead me to milk and honey
But a land of drambuie and icebergs of cream.

27

The Palm Court Planet's orchestra whines
The Money Spangled Money
And The Red Money. In my silver chains
I always stand when I hear the band
Play Money Save the Money.

South Kensington Is Much Nicer

London, you hurt me. You're the girl
With hair fresh-permed and every curl
A gold ring in its proper place,
But spread across your poker face
A net of scars. A dress of smoke,
Your body an unfinished joke.
I love you, but I cannot sing
That money–splendoured hair is everything.
For I've walked through the alleys of Poison Town,
They led me up, they led me down.
The colour of the air was brown.

Reply to a Canvasser

Cats are spies for something dark.
Rabbits are wiped out.
Captain Cousteau scares the shark
With an underwater shout.

Snakes slide over jagged ground
Making the same sound as grass.
Elephants are pushed around.
Fish are hooked, or circle worlds of glass.

Hyenas have a nervous laugh,
Corruption is their only need.
Worms get fat, then cut in half.
A dog's a footman on a lead.

I'd rather be a stag at bay
Daubed in colours brown and gory,
Or any creature any day
Than be a bloody Tory.

Look at the View

Like the memory of a long-dead clerical uncle
Reclines St Paul's Cathedral
In the blue smoke from London's frying-pan.
Climb to the dome, and then you can
Watch the dull length of Blackfriars Bridge.
See the flat girl approach the edge,
Jump, fall, splash, vanish, struggle, cease.
Do you bet she'll be saved by the River Police
Who ride the tides in a humming launch?
Or an oil millionaire without a paunch
Will dive and take her wet to lunch?
Save her and leave her, and she'll be seen
Next day on the bridge near that tarnished tureen
St Paul's Cathedral, glowering in the rain.
She will take off her shoes and fall again

The Observer

A tattooed Irishman still
Shaking from his pneumatic drill.
    From his mouth
    Saunters sweet talk
    As he stretches the chained spoon
    To his mug of tea again.
    Talk as sweet and warm as tea
    Floats in bubbles from his mouth.
    As he counts fivepence he's reminded
    That his working life has ended.

Bubbles burst. His tongue's light tune
Stumbles and does not rise. Deep in his belly
The molten tea solidifies.
His tall face lowers slowly
Like a red wall collapsing in the rain.

A young Guards officer
Shaking with long-imprisoned anger.
  From his mouth
  Marches, in step, his conversation
  As he taps a silver plate
  With his menthol cigarette.
  Talk as white and soft as smoke
  Pours from his educated mouth.
  His Colonel claims that the Brigade
  Might well recruit the unemployed.
  The young man's facial veins inflate,
  His talk moves at the double, sweating,
  Mad keen, but disciplined at that,
  As his whole face opens letting
  Free a smile bright as a bayonet.

In the café and the mess
A liberal hears what each man says.
  He notes the navvy's imagination
  And he smiles.
  Notes the Guard's well-drilled conversation
  And he smiles.
  With memories of Wimbledon
  He says under his pleasant breath:
  'Why don't both men just jump the net,
  Shake hands, and say the class war's won?'
  He lights a Woodbine from a Ronson.
  His eyes bulge, large with vision,
  Seeing both sides of every question,
  One with his left eye,
  One with his right,
  The cross-eyed, doomed hermaphrodite.

Song About Mary

Mary sat on a long brown bench
Reading *Woman's Own* and *She*,
Then a slimy-haired nit with stripes on his collar
Said: 'What's the baby's name to be?'

She looked across to Marks and Spencers
Through the dirty window-pane,
'I think I'll call him Jesus Christ,
It's time he came again.'

The clerk he banged his ledger
And he called the Cruelty Man
Saying: 'This bird thinks she's the mother of Christ,
Do what you bleeding well can.'

They took Mary down to the country
And fed her on country air,
And they put the baby in a Christian home
And he's much happier there.

For if Jesus came to Britain
He would turn its dizzy head,
They'd nail him up on a telegraph pole
Or he'd raise the poor from the dead.

So if you have a little baby
Make sure it's legitimate child,
Bind down his limbs with insurance
And he'll grow up meek and mild.
    Meek and mild...meek and mild...meek and mild.

We Call Them Subnormal Children
(FROM *The Body*)

They are here, they are here,
they are very far away.

Perhaps they see exciting visions
in the hollows of their hands.
Perhaps they can hear music we are deaf to

but I think their hearts trudge
and that their days trudge

for the way they sort of stand
the way they sort of speak

laboriously expresses one word only
wounded   wounded   wounded

We are taking a deep breath before the long slow dive through space to Mars.

We have not yet explored these island people.

They are here.
They will not go away.

In Other Words, Hold My Head

'Capitalism – ,' I started, but the barman hopped out of a pipkin.
'Capitalism,' he countered, 'that's a flat and frothless word.
I'm a good labourman, but if I mentioned capitalism
My clientèle would chew off their own ears
And spit them down the barmaid's publicised cleavage.'
'All right,' I obliged, 'don't call it capitalism,
Let's call it Mattiboko the Mighty.'

'Exploitation – ,' I typed, but the Editor appeared unto me,
A spike in one hand, a fiery pound note in the other.
'I'm a good liberal, but you're going out on a lamb –
You don't catch Burnem Levin writing about exploitation –
A million readers would gouge their eyes out,
Think of that, like two million pickled onions in the cornflakes.'
'Hold the back page,' I surlied, 'sod exploitation,
I'll retitle it The Massimataxis Incorporated Supplement.'

'Oppression and mass-murder – ,' I opined straight into the camera.
'Cut!' yelled the director, cutting off his head with a clapperboard.
'I'm a good fascist, but if you use that language
Half your viewers are going to
Tear the lids off their TV sets,
Climb inside, pour Horlicks over their heads
And die of calculated combustion.

Too late now to balance the programme
With a heartsofoak panel of our special experts
Who are all oppressors and mass-murderers.'
'You know the market,' I wizened,
'Oppression and mass-murder are out this year –
I'll christen them Gumbo Jumbo the Homely Obblestrog Spectacular.'

This was my fearless statement:
The Horror World can only be changed by the destruction of
Mattiboko the Mighty,
The Massimataxis Incorporated Supplement
And Gumbo Jumbo the Homely Obblestrog Spectacular.

Audience reaction was quite encouraging.

A Party Political Broadcast on Behalf of the Burial Party

SPOKESMAN:

Already our government has enforced the four freedoms:
Freedom to speak if you have nothing to say.
Freedom from fear if you stay in your shelter.
Freedom from want if you do what we want
And freedom from freedom.

But yesterday we, the British Government,
Detected, thanks to our spider's web of sundaypapers
And bloodshot radar traps,
Two mutineers scowling from your moderate ranks.

POLICE CONSTABLE BOOTHEAD:

At two in the morning I found the accused,
A man and a woman, both unclothed,
Sprawling across their mammoth bed.
(The mammoth is being held in custody at Disneyland.)
Their eyes were shut, and they grinned
Like a couple of pink grand pianos.
When asked why they were smiling with their eyes shut,
The accused informed me (in song):
'We are happy.'
I made a note of that at the time.

JUDGE:

What was that word again?

PROSECUTOR:

Happy, milord,
An expression common among delinquents.
It means – irresponsible.
Extensive chromosome and corpuscle counts,
Exhaustive spiritual testing
And a touch of the old Doctor Scholl revealed
That the male and female citizen were both addicted
To one of the most dangerous drugs on the list –
Exhibit A – Love –
Highly addictive, producing hallucinations,
For example:
Fats Waller fornicating downwards
At the wheel of a purple-striped cloud
To play *The Resurrection of South America* –
This love-drug can remove
The user's interest in moneyandproperty
And in killing in order to defend
Moneyandproperty.

JUDGE:

Stop it, I can't bear it.

SPOKESMAN:

The lovers were found guilty of not being guilty.
Their obscene craving was hard to cure
But a succession of secret licemen did their best.
They can hardly be blamed if the gasping lovers died
After ten days apart, ten days apart.
They died with their grins on, both of them drowned
In the same daydream,
The same degenerate lagoon.

Freedom to speak if you have nothing to say.
Freedom from fear if you stay in your shelter.
Freedom from want if you do what we want.
Freedom from freedom, freedom from sanity
And freedom, finally, from life.

IT IS LIKELY THAT DURING THE NEXT TEN YEARS
YOU WILL BE CALLED UPON TO DIE FOR FREEDOM.

Old Age Report

When a man's too ill or old to work
We punish him.
Half his income is taken away
Or all of it vanishes and he gets pocket-money.

We should reward these tough old humans for surviving,
Not with a manager's soggy handshake
Or a medal shaped like an alarm clock –
No, make them a bit rich,
Give the freedom they always heard about
When the bloody chips were down
And the blitz or the desert
Swallowed their friends.

Retire, retire into a fungus basement
Where nothing moves except the draught
And the light and dark grey figures
Doubling their money on the screen;
Where the cabbages taste like the mummy's hand
And the meat tastes of feet;
Where there is nothing to say except:
'Remember?' or 'Your turn to dust the cat.'

To hell with retiring. Let them advance.
Give them the money they've always earned –
or more – and let them choose.
We could wipe away some of their worry,
Some of their pain – what I mean
Is so bloody simple:
The old people are being robbed
And punished and we ought
To be letting them out of their cages
Into green spaces of enchanting light.

Now We Are Sick

Christopher
      Robin
          goes
              hippety
immigrants   hoppety
       bring down
             the value of
                 property

Involvement

QUESTION (from the *London Magazine*): In most European countries, and in America, writers are becoming involved, one way or another, in public mani-festations of protest. As an English writer, do you feel that working on your own terms is more important than taking a practical part in organising public opinion?

In other words, in the continuing debates – about race, class, violence, war, financial priorities – that crucially affect our lives, are you for the writer in any way as polemicist, or do you believe that his instinct as an artist is ultimately the real test of his integrity?

ANSWER:

SCENE: an alley.

(*A* MAN *is being beaten up by* TWO POLICEMEN. *An* ENGLISH WRITER *approaches*.)

MAN: Help!

ENGLISH WRITER: Well, that may be what you think you want. But I've got to work on my own terms.

MAN: Help!

(TWO POLICEMEN put the boot in.)

ENGLISH WRITER: Look, I don't like this any more than you do. But I've got to follow my own instinct as an artist

MAN (*spitting teeth*): Yes, well that's ultimately the real test of your integrity.

(The beating up continues. ENGLISH WRITER pisses off to write a poem about ants.)

CURTAIN

Divide and Rule for as Long as You Can

Glasgow.
Trade Unionists march through the Square
Towards the City Chambers.

Police. Police. Police.

And in the streets leading off the Square –
Scottish soldiers with rifles.
Live ammunition.
They may be ordered to shoot into the crowd.

And behind the Scottish soldiers –
English soldiers with rifles.
Live ammunition.
If the Scottish soldiers refuse to shoot into the crowd
The English soldiers will be ordered
To shoot the Scottish soldiers.

Oh, but that was long ago.

That was in the future.

The Ballad of Sally Hit-and-Run

A train pulls into town and a woman jumps down
Her leathers are shining and her eyes are shining
With the body of a goddess and the cool of a nun
Everywhere she goes they call her Sally Hit-and-Run.

She moves down the street with a shuffle and a beat
Of her feet on the concrete – she's a creature
With senses that respond to every sound in town
And a hit-and-run habit when the sun goes down.

Sally Hit-and-Run on a barstool perch
Glances round the bar like a rector in church
Then she points one finger like a sensitive gun
And another guy topples to Sally Hit-and-Run.

Holiday Inn, Room three hundred and three,
Sally got him wrapped around the colour TV!
She shakes him and she bangs him like a tambourine,
Then she spreads him on the carpet like margarine.

Up comes the dawn – Sally's gone like a dream
Riding Inter-City drinking coffee and cream
Guy's left counting up the things he's done
Trying to give his goodness to Sally Hit-and-Run.

Dear Sir

I have read your Manifesto with great interest but it
says nothing about singing.

English Scene

You sit at a table with two other men

Your left wrist slants in front of your throat
Your right incisors chew the nail on your left little finger
Your right index fingernail ploughs across the grain of the tabletop
You are nervous, obviously

You are right to be nervous, obviously

The man on one side of you has less money than you
He wants your money

The man on the other side of you has more money than you
He wants your money

Your left arm protects your throat
They usually go for the throat

Under Photographs of Two Party Leaders, Smiling

These two smiled so the photographer
Could record their smiles
FOR YOU

As they smiled these smiles
They were thinking all the time
OF YOU

They smile on the rich
They smile on the poor
They smile on the victim in his village
They smile on the killer in his cockpit

Yes, Mummy and Daddy
Are smiling, smiling
AT YOU

please try to smile back.

Saw It in the Papers

Her baby was two years old.
She left him, strapped in his pram, in the kitchen.
She went out.
She stayed with friends.
She went out drinking.

The baby was hungry.
Nobody came.
The baby cried.
Nobody came.
The baby tore at the upholstery of his pram.
Nobody came.

She told the police:
'I thought the neighbours would hear him crying,
and report it to someone who would come
and take him away.'

Nobody came.

The baby died of hunger.

She said she'd arranged for a girl,
whose name she couldn't remember,
to come and look after the baby
while she stayed with friends.
Nobody saw the girl.
Nobody came.

Her lawyer said there was no evidence
of mental instability.
But the man who promised to marry her
went off with another woman.

And when he went off, this mother changed
from a mother who cared for her two-year-old baby
into a mother who did not seem to care at all.
There was no evidence of mental instability.

The Welfare Department spokesman said:
'I do not know of any plans for an inquiry.
We never become deeply involved.'
Nobody came.
There was no evidence of mental instability.

When she was given love
she gave love freely to her baby.
When love was torn away from her
she locked her love away.
It seemed that no one cared for her.
She seemed to stop caring.
Nobody came.
There was no evidence of mental instability.

Only love can unlock locked-up-love.

Manslaughter: She pleaded Guilty.
She was sentenced to be locked up
in prison for four years.

Is there any love in prisons?

She must have been in great pain.

There is love in prisons.
There is great love in prisons.
A man in Gloucester Prison told me:
'Some of us care for each other.
Some of us don't.
Some of us are gentle,
some are brutal.
All kinds.'

I said: 'Just the same as people outside.'
He nodded twice,
and stared me in the eyes.

What she did to him was terrible.
There was no evidence of mental instability.
What was done to her was terrible.
There is no evidence of mental instability.

Millions of children starve, but not in England.
What we do not do for them is terrible.

Is England's love locked up in England?
There is no evidence of mental instability.

Only love can unlock locked-up love.

Unlock all of your love.
You have enough for this woman.

Unlock all of your love.
You have enough to feed all those millions of children.

Cry if you like.
Do something if you can. You can.

Ten Ways to Avoid Lending Your Wheelbarrow to Anybody

1 *Patriotic*

May I borrow your wheelbarrow?
I didn't lay down my life in World War II
so that you could borrow my wheelbarrow.

2 *Snobbish*

May I borrow your wheelbarrow?
Unfortunately Samuel Beckett is using it.

3 *Overweening*

May I borrow your wheelbarrow?
It is too mighty a conveyance to be wielded
by any mortal save myself.

4 *Pious*

May I borrow your wheelbarrow?
My wheelbarrow is reserved for religious ceremonies.

5 *Melodramatic*

May I borrow your wheelbarrow?
I would sooner be broken on its wheel
and buried in its barrow.

6 *Pathetic*

May I borrow your wheelbarrow?
I am dying of schizophrenia
and all you can talk about is wheelbarrows.

7 *Defensive*

May I borrow your wheelbarrow?
Do you think I'm made of wheelbarrows?

8 *Sinister*

May I borrow your wheelbarrow?
It is full of blood.

9 *Lecherous*

May I borrow your wheelbarrow?
Only if I can fuck your wife in it.

10 *Philosophical*

May I borrow your wheelbarrow?
What is a wheelbarrow?

Vroomph! *or* The Popular Elastic Waist

(A cut-up of sentences from the Sunday Times Colour Magazine of 9 December 1967, which featured Civil Defence, Famous Footballers, The Girls of Thailand, Gangsters, and several advertisements.)

Juliet sighs. Romeo speaks.
Deep shelters are out of most people's reach.
The white tin is a simple gadget for pinpointing the size and position of
    nuclear bursts.
Simply push the needle in, pump the handle, and
You haven't seen anything till you've seen the 200 pounds of beautiful Louise
Tucked away in the secret, hardened, national seat of government,
Or balanced on bicycles while removing 12 shirts.
Yet, even when we made love, at a time when most
      women are feeling romantic, she would start to
          prattle away about
The Royal State Trumpeters of the Household Cavalry.

Stimulated by these breaks in the nuclear overcast,
      the Sunday Times here offers what is probably the
          first complete review of our Civil Defence
              preparations,
A symbol of the virile, aggressive, muscular game which
      one associates with a man who has twice broken the
          same leg – and twice returned to the game.
This is the problem: whether to drink Cointreau neat
    and slowly savour every warming sip,
Or hang from the tops of palm trees by our feet.

While we have the bomb it seems ridiculous not to be honest.
It works like this: the motor is powered by ordinary torch batteries.
The slightly wounded will be sent on their way, the severely wounded left to
The Marquis de Ferrara.
Fill out the Panic Sheet.
Neither the Sunday Times nor its agents accepts any liability for loss or
The gruesome electric chair.
You see, we are unashamedly devoted to the kind
  of quiet courtesy
    which gets rarer
      every
        day.

Leaflets

(for Brian Patten and my twelve students at Bradford)

Outside the plasma supermarket
I stretch out my arm to the shoppers and say:
'Can I give you one of these?'

I give each of them a leaf from a tree.

The first shopper thanks me.
The second puts the leaf in his mack pocket where his wife won't see.
The third says she is not interested in leaves. She looks like a mutilated willow.
The fourth says: 'Is it art?' I say that it is a leaf.
The fifth looks through his leaf and smiles at the light beyond.
The sixth hurls down his leaf and stamps it till dark purple mud oozes through.
The seventh says she will press it in her album.
The eighth complains that it is an oak leaf and says he would be on my side if
I were also handing out birch leaves, apple leaves, privet leaves and larch leaves.
I say that it is a leaf.
The ninth takes the leaf carefully and then, with a backhand fling, gives it its
  freedom.
It glides, following surprise curving alleys through the air.
It lands. I pick it up.
The tenth reads both sides of the leaf twice and then says: Yes, but it doesn't
  say who we should kill.'

But you took your leaf like a kiss.

They tell me that, on Saturdays,
You can be seen in your own city centre
Giving away forests, orchards, jungles.

The Obliterating Prizes

A gruesome occurrence fell on me once
    When I was a sammy at oxford
They chose me to be the college's dunce
    O I was the lubber of oxford

A conical hat they plunked on my head
    Those grievous old gories in oxford
With a D for Dunce wrote upon it in red
    Yes I was downderried at oxford

Now underbred dunderheads romp round the town
    Through the blithering weather of oxford
Each wears a gold cap and a silvery gown
    Each moocher but adrian in oxford

And I cautiously watch their regalia flap
    As I stand in the corner in oxford
For now I've been wearing that overhead hat
    For twenty dark blue years of oxford

Ode to Enoch Powell

The vulture is an honest man
He offers no apology
But snaps the fingers from the hand
And chews them with sincerity

Birmingham Council are bidding for the Berlin Wall.
There's swastikas sprouting in the ground round Bradford Town Hall
Callaghan and Thatcher are dancing cheek to cheek –
Everybody getting ready for Kindness to Vultures Week

The vulture is a gentleman
He does not stoop to kill
But watches murders from a height
Then drops to eat his fill

The Press is so excited that the Press can hardly speak
There's red stuff dripping from the corner of the *Telegraph*'s beak.
You can say that white is right but it looks like black is bleak
Everybody getting ready for Kindness to Vultures Week.

The vulture is a Christian man
Goes to church on Sunday
Prays to God to give him strength
To tear a corpse on Monday...

But when Mr Enoch Powell
Emigrates from this life
And the media forget to mention
That his tongue was a poison knife
When they lay him out in state
With a lipstick job
And an aura of after-shave
And twenty-one guns have farted Goodbye –
We'll dance on the bugger's grave

Dance on the earth that's hotter than his life
His blood was chilled
Dance to the music of the human beings
That liar killed

We'll stomp – 1, 2, 3, 4, 5, 6
Stomp – 7, 8, 9, 10.
Yes we'll stomp all night till the soil's right tight
So Enoch never rises again.

The Blackboard

Five foot by five foot,
(The smalls have measured it.)
Smooth black surface,
(Wiped by a small after every class.)
Five different colours of chalk
And a class of thirty-five smalls,
One big.

Does the big break up the chalk
Into thirty-five or thirty-six
And invite the smalls to make
A firework show of colours
Shapes and words
Starting on the blackboard
But soon overflowing
   All over the room
   All over the school
   All over the town
   All over the country
   All over the world?

   No.
The big looks at the textbook
Which was written by a big
And published by a big.
The textbook says
The names and dates of Nelson's battles.
So the big writes, in white,
Upon the black of the blackboard,
The names and dates of Nelson's battles.
The smalls copy into their books
The names and dates of Nelson's battles.

   Nelson was a big
Who died fighting for freedom or something.

Question Time in Ireland

1. If the Devil had used all his ingenuity to damn Ireland, could he have invented a more devastating trinity than the Roman Catholic Church, the Protestant Church and the English Houses of Parliament?
2. Why is it possible to withdraw from India, Kenya and Aden – but impossible to withdraw from Ireland?

3. Did Jesus say: Blessed are the poor, for they shall tear each others' throats out? Blessed are the rich, for they shall watch the tearing out of the throats and shall place bets upon the outcome?

4. What's wrong with torture in a good cause so long as it's not reported on television?

5. What is the answer to the English Question?

The Savage Average

I feel like a little girl of six
In a school built of two hundred thousand bricks
And every day, in the purple playground,
One child is chosen and killed by the other children.

Loose Leaf Poem

(This is a diary of good and bad things, mostly for friends and allies but with a few sections for enemies as well. It was written in a peaceful room with a view of the Yorkshire Dales. In reading it aloud, I often change the order of sections, talk in between sections and leave out any part which doesn't seem relevant at the time.)

*

There was a child danced with a child
The music stopped

*

I stopped reading The Wretched of the Earth
Because you cannot read it all the time.

My stomach felt like outer space.
The sunday papers all sounded
Like bidders in a slave market.

I ate rapidly, alone,
Because I couldn't sit and eat with anyone,
Or look at anyone.

I glanced into the television's eye.
it was both bright and blind.

I was full of useless tears.
I did not use them

*

Who was the hooligan who ripped off all your skin, madam?
The North Atlantic Treaty Organisation.

*

Below my window, a stone wall begins,
swerves past a tree, drags its weight
upwards, almost collides with a second tree,
breaks for a gate, resumes,
and skitters over the horizon.
I watch the way it rides,
blonde stone in the blonde light of Yorkshire.

*

Are you bored by pictures of burning people?
You will be bored to death.

They did the dying.
You did nothing.

Not a gesture, not a word, not a breath,
Not a flicker of one line of your face.

You said: There is nothing I can do.
As you said it you seemed so proud.

*

There was a wretched danced with a wretched
The music began to burn.

*

In the chapel-cold porridge of fear
Crouched the spirit of Edward Lear
   Through the hole in his head
   His agony bled
   Till he changed to a Whale
   And spouted a hail –
Cholomondley Champagne and the best Babylonian Beer.

*

To   Ian Hamilton and A. Alvarez, Poetry Reviewers –
   Get your blue hands
   off the hot skin of poetry

*

(to dogmatic men and automatic dogs)

I'm an entrist, centrist, Pabloite workerist
– Sweet Fourth International and never been kissed,
I've got a mass red base that's why I'd rather sit on the floor,
If you want to be a vanguard, better join Securicor.

My daddy was opportunistic
My mama was mystified
I want to be a movement
But there's no one on my side...

50

NO REVOLUTION WITHOUT COMPASSION

*

Never look out
You might see something bigger than you
Never go out
You might get your iambics dirty

Wine is a river
Flowing down to sleep
So climb in the boat
With your legitimate wife
No sharks   No storms
No underwater explosions

Never look out
The sun might punch you in the eye –

Say home.

*

I pulled on my solid granite gargoyle suit, borrowed a hunch from
    Sherlock Holmes and swung down from the turrets of Notre
        Dame just in time to rescue the naked Andromeda who was
            chained to King Kong in the middle of Red Square,
                Milwaukee.

Mark Antony immediately denounced me to a mob of Transylvanian
    peasants, who hurried me to the nearest oasis for a good
        guillotining.

Luckily for me the Flying Nun was power-diving down for a
    suicide raid on Moby Dick.

She noticed my plight, shot out a tentacle and scooped me into an
    echo chamber full of Dusty Springfields, thus foiling the
        machinations of Edgar Allen Fu Manchu, the Jackdaw of Zenda.

So you will understand why I am delighted to be here tonight to
    introduce a fourth member of fiction's Trolleybus Trinity –
        ladies and gentlemen, let's hear it for Miss Marlene Brontë.

*

At the end of each adventure

Mighty Mouse stands, arms folded, on a pedestal,
Cheered by a crowd of infant mice.

Every Sunday
God is praised
In several million churches.

Mighty Mouse saved us from the Monster Cat!!!!

*

In case the atmosphere catches on fire
The first thing to do will be to burn

My brain socialist
My heart anarchist
My eyes pacifist
My blood revolutionary

*

The man who believes in giraffes would swallow anything.
There's been nothing about ostriches in the papers for months,
    somebody's either building an ostrich monopoly or
    herding them into concentration camps.
Butterflies fly zigzag because they want to fly zigzag.
I have looked into a hedgehog's face and seen nothing but goodness.
A huge ram stamps his foot – a million sheep charge and occupy
    the Bradford Wool Exchange.

*

           pip
           pop
           pip
           pop
    pip   pip   pip
           pop

i am either a sound poet
or a bowl of Rice Crispies

*

(to a friend who killed himself)

All that pain
double-bulging under your forehead
I wish you could have taken
a handful of today's Yorkshire snow
and pressed it to that pain.
You rummaged for peace
in the green country, in the eye of the sun,
in visions of Tibet,
brain-shaking drugs, black magic,
police stations, among the stones,
beneath the stones.
But the stones, which seemed so calm,
screamed into life in your hurt hands.
Simpler than you
I simply wish you were alive
walking among this snowfall.
I'm glad that all your pain is dead.

*

Your breath is like deodorant, your blood like Irish lager,
Your idea of paradise an infinite Forsyte Saga,
Your head belongs to Nato and your heart to the Playboy Club,
You're the square root of minus zero, playing rub-a-dub-dub in a Fleet Street pub.

Sit tight in your tower of money...

You've got a problem of identity, ooh what an intellectual shame,
You've got a million pseudonyms and can't recall your maiden name,
You cannot tell your face from your arse or your supper from your sex,
But you always remember who you are when it comes to signing cheques –

Sit tight in your tower of money...

In case England catches on fire
The first thing to do will be to form a committee
To organise a weekend seminar
On Little-Known Conflagrations in Italian History
Or The Rise and Fall of the Safety Match in Literature and Life.

*

Many thin men
saying: No.

But of course we've got to inside-out ourselves
and splash around in our own juice,
and the juice can't shine if you don't throw it up into the light,
and of course you're hard to hit if you keep dancing
and harder to hit if you make up your own dance as you dance,
and of course Tarzan is more exciting than Anthony Trollope
because he can MOVE, swinging through jungles of clubfooted prose,
into your eye and out your navel,
and of course there's no perfect music,
no perfect words,
only the ridiculous beauty of man and woman
silly with each other,
pulling off their skins and swinging them round their heads,
becoming incredible fountains upon legs –

Many thin men
saying: No.

*

There's a factory for making factories,
A sinking pool for learning to drown,
A university like a pencil sharpener
To whittle you down to a pinpoint.
There's a mean old weather machine
Churning out crapstorms
And a generation gap between
Me and what I used to be.
But the cities of horror,
Skull pavements, murder girders –
They're going to crumble away in our hands.

*

The ice-cubes in my bloodstream decided to melt today.
I'd buy a moustache like everyone else
But I'm too attached to golden syrup.
There are hailstones big as hailstones, but I'm sure
They're not aimed at me.
Yes, Timbuctoo. I suddenly want to go to Timbuctoo.

*

Grass pours down the hillside.
The stone wall gradually turns green.
A dead tree can keep its balance for years.

*

You can't win
Mary Queen of Scots invented high-heel shoes to make her-
self look taller they cut her bloody head off. (John Walton)

*

Suddenly it hits me that it's May Day and I hadn't even noticed it was April,
And was gazing over the floodlit fields at a group of socially-minded cows,
And laughing to myself about the time Allen Ginsberg bared his arse to the
    people in a whizzing-by train,
And marking passages in a book of Fidel Castro's speeches –
Quote – And then you hear a revolutionary say: They crushed us,
They organised 200 radio programmes, so many newspapers,
    so many magazines, so many TV shows,
    so many of this and so many of that – and one wants to ask him,
What did you expect?
That they would put TV, radio, the magazines, the newspapers,
    the printing shops –
All this at your disposal?
Or are you unaware that these are the instruments of the ruling class
Designed explicitly for crushing the Revolution? – unquote.
And I was also thinking of the pirhana fish grinning in the depths of my bank
    manager's soul,
And I was looking through the BBC Folk Club magazine and trying to
    imagine the BBC Folk,
And I was looking forward to a bit of bed with Celia in the afternoon,
And my eyes kept returning to a letter from the poet Tim Daly,
Liquid blue handwriting between strict blue lines,
His words saying – quote –
As a whole, the support I have received has amazed me,
I had anticipated only antagonism.
Love be praised, I was wrong – unquote –
And I look again at his address:
Her Majesty's Prison, County Road, Maidstone, Kent.
Tim, aged twenty-one, who took his petrol bombs
To the Imperial War Museum
Because the Museum was teaching children war...
And so when it suddenly hits me that it's been May Day all day
And I should be feeling solidarity,
I think yes so I should, and yes I do, and so yes I write this down
As a demonstration of solidarity –

With the cows, who have now moved on,
With Allen Ginsberg, who has now moved on,
With Fidel Castro as he moves socialism onwards,
With Celia who moves me as we move together,
And with Tim Daly the poet,
Locked away for four years
So that England may be safe for the dead.

Back in the Playground Blues

I dreamed I was back in the playground, I was about four feet high
Yes dreamed I was back in the playground, standing about four feet high
Well the playground was three miles long and the playground was five miles wide

It was broken black tarmac with a high wire fence all around
Broken black dusty tarmac with a high fence running all around
And it had a special name to it, they called it The Killing Ground

Got a mother and a father, they're one thousand years away
The rulers of The Killing Ground are coming out to play
Everybody thinking: 'Who they going to play with today?'

    Well you get it for being Jewish
    And you get it for being black
    Get it for being chicken
    And you get it for fighting back
    You get it for being big and fat
    Get it for being small
    Oh those who get it get it and get it
    For any damn thing at all

Sometimes they take a beetle, tear off its six legs one by one
Beetle on its black back, rocking in the lunchtime sun
But a beetle can't beg for mercy, a beetle's not half the fun

I heard a deep voice talking, it had that iceberg sound
'It prepares them for Life' – but I have never found
Any place in my life worse than The Killing Ground.

The Swan

The anger of the swan
Burns black
Over ambitious eyes.

The power of the swan
Flexes steel wings
To batter feeble air.

The beauty of the swan
Is the sermon
Preached between battles.

Farm Animals

Clotted cream sheep
We troop in a dream
Through the steep deep wool
Of a yellow meadow
We are oblong and boring
We are all alike
Liking to be all alike

And the grass-like grass
Is alike, all alike, and all we think
Is grass grass grass
Yes grass is all we think
And all we do
Is wool

But that's the deal, the ancient deal,
The wonderful deal between sheep and men

Men give grass
We come across with wool

That agreement was signed
On the green baize table in Eden

What would happen if we broke the contract?
Oh that would be mutiny, we would be punished
By being eaten, we would deserve to be eaten.
But of course we never rebel, so we are never eaten.

On the Verses Entitled 'Farm Animals'

The stereotypical tra-a-avesty opposite
Purports to speak for sheep
Nothing could be more cra-a-assly human

Despite our similar coiffures
Each sheep's a separate planet
With its own opinions and visions

All that we share is the furnace heart
Of all long-distance serfs
We're hot and getting hotter
So shepherds, you better watch your flocks

A. Ram

Commuting the Wrong Way Round Early Morning

Caught the Gospel Oak train
At the dog-end of Tuesday night.
Camden Town darkness
Laying like gravy on a plate...
But at Liverpool Street Station
They've got a smudgey brand of blue daylight.

Here comes half the Essex population
Tensed up for their desky work.
I'm struggling up a waterfall –
Bubbling secretaries, rocky clerks.
For I'm off to Billericay
Like a sausage on a fork.

For My Son

'The next best thing to the human tear'

ADVERTISING SLOGAN FOR AN EYEWASH

The next best thing to the human tear
Is the human smile
Which beams at us reflected white
For a lunar while.
But smiles congeal. Two eyes alight
With water cannot glow for long,
And a better thing than the human tear
Is the human song.

If cigarette or city burn
The smoke breaks into air.
So your breath, cries and laughter turn
And are abandoned there.
Once I had everything to learn
And thought each book had pretty pages.
Now I don't even trust the sun
Which melts like butter through the ages.

Nevertheless, crack-voiced I'll sing
For you, who drink the generous light
Till, fat as happiness, you sing
Your gay, immortal appetite.
I bring you air, food, grass and rain,
Show you the breast where you belong.
You take them all and sing again
Your human song.

Four Sorry Lines

Sixteen years old, and you would sneer
At a baby or a phoenix.
Mock on, mock on, in your blue-lidded splendour –
Most well-paid jobs are reserved for cynics.

Action and Reaction Blues

Further back you pull a bow-string
    the further the arrow goes whooshin
Further back Maggie drags us
    the further the revolution

Screws and Saints

What's worse than the uniformed devils
When they trap you in a concrete hell?
The claws and boots of the angels
When you're savaged in a golden cell.

New Skipping Rhymes

Good little Georgie
Worked like a madman
Three years at Oxford
Five years an Adman
Went on Mastermind
Did so well on that show
Now he's the Host
Of a TV Chat Show

      My savings are my baby
      Money is my boss
      My mummy and my daddy
      Were profit and loss
      One thousand, two thousand, three
      thousand, four...

Meat on the hook
Powder in the jar
Mickey Jagger is a Star
S-T-A-R spells Star
He can whistle
He can hum
He can wriggle his umpumbum

      Pretty little Pam
      Passed her exam
      What shall we give her?
      Doughnuts with jam

      Stupid little Sam
      Failed his exam
      What shall we give him?
      Who gives a damn?

Staying Awake

Monday came so I fucked off to school
School is a big huge building
Where you're not supposed to get any fucking sleep
We hung around till they counted us in a room
With pictures of fucking owls and bats
Then we hung around some more

Miss Harburton ponced in and yelled about
How her fucking bike's gone missing who cares
Then we all fucked off to another room

It was Mister Collins from Outer Space
Talked about not leaving gum stuck around
And Queen Victoria up the Suez Canal
And how he wouldn't let us act out
The Death of General Gordon again
Not ever and no he never saw *Chainsaw Massacre*
And no didn't want to even free
On Goodgeman's sexy mother's video
And Beano Black said his mother was poorly
And started to give us the fucking grisly details
Saved by the bell and we hung around
Smoking in the bog and not getting any sleep

Then we all fucked off to another room
And it was Mrs Grimes Environmental Studies
So I finally got my fucking sleep.

I stay out of trouble but in my head
I'm bad I'm fucking bad as they come
When I die they'll punish me
For the things I done in my fucking head.
They'll send me off to a big huge building
And they won't let me get any fucking sleep.
Well that's what I reckon
Death is like fucking off
To another fucking school.

Bring Out Your Nonsense

A detective-sergeant walks into the police station
A woman with a floor at home inspects the carpet store
A train stops at the platform after deceleration
Librarians enter the library through the library door
Telephonists at the switchboard are answering telephones
A *Telegraph* reader buys the *Telegraph* from the paper shop
Cars drive, pedestrians walk and my heart groans
As out of the Billericay copshop steps a cop

But I'm wrong – the cop debags himself to give birth to a phoenix
Which zips down the High Street with Dizzy Gillespian squeals
And the silver and gold melts in all the jewellers' windows
And the town is crotch-deep in whirlpools of syrup
And you sail over the horizon in a pea-blue schooner
Bearing the wild good news you sail bearing the good wild food
Over the horizon with a ton of friends playing magical banjoes
And the people of Billericay dance in delirious dozens

Give It to Me Ghostly

give it to me ghostly
close-up and long-distance
i've an open policy
of misty non-resistance
so give it to me ghostly
shudder up and lisp a
bogey-woman promise
to your will o' the whisper

give it to me ghostly
spook it to me somehow
haunt me haunt me haunt me
oooo thanks i've come now

Bury My Bones with an Eddy Merckx

live people don't often
have eyes for the overhead stars
but gloom down roads
in microwave cars

they dunno how the rippling
of the wild air feels
frowning round town
in tombs on wheels
but ghosts ride bikes
free-wheeling mostly
singing songs like
Give It To Me Ghostly

ghosts got no rooty-tooty
duty to be done
cars are for bloody business
bikes for fun

Remember Red Lion Square?

I haven't heard any Moderates lately
Mention the name of Kevin Gateley,
The student who, so the Coroner said,
Died from 'a moderate blow to the head'.

Ode to Her

You so draggy Ms Maggie
The way you drag us down
The way you shake your finger
Way you frown your frown
But a day's soon dawning
When all the world will shout
We're gonna catch yer Ms Thatcher
You'll be dragged out

You so draggy Ms Maggie
You tore this land apart
With your smile like a laser
And your iceberg heart
You teach the old and jobless
What poverty means
You send the young men killing
The Irish and the Argentines
You so draggy Ms Maggie
With your million cuts
You slashed this country
Till it spilled its guts
You crucified parents
And their children too
Nailed 'em up by the million
Here's what we'll do

You so draggy Ms Maggie
Madonna of the Rich
We're gonna introduce you
On the Anfield pitch
Oh you can talk your meanest
But you as good as dead
When Yosser Hughes butts you
With his poor old head...

On the Beach at Cambridge

I am assistant to the Regional Commissioner
At Block E, Brooklands Avenue,
Communications Centre for Region 4,
Which used to be East Anglia.

I published several poems as a young man
But later found I could not meet my own high standards
So tore up all my poems and stopped writing.
(I stopped painting at eight and singing at five.)
I was seconded to Block E
From the Ministry for the Environment.

Since there are no established poets available
I have come out here in my MPC
(Maximum Protective Clothing)
To dictate some sort of poem or word-picture
Into a miniature cassette recorder.

When I first stepped out of Block E on to this beach
I could not record any words at all,
So I chewed two of the orange-flavoured pills
They give us for morale, switched on my Sony
And recorded this:
I am standing on the beach at Cambridge.
I can see a group in their MPC
Pushing Hoover-like and Ewbank-like machines
Through masses of black ashes.
The taller men are soldiers or police,
The others, scientific supervisors.
This group moves slowly across what seems
Like an endless car park with no cars at all.

I think that, in one moment,
All the books in Cambridge
Leapt off their shelves,
Spread their wings
And became white flames
And then black ash.
And I am standing on the beach at Cambridge.

You're a poet, said the Regional Commissioner,
Go out and describe that lot.

The University Library – a little hill of brick-dust.
King's College Chapel – a dune of stone-dust.
The sea is coming closer and closer.

The clouds are edged with green,
Sagging low under some terrible weight.
They move more rapidly than usual.

Some younger women with important jobs
Were admitted to Block E
But my wife was a teacher in her forties.
We talked it over
When the nature of the crisis became apparent.
We agreed somebody had to carry on.
That day I kissed her goodbye as I did every day
At the door of our house in Chesterton Road.
I kissed my son and my daughter goodbye.
I drove to Block E beside Hobson's Brook.
I felt like a piece of paper
Being torn in half.

And I am standing on the beach at Cambridge.
Some of the men in their MPC
Are sitting on the ground in the black ashes.
One is holding his head in both his hands.

I was forty-two three weeks ago.
My children painted me
Bright-coloured cards with poems for my birthday.
I stuck them with Blu-Tack on the kitchen door.
I can remember the colours.

But in one moment all the children in Cambridge
Spread their wings
And became white flames
And then black ash.

And the children of America, I suppose.
And the children of Russia, I suppose.

And I am standing on the beach at Cambridge
And I am watching the broad black ocean tide
Bearing on its shoulders its burden of black ashes.

And I am listening to the last words of the sea
As it beats its head against the dying land.

RELIGION, ROYALTY AND THE ARTS

The Liberal Christ Gives a Press Conference

I would have walked on the water
But I wasn't fully insured.
And the BMA sent a writ my way
With the very first leper I cured.

I would've preached a golden sermon
But I didn't like the look of the Mount.
And I would've fed fifty thousand
But the Press wasn't there to count.

> And the businessmen in the temple
> Had a team of coppers on the door.
> And if I'd spent a year in the desert
> I'd have lost my pension for sure.

> I would've turned the water into wine
> But they weren't giving licences.
> And I would have died and been crucified
> But like – you know how it is.

I'm going to shave off my beard
And cut my hair,
Buy myself some bulletproof
Underwear
I'm the Liberal Christ
And I've got no blood to spare.

Miserable Sinners

Now I know that revolutionary Catholic priests have died fighting for freedom and socialism in South America, and Quaker schools are smashing, and Donald Soper's all right in his place, and some of the sayings of Jesus are worthy of William Blake – but to hell with organised religion.

In Ireland, the basic human needs of liberty, equality and fraternity go to blazes while the two big local superstitions fight it out.

If the professionals in the churches believe in Christ, why don't they work as he did? Jesus didn't take scholarships so he could study to become a rabbi. He didn't ask for a temple and a vicarage and a salary and a pension scheme. He didn't push for exclusive propaganda rights in schools.

To Jesus, the Churches of England and Rome would have been strictly science fiction. Vast, rich propaganda machines, thriving on spiritual blackmail.

He worked differently. He told as much of the truth as he could until they killed him – like many other good men, religious and irreligious. I've met many people like that, most of them members of no church, most of them completely unknown.

If the churches cared for this world, they would extract their hooks from their people, disestablish, disperse and house the people instead of God. De-escalate organised religion and some of the most hopeless political situations in the world would become clearer, even soluble. Even Ireland. Even the Middle East.

If you detect personal bitterness in the above, you are damn right. I will declare my interest. For a few years I attended a school where evangelism was the dominant religion. We used to go to camp in North Wales for intensive Bible readings and declarations of conversion.

The message sank in deep, and the message was guilt. And the punishment for guilt was Hell. I was taught the ugliness and vileness of the body. I was taught terror. The Hell we were threatened with was the Hell of the sermon in *Portrait of the Artist as a Young Man*.

In short, we were children with no defences, and we were violated by holy Hitchcocks. It took me about fifteen years to shake off most of that fear and disgust. I don't know what happened to the others.

Sure, this was an extreme case. Sure, it was way back in the nineteen-forties. But Frankenstein's monster (alias the Church of Christ) keeps rolling along, crushing children as it rolls.

QUESTION: But what would you put in the place of organised religion?

ANSWER: Omnicreed.

QUESTION: What is Omnicreed?

ANSWER: A custom-built religion, which incorporates the most imaginative ideas of all religions and rejects the boring, terror-laden and anti-imaginative concepts.

QUESTION: Can you give me some examples?

ANSWER: You bet your sweet soul. The Anti-Imagination, known and rejected among Omnicreed initiates as The Brown Lump, embraces such concepts as the Sabbath, clergymen, popery, no popery and Cliff Richard in Westminster Abbey. On the other hand, Omnicreed awards its Good Church-keeping Certificate to such doctrines as The Immaculate Unction of Pope Joan, Nirvana as a Motel, the Bank of England Formation Dancing Team, Bulldozer Rallies, Calvin as the Inventor of Milk Chocolate, Nationalised Delicatessens, Zen Washing Lines and the Company of Dogs.

QUESTION: Have you got a light?

Sunday Poem
(to the Christians)

Eat this: God has a place,
Incense-deodorised, a vaulted mouth
Where the good dead always
Alleluia among towers of teeth.
Boring? In that honey of saliva?
They tell me male sharks come for seven
Or eight hours. Multiply forever –
You still can't count the heaven of Heaven.

Eat this: God has another place,
A gaol-hole. Walls contract and crush
Necks on to legs, bellies into faces
And all parts in a constipated hash
Of cancered madmen, vomiting and skinned,
Skewered in flames which rot, restore and rot,
Breathing only the tear-gas of their sins –
That's what the bad dead get.

Quite Apart from the Holy Ghost

I remember God as an eccentric millionaire,
Locked in his workshop, beard a cloud of foggy-coloured hair,
Making the stones all different, each flower and disease,
Pulling the Laps in Lapland, making China for the Chinese,
Laying down the Lake of Lucerne as smooth as blue-grey lino,
Wearily inventing the appendix and the rhino,
Making the fine fur for the mink, fine women for the fur,
Man's brain a gun, his heart a bomb, his conscience – a blur.

Christ I can see much better from here,
And Christ upon the Cross is clear.
Jesus is stretched like the skin of a kite
Over the Cross, he seems in flight
Sometimes. At times it seems more true
That he is meat nailed up alive and pain all through.
But it's hard to see Christ for priests. That happens when
A poet engenders generations of advertising men.

The Eggs o' God

Last Thursday God manifested himself as a barrage balloon with varicose veins and descended on the Vatican. I'm shrivelling, he shouted to the Pope, once I was bigger than the Universe but now I'm shrinking fast. The bulk of God lolled in St Peter's Square, deflating soon to the size of a double-decker bus. Quick, cried God, before I vanish, one last request. When I've disappeared, put my eggs in a jar, keep in a cool place and run a world-wide search for a warm-hearted virgin. Let her hatch the eggs and then you'll find –

But by now God is a hissing football, and now he is a grapefruit, now a grape, and now the grape has exploded and nothing is left in the Square but the Eggs of God.

Four Switzers armed with money-trowels shovelled the golden spawn into a lucent white container and bore it to the Papal fridge.

At two in the morning a whisky cardinal staggered in, his stomach growling for a snack. Unfortunately he fancied caviar...

> The Pope has risen frae his bed
> On his twa holy legs
> And doon the marble staircase gaed
> Tae see the sacred eggs
>
> O wha has stolen the Eggs o' God
> Gae seek him near and far
> O wha has stolen the Eggs o' God
> Frae the Gentleman's Relish jar
>
> Then up and spak the Cardinal
> His voice was like a Boeing
> O I hae eaten the Eggs o' God
> And I'm eight miles tall, and growing...

ROYAL POEMS

Another Prince Is Born

Fire off the bells, ring out wild guns,
Switch on the sun for the son of sons.
For loyal rubbernecks who wait
Stick a notice on the gate.
Thrill to frill and furbelow,
God Save Sister Helen Rowe.
Lord Evans, Peel, Hall and Sir John
Guard the cot he dribbles on.
An angel in a Hunter jet
Circles round his bassinet.
Inform *The Times, Debrett, Who's Who*,
Better wake C. Day Lewis too.

Comes the parade of peers and peasants,
The Queen bears children, they bear presents –
Balls and toy guardsmen, well-trained parrots,
A regal rattle (eighteen carats),
And one wise man with myrrh-oiled hair
Brings a six-foot teddy bear
From the Birmingham Toy Fair.

Lying in State

He's dead. Into the vault and out
Shuffles the reverent conga.
With his intestines taken out
He will stay sweeter longer.

Poem on the Occasion of the Return of
Her Majesty the Queen from Canada

Some love Jesus and some love brandy
Some love Schweitzer or the boys in blue
Some love squeezing that Handy Andy
But I love model airplane glue
    Gloucester Gladiator
    Super-Constellation
    U2 U2 U2
I can see all of Russia from up here

Once upon a time I couldn't leave the ground
My wings were warping and my props were through
No elastic could turn them round
Till I found model airplane glue
    Supermarine Spitfire
    Vickers Viscount
    Junkers Junkie
Come fly with me

Take one sniff and my engines start
Second sniff I'm Blériot and Bader too
Holds me together when I'm flying apart
So I love model airplane glue
    BOAC
    El-Al
    Sputnik
I am Eagle I am Eagle

Some love a copper and some love a preacher
Some love Hiroshima and Waterloo
Some love the Beatles and some love Nietzsche
But I love model airplane glue
    A bit of wire
    A rubber band
    Balsa wood
    That's man
And a man needs glue.

My Shy Di in Newspaperland

(All the lines are quoted from the British Press on Royal Engagement day,
the only slight distortions appear in the repeats of the four-line chorus.
Written in collaboration with Alistair Mitchell.)

Who will sit where in the forest of tiaras?
She is an English rose without a thorn.
Love is in their stars, says Susie.
She has been plunged headfirst into a vast goldfish bowl.

Did she ponder as she strolled for an hour through Belgravia?
Will they, won't they? Why, yes they will.
They said so yesterday.
He said: 'Will you?'
She said: 'Yes.'
So did his mother – and so say all of us.

Who will sit where in the head of the goldfish?
She is an English forest without a tiara.
Love is in their roses, says Thorny.
She has been plunged starsfirst into a vast susie bowl.

Most of the stories in this issue were written
By James Whitaker, the *Daily Star* man
Who has always known that Diana and Prince Charles would marry.
He watched them fishing on the River Dee –
And Lady Diana was watching him too.
She was standing behind a tree using a mirror
To watch James Whitaker at his post,
James Whitaker, the man who always knew.

Who will sit where in the stars of Susie?
She is an English head without a goldfish.
Love is in their forests, says Tiara.
She has been plunged rosefirst into a vast thorn bowl.

All about Di.
Shy Di smiled and blushed.
Lady Di has her eyelashes dyed.
My shy Di.

She descends five times from Charles II –
Four times on the wrong side of the blanket
And once on the right side.

Who will sit where in the rose of thorns?
She is an English star without a susie.
Love is in their heads, says Goldfish.
She has been plunged forestfirst into a vast tiara bowl.

Flatmate Carolyn Pride was in the loo
When she heard of the engagement.
'Lady Diana told me through the door,' she said last night.
'I just burst into tears. There were floods and floods of tears.'

Who will sit where in the forest of tiaras?
She is an English rose without a thorn.
Love is in their stars, says Susie.
She has been plunged headfirst into a vast goldfish bowl.

THE ARTS

Goodbye

He breathed in air, he breathed out light.
Charlie Parker was my delight.

Jimmy Giuffre Plays 'The Easy Way'

A man plodding through blue-grass fields.
He's here to decide whether the grass needs mowing.
He sits on a mound and taps his feet on the deep earth.
He decides the grass doesn't need mowing for a while.

Buddy Bolden

He bust through New Orleans
On his cornet night and day,
Buddy kept on stompin'
Till he was put away.

He chose his girls like kings do
And drank like earth was hell,
But when they tried to cut him
He played like Gabriel.

The notes shot out his cornet
Like gobs come off a ship.
You felt the air get tighter
And then you heard it rip.

They threw him in the bughouse
And took away his horn.
He hadn't felt so mean since
The day that he was born.

Some say corn liquor done it
Or layin' a bad whore
But I guess he blew so much out
He couldn't think no more.

Bessie Smith in Yorkshire

As I looked over the billowing West Riding
A giant golden tractor tumbled over the horizon
The grass grew blue and the limestone turned to meat
For Bessie Smith was bumping in the driver's seat.

Threw myself down on the fertilised ground and cried:
'When I was a foetus I loved you, and I love you now you've died.'
She was bleeding beauty from her wounds in the Lands of Wrong
But she kept on travelling and she spent all her breathing on song.

I was malleted into the earth as tight as a gate-post
She carried so much life I felt like the ghost of a ghost
She's the river that runs straight uphill
Hers is the voice brings my brain to a standstill

Black tracking wheels
Roll around the planet
Seeds of the blues
Bust through the concrete

My pale feet fumble along
The footpaths of her midnight empire

What to Do if You Meet Nijinsky

The special child
Remains a child
Knowing that everything else
Is smaller, meaner and less gentle.

Watch the creature standing
Like a fountain in a photograph.
He's moving carefully as a leaf
Growing in a hothouse.
What are the roots?
What is the stem?
What are the flowers?
Nijinsky
Dancing too much truth.

If you don't kill Nijinsky
He's going to turn you into Nijinsky.
You'll live like a leaf, die like a leaf,
Like Nijinsky.

Sweet magical
Skinned
Alive
Animal

You must decide for yourself how you're going to kill Nijinsky.

Leave him in the prison
Whose stones are cut so cleverly
They fit every contour of his skin exactly.

Leave him collapsing
In the foreign forest clearing
While the pine trees burn around him like a circle of matches.
Climb into your car and drive like a rocket right out of the world of feeling.

Leave Nijinsky dancing
The dance of lying very still

To the Statues in Poets' Corner, Westminster Abbey

You stony bunch of pockskinned whiteys,
Why kip in here? Who sentenced you?
They are buying postcards of you,
The girls in safety knickers.
Tombfaces, glumbums,
Wine should be jumping out all of your holes,
You should have eyes that roll, arms that knock things over,
Legs that falter and working cocks.
Listen.
On William Blake's birthday we're going to free you,
Blast you off your platforms with a blowtorch full of brandy
And then we'll all stomp over to the Houses of Parliament
And drive them into the Thames with our bananas.

Crusoe Dying in England

Always the seagulls cry on me
Weak from the waves. They tell me tales,
Say: Now you breathe the English sky;
You have been rescued from the toils
Of the black island. All the day
They speak fair times. But constantly
Caged in my chest a huge fowl wails
And screams the truth above the lie:
England is drowned. Old age despoils
My senses. I am cast away.

My body is a breathing weight
Obscenely formed to be my shame.
I cannot show it to the light
But hide it in my hollow room;
For now the rooted traps are set,
The springs are sour and my estate
Is lost to me. I have no name.
Thick grow the poison weeds, no flight
Is possible. The branches loom
Shining above with lazy sweat.

Fruit hangs and drops upon the hut
Endlessly from heavy trees.
I have no will to hook or net
Fantastic fish I used to prize.
Shuddering skies melt in the heat
To soak my limbs. My heart is shut
And locked to hope. My silly knees
Kissing the earth, let me forget
The ghosts who turn before my eyes,
Companions of sea and street.

We would go, swaggering and fine,
To rake the taverns of a port.
My storming friends, we loved in vain
For now your eyes are all put out.
Shackled along the rusty chains
Of thought, you are not truly mine.
Captives, but you will not be taught
To sing, or move, or speak again.
Bad air invades me from without
My friends lie sullen in my brains.

Crusoe? I am some other thing,
A city caught in evil days
Of plague and fire: I am a throng
Of shaking men: I am a race
Undone by fear, for I was born
In a cursed country. Who is King?
Who is the ruler of this shattered place
Myself? The Bible God? But strong
Crusoe is dead. I have no face;
An old mad god, my powers gone.

Whitman on Wheels

Fanfare: in transports over transport
I salute all passenger-carrying machines –
The admirable automobile, the glottal motor-cycle,
The womby capsule bound for Mars.
The tube train (see how well it fits its tube).
The vibrant diesel, the little engine that could
And all manner of airplanes whether they carry
Hostesses, hogs or horror.
Gargantuan traction engines.
Curmudgeonly diggers, bulldozers, dinosauric tank-tracked cranes.
Zoomers, splutterers, purrers and gliders
I salute you all,
And also the reliable tricycle.

Canine Canto

Dogs thurber through the whitman grass
On wild shakespearean excursions.
They have no waugh or corneille class
In their laurence sterne diversions.
They sniff blake blooms and patchen weeds,
They have no time for strindberg doom,
Or walks on firm jane austen leads,
Formal pope gardens or the baudelaire room.
As for donne love, while going it,
They lawrence without knowing it.

Thank You Dick Gregory

King Lear kept shouting at his Fool:
'These children squeeze, bruise and knot my arteries.
I ache and shake with fatherhood.
Sex can't ache or shake me now
But bawdiness makes my old eyes shine.
So make me jokes that jump, and tumble,
A whole crowd of jokes, a courtful of pretty people jokes
So I can meet each one just once
And then forget, meeting another joke.'
But the Fool made a face like an expensive specialist,
He put one hand on the king's pulse, one on his own heart
And said: 'Your Majesty, you're dying, man.'

Dick Gregory, the funny man, left the glad clapping hands
Of San Francisco, where tigers still survive,
To walk in the dust of Greenwood, Mississippi.
He walked as Gary Cooper used to walk
In Westerns, but Gregory walked blackly, seriously, not pretending.
He burned as Brando burns in movies
But the flames behind his eyes were black
And everything his eyes touched scorched.
His jokes crackled in the air,
Gags like Bob Hope's, but these were armed and black.
Liberals realised that they were dwarfs,
Colonels got blisters, and Gregory laughed.

When Dick Gregory reached the South
They told him his two-month son was dead.
I heard that today.
I had to write and say:
Thank you Dick Gregory,
I send as much love as you will take from me,
My blackest and my whitest love.
King Lear is dying of your jokes,
Of your flames, of your tall walking –
Thank you Dick Gregory.

Lullaby for William Blake

Blakehead, babyhead,
Your head is full of light.
You sucked the sun like a gobstopper.
Blakehead, babyhead,
High as a satellite on sunflower seeds,
First man-powered man to fly the Atlantic,
Inventor of the poem which kills itself.
The poem which gives birth to itself,
The human form, jazz, Jerusalem
And other luminous, luminous galaxies.
You out-spat your enemies.
You irradiated your friends.
Always naked, you shaven, shaking tyger-lamb,
Moon-man, moon-clown, moon-singer, moon-drinker,
You never killed anyone.
Blakehead, babyhead,
Accept this mug of crude red wine –
I love you.

For David Mercer

I like dancers who stamp.
Elegance
Is for certain trees, some birds,
Expensive duchesses, expensive whores,
Elegance, it's a small thing
Useful to minor poets and minor footballers.
But big dancers, they stamp and they stamp fast,
Trying to keep their balance on the globe.
Stamp, to make sure the earth's still there,
Stamp, so the earth knows that they're dancing.
Oh the music puffs and bangs along beside them
And the dancers sweat, they like sweating
As the lovely drops slide down their scarlet skin
Or shake off into the air
Like notes of music.
I like dancers, like you, who sweat and stamp
And crack the ceiling when they jump.

Hear the Voice of the Critic

There are too many colours.
The Union Jack's all right, selective,
Two basic colours and one negative,
Reasonable, avoids confusion.
    (Of course I respect the red, white and blue)

But there are too many colours.
The rainbow, well it's gaudy, but I am
Bound to admit, a useful diagram
When treated as an optical illusion.
    (Now I'm not saying anything against rainbows)

But there are too many colours.
Take the sea. Unclassifiable.
The sky – the worst offender of all,
Tasteless as Shakespeare, especially at sunset.
    (I wish my body were all one colour).

There are too many colours.
I collect flat white plates.
You ought to see my flat white plates.
In my flat white flat I have a perfect set,
    (It takes up seven rooms).

There are too many colours.

The Ballad of the Death of Aeschylus

Eagle flying along
hey hey
Eagle flying along
Swinging his golden all along the hey hey sky

Tortoise rumbling along
hey hey
Tortoise rumbling along
Dreaming of salad if you want the hey hey truth

But that was one heap of an
Astigmatic eagle
Astigmatic eagle
The kind of person
Who looks at a tortoise
And believes he's seeing casserole

Eagle swivelling down
hey hey
Eagle swivelling down
Clamping that tortoise into his beak
Dragging him up into a neighbouring cloud
And shutting the hey hey door

 Aeschylus was steaming through Athens
 Somewhere near the Parthenon Gents
 It is believed
 Aeschylus was steaming through Athens
 Out to get his tragical propens-
 ities relieved

That's the hey hey set up so remember it love
Man down below and an eagle plus a tortoise up above
Better carve that message in a durable cheese
And let it learn you a bit of manners please

It wasn't one of your charter flights
The eagle got Aeschylus in his sights

It was tortoise away and super-zap
Doing kerflumph and possibly BAP
Does anyone want a flat-headed tragedian?

Poor old bloody Aeschylus
hey hey
Poor old bloody Aeschylus
Come to that poor old bloody tortoise

Gaston the Peasant

Gaston liked being a peasant. He enjoyed all the things which peasants usually like, elemental things like being born, living and, something he looked forward to with oafish optimism, dying. Often, seated on a sack of blackened truffles in the steam of the peat fire, he would speak of these things:

'We peasants are almost excessively privileged,' he would vouch, in the expressive dialect of the Basques, 'in that not only do we delight in the elemental joys of Mankind, but also in that we are denied the manifold responsibilities accorded will-he nill-he to the holder of high office.'

Gaston had lived a long time, seen much, known many, done little. He was sketched eating turnips by Van Gogh. D.H. Lawrence dropped in to talk to him about the blood. He once tried to cheer up Emile Zola. Orwell slept with his pigs for the experience. Ernest Hemingway borrowed his pitchfork He did not return. He did not return the pitchfork.

Lady Macbeth in the Saloon Bar Afterwards

It was all going surprisingly well –
Our first school matinee and we'd got up to
My sleepwalking scene with the minimum of titters…
Right, enter me, somnambulistically.
One deep sigh. Then some lout tosses
A banana on to the fore-stage.
It got a round? Darling, it got a thunderstorm!
Of course, we carried on, but suddenly
We had a panto audience
Yelling out: 'Look out! He's behind you!'
Murders, battles, Birnam Wood, great poetry –
All reduced to mockery.
The Bard upstaged by a banana.
Afterwards we had a flaming row in the Grenville
About just who should have removed it
And just when –
One of the servants, obviously.
And ever since, at every performance:
Enter myself in those exquisite ribbons
And – plomp – a new out-front banana.

Well, yes, it does affect all our performances
But actually, they seem to love it.
And how, now Ben's in Canada
Doling out Wesker to the Eskimos,
Can we decide who exits with banana?
You can't expect me to parade down here,
Do a sort of boob-baring curtsey and announce:
'Is this a banana that I see before me?'
Anyway, darling, we may have egg on our faces –
But we've got a hit on our hands.

To the Organisers of a Poetry Reading by Hugh MacDiarmid

You chose the wrong place –
A neutral room with tawny blinds pulled down.
You pulled the wrong audience –
The gabbiest cultural bureaucrats in town.
You picked the wrong poet –
Too clever too daft too great for you to deserve his spittle

And you brought the wrong whisky
And you only bought him half a bottle.

Private Transport

round and round
his private roundabout
drives the little critic's car –
a sneer on four square wheels

What the Mermaid Told Me

(for the Fiftieth Anniversary of the British Broadcasting Corporation.)

Every sentence in the middle section of the piece was broadcast
by BBC TV during the period 13 July – 12 August 1972.

Strapped on my aqualung and flippered my way
To the bed of the electric ocean.
The water was flickering white and grey
And thick as calamine lotion.
Groped along the rocks till my hand came to rest
On the lukewarm pudding of a mermaid's breast.
She was British, broad, corporate and fiftyish
With a hint of aristocracy
Her top was woman and her arse was fish
And this is what she said to me:

    'How dangerous are these cable cars?
    We have a lot of fun on this show.
    When is all this killing going to stop?
    I think they deserve some applause, don't you?

    'We are very environment-conscious
    This is like a bloody Xmas grotto.
    What if everyone else refused to obey
    The laws of which they don't approve?

    'What does Muswell Hill mean to you?
    Will the ceasefire stick?
    He was not the man to embarrass the police.
    I think they deserve some applause, don't you?

    'I came to an arrangement with him
    To come up with 40 million dollars.
    When I sing my songs you can't sit still,
    Your big toe shoot up in your boot.

    'If only women could get on with women
    Like men get on with men.
    It's lovely for me to be sitting
    In a seat like this again

    'Just in one day our lives were crushed.
    I don't want to be an old curmudgeon.
    Are the five senses enough any more?
    I think they deserve some applause, don't you?

'You're doing to this country what Hitler failed to do.
Has he been the victim of a personal witch-hunt?
He makes no bones about carrying the can
For Rio Tinto Zinc.

'There is going to be a very high attrition rate
In this field of 26 starters,
Look all around, there's nothing but blue skies.
We'll kill 'em all or get back into Cambodia.

'I've had people who've had conversion experiences
Following leucotomy.
You can never be certain of anything in Ireland.
I think they deserve some applause, don't you?

'British public life is singularly free from any taint of corruption at all.
Our towns are almost ready to be destroyed, they are uninhabitable,
They are completely contrary to human life
The British found it necessary to intervene to protect their interests.

There are so few young women in Highbury who are in any way suitable
What has become of your traditional British phlegm and common sense?
We're only giving the public what they want.
I think they deserve some applause, don't you?'

The mermaid was ten thousand times as heavy as me
And the scales of her tail were moulting.
But since she was the hottest thing in the sea
She was also the least revolting.
I proposed a little sexual action
And she smiled (which was mostly gaps),
And she wriggled her satisfaction
As she whispered to me: 'Perhaps.'

A Blessing for Kenneth Patchen's Grave

may hummingbirds
forever hover over
white and purple domes of clover

89

Discovery

Unpopular, Tibetan and four foot two,
He ran an underground cocktail bar
Near the pit-face of a Congolese coal-mine.
Nobody would listen to his stories
So he scribbled them on the backs of beer-mats,
One sentence on each mat.
Because he hated coal
He wrote, mostly, about the sea.

Years later two critics from Cambridge
Spent their honeymoon at the same colliery.
They discovered a black chamber
Empty but for a hundred thousand beer-mats.

After years of beer-mat shuffling and transcription
The critics published the text
As The Fictional Works of Joseph Conrad.
Three cheers for the critics!
Three cheers for Cambridge!
Where would Joseph Conrad be without them?
Down the mine.

Where be Joseph Conrad?
Two hundred yards down in the same Congolese pit,
Serving mint juleps to the husky miners,
Speaking when he is spoken to.

There Are Not Enough of Us

How much verse is magnificent?
Point oh oh oh one per cent.
How much poetry is second-rate?
Around point oh oh oh oh eight.
How much verse is a botched hotch potch?
Ninety-eight per cent by my watch.
How much poetry simply bores?
None of mine and all of yours.

Oscar Wilde in Flight

motherofpearlcoloured feathers
preposterous wingspan
glides over earthscapes waterscapes icescapes
dropping a trail of surprise green blossoms

and archangel Oscar
rolls with laughter as he dives
through the sunset revolving door
of a cloud decked out like the Café Royal

only once in every thousand years
he downs a glass of liquid granite
and privately weeps with memory
for the butchers chopped his wings to stumps
and threw him into Reading Gaol
with the other amputees
he weeps for them
not for himself
then he shakes away his tears

and up he soars again
swinging his way
throughout the blue and white in happy flight

John Keats Eats His Porridge

It was hot enough to blister
The red paint of his mouth.
But if he let it lie there, glistening,
then clipped segments from the circumference,
it slid down like a soggy bobsleigh.

Grey as November, united as the kingdom,
but the longer he stared into that dish of porridge
the more clearly he traced
under the molten sugar
the outline of each flake of oatmeal...

When the milk made its slow blue-tinted leap from jug to bowl
the porridge became an island.
John's spoon vibrated in his hand.
The island became a planet.
He made continents, he made seas.

This is strange porridge.
Eat it all up.

Forster the Flying Fish

Forster the Flying Fish
In a purple tank did dwell.
I say dwell, it sounds damper than 'lived'
And also I would be the first to inform you
Were Forster the Flying Fish to be dead.
And 'did dwell' gives a quirky kind of antiquated
Twist of the wrist to the opening lines,
Good.
I mean the bones of this poem to show
And I make no bones about it.

Forster was named Forster by his master
After the liberal novelist.
Forster the Flying Fish was born to stunt,
At least he thought of himself as a stunt fish
But he never learned the knack of stunting.

Look, I promise you the critics will hate this poem.
They hate all poems they haven't read already.
However, the audience of gentle, wealthy readers
Who drooled over Tarka the Otter, Hazel the Bunny,
Jonathan Livingstone Vulture,
Bebop the Hobbit and Dolly the Wet Hen –
Surely they will salute
Forster the Flying Fish,
The latest Literary animal hero.

Forster the Flying Fish
Had a sidekick –
A slick amphibian called Cissy the Coelacanth.
Together they paddled and lapped round the globe,

Righting the wrongs of the animal kingdom –
Forster taking care of war in the air,
Cissy looking after land jobs.
If you have intelligent pets
Ask them to complete this poem.
I've got stomach ache.

The Oxford Hysteria of English Poetry

Back in the caveman days business was fair.
Used to turn up at Wookey Hole,
Plenty of action down the Hole
Nights when it wasn't raided.
They'd see my bear-gut harp
And the mess at the back of my eyes
And 'Right,' they'd say, 'make poetry.'
So I'd slam away at the three basic chords
And go into the act –
A story about the sabre-toothed tigers with a comic hero,
A sexy one with an anti-wife clubbing twist –
Good progressive stuff mainly,
Get ready for the Bronze Age, all that.
And soon it would be 'Bring out the woad!'
Yeah, woad. We used to get high on woad.

The Vikings only wanted sagas
Full of gigantic deadheads cutting off each other's vitals
Or Beowulf Versus the Bog People.
The Romans weren't much better
Under all that armour you could tell they were soft
With their central heating
And poets with names like Horace.

Under the Normans the language began to clear
Became a pleasure to write in,
Yes, write in, by now everyone was starting
To write down poems.
Well, it saved memorising and improvising
And the peasants couldn't get hold of it.
Soon there were hundreds of us
Most of us writing under the name
Of Geoffrey Chaucer.
Then suddenly we were knee-deep in sonnets.

Holinshed ran a headline:
BONANZA FOR BARDS.
It got fantastic –
Looning around from the bear-pit to the Globe,
All those freak-outs down the Mermaid,
Kit Marlowe coming on like Richard the Two,
A virgin Queen in a ginger wig
And English poetry in full whatsit –
Bloody fantastic, but I never found any time
To do any writing till Willy finally flipped –
Smoking too much of the special stuff
Sir Walter Raleigh was pushing.

Cromwell's time I spent on cultural committees.

Then Charles the Second swung down from the trees
And it was sexual medley time
And the only verses they wanted
Were epigrams on Chloe's breasts
But I only got published on the back of her left knee-cap.

Next came Pope and Dryden
So I went underground.
Don't mess with the Mafia.

Then suddenly – WOOMF –
It was the Ro-man-tic Re-viv-al
And it didn't matter how you wrote,
All the public wanted was a hairy great image.
Before they'd even print you
You had to smoke opium, die of consumption,
Fall in love with your sister
And drown in the Mediterranean (not at Brighton).
My publisher said: 'I'll have to remainder you
Unless you go and live in a lake or something
Like this bloke Wordsworth.'

After that there were about
A thousand years of Tennyson
Who got so bored with himself
That he changed his name
To Kipling at half-time.
Strange that Tennyson should be
Remembered for his poems really,
We always thought of him
As a golfer.

There hasn't been much time
For poetry since the Twenties
What with leaving the Communist Church
To join the Catholic Party
And explaining why in the *CIA Monthly*.
In 1963, for one night only,
I became the fourth Liverpool Marx Brother.
There was Groucho McGough,
Chico Henri, Harpo Patten
And me, I was Zeppo,
Yer, I was Pete Best.
Finally I was given the Chair of Comparative Ambiguity
At Armpit University, Java.
It didn't keep me busy,
But it kept me quiet.
It seemed like poetry had been safely tucked up for the night.

What Is Poetry?
(for Sasho, Daniella, Vladko and Martin Shurbanov)

Look at those naked words dancing together!
Everyone's very embarrassed.
Only one thing to do about it –
Off with your clothes
And join in the dance.
Naked words and people dancing together.
There's going to be trouble.
Here come the Poetry Police!

Keep dancing.

Autumnobile

The forest's throat is sore.
Frost-work. Echoing shouts of friends.
October, in her gold-embroidered nightie,
Floating downstream, little mad flowers shimmering.

The silky fur of her
And her hot fingers curling,
Uncurling round and a sudden shove –
There goes my heart tobogganing,

Down snow, slush, ending stuck in the mud,
That's love! O dig me out of here
And glide me off down Pleasure Street
To the sparkle rink where bears go skating.

I ate pancakes at the funeral.
I ate pancakes and ice-cream too.
The mourners drank like musty flies,
All round Summer's coffin, sucking and buzzing.

The days of dust and nights of gnats
Are over and, covered with raindrop warts,
My friend, the most unpopular Season in school,
Smoking and spitting – Autumn's coming.

How do I love that fool, the Fall?
Like Paraquatted nettles. Like
A two-headed 50p. Like a sick shark.
Like a punchy boxer who can't stop grinning.

Sunshine's rationed. Get in the queue
For a yard of colour, a pound of warm.
Deathbed scenes on the video-sky,
Sunsets like Olivier acting dying.

I feel weightless as a child who's built
Out of nursery bricks with ducks and clocks on.
I eat more sleep. I slap more feet.
Autumn – my marzipan flesh is seething.

I open a book and splash straight into it.
The fire reads all my old newspapers.
I freak across the galaxy on Pegasus
And see the cracked old world, rocking and bleeding.

The saloon doors in my skull swing open,
Out stride a posse of cowboy children
Bearing a cauldron of the magic beans
Which always set my poems quivering.

Now my electric typer purrs,
And now it clackers under my fingers'
Flickering. And now the oily engine
Throbs into hubbub. The Autumnobile is leaving.

Nobody on earth knows where on earth they're going
......

(a hell of a long way after Pushkin and Derzhavin)

Land of Dopes and Loonies

William Shakespeare was loony
Burns was a maniac too
Milton was thoroughly crackers
Yeats was a loony all through
Edward Lear, Shelley and Coleridge,
Whitman and Lawrence and Blake
What a procession of nutters
Looning for poetry's sake
All of the poets were dafties
Dafter when the going got rough
All except William Wordsworth
Who wasn't nearly crazy enough

Leonardo was loopy
So was Toulouse Lautrec
Bosch had all of his screws loose
Van Gogh's head was a wreck
Pablo Picasso was batty
Just take a look at his work
Rembrandt was out of his windmill
Brueghel was bloody berserk
All of the painters were bonkers
In the barmy army of art
All except Sir Joshua Reynolds
And he was a wealthy old Humpty Dumpty...

To a Critic

You don't go to Shakespeare for statistics
You don't go to bed for a religious service
But you want poems like metal mental mazes –
Excuse me while I nervous.

A song can carry so many facts
A song can lift plenty of story
A song can score jokes and curses too
And any amount of glory

But if you overload your dingadong song
With theoretical baggage
Its wings tear along the dotted line
And it droppeth to earth like a cabbage

Yes it droppeth to earth like a bloody great cabbage
And the cabbage begins to rot.
My songs may be childish as paper planes
But they glide – so thanks a lot.

A Sunset Cloud Procession Passing Ralph Steadman's House

1. A cigar-smoking porker drags a small hay-cart from which a jewelled crocodile smiles and waves.

2. A black fried egg struts by, one woolly eyebrow raised like Noel Coward.

3. An emaciated caribou clanks along.

4. An ant-eater inflates a smoker's-lung balloon.

5. Eskimo Jim pulls Auntie Hippo tail-first, but she hangs on to her perambulator full of hippolets.

6. They are pursued by a neolithic Hoover.

7. And followed by Leonardo's Tin Lizzie and Michelangelo as a tumescent frogman, pride of the Sexual Boat Service.

8. A simple mushroom shape, rising one inch every four seconds.

9. Father Time with a crumpled scythe.

10. A whale spouting black shampoo all over its own humpy head.

11. A cocker spaniel taking a free ride on the backbone of a boa-constrictor.

12. And up from out of the dark hill's shoulders rise the shoulders of another, larger, darker hill.

Ode to George Melly

If Bonzo the Dog got resurrected he could leap like you
If Satan the Snake ate Adam's birthday cake he would creep like you
If Liz Bat Queen wasn't pound-note green she'd hand the Crown to you –
For nothing on earth falls down like George Melly do.

For the Eightieth Birthday of Hoagy Carmichael
(*22 November 1979*)

Hoagland – white waterfall piano keys!
Old rockin' chairs to help us all think mellow!
Always-Fall forests of star-tall trees
Growing chords of gold, brown, red and yellow!
Yes, Hoagland, friendliest of all countries.

Casual is, I guess, as casual does,
And you casually sing and casually knock us sideways.
Rolling songs riding the river's tideways,
Mist-songs gliding, city-songs that buzz.
I wander Hoagland pathways when dusk falls.
Celia strolls with me as wild and tame
Hoagland bird-folk enchant us with their calls.
Anyone who has ears grins at your name.
Eighty years of great songs! I wish you would
Live on as long as your good Hoagland life feels good.

NOTES: *a. Hoagland is Mr Carmichael's official Christian name.*
b. Celia is my wife's name.

Happy Fiftieth Deathbed

D.H. Lawrence on the dodgem cars
Sniffing the smell of the electric stars
Cool black angel jumps up beside
Sorry David Herbert it's the end of your ride

Thank you very much Mr D.H. Lawrence
Thank you very much
Thank you very much Mr D.H. Lawrence
For *The Rainbow* and such

D.H. Lawrence with naughty Mrs Brown
Trying to play her hurdy-gurdy upside-down
In comes Mr Brown and he says Veronica
May I accompany on my harmonica

Thank you very much Mr D.H. Lawrence
Thank you very much
Thank you very much Mr D.H. Lawrence
Back to your hutch

D.H. Lawrence met Freud in a dream
Selling stop me and buy one Eldorado ice cream
Siggie says you ought to call your stories
Knickerbocker Splits and Banana Glories

Thank you very much Mr D.H. Lawrence
Thank you very much
Thank you very much Mr D.H. Lawrence
Keep in touch

The Call
(*or* Does The Apple Tree Hate Plums?)

i was standing in my room
the whirling tape was singing:
i'm never going back
i'm never going back.

i read four lines by Elaine Feinstein
the tears jumped in my eyes.
i read eight lines by Allen Ginsberg
and electricity sprang
from the soles of my feet
and the electric flames
danced on the roof of my skull.

someone calling
my self calling to myself
the call i'd been hoping for

let yourself sing it said
let yourself dance
let yourself be
an apple tree

i wrote this daftness down
then smiled and smiled
and said aloud
thank you thank you

you may want money
you may want pears
you may want bayonets
or tears

shake me as hard as you like
only apples will fall
apples   apples   and apples

Lament for the Welsh Makers

WILLIAM DUNBAR sang piteously
When he mourned for the Makers of poetry.
He engraved their names with this commentary –
Timor mortis conturbat me.

DUNBAR, I'm Scot-begotten too,
But I would celebrate a few
Welsh masters of the wizardry –
The fear of death moves inside me.

'After the feasting, silence fell.'
ANEIRIN knew how the dead smell.
Now he has joined their company.
The fear of death moves inside me.

TALIESIN, born of earth and clay,
Primroses, the ninth wave's spray
And nettle flowers, where is he?
The fear of death moves inside me.

LLYWARCH's sons numbered twenty-four.
Each one was eaten by the war.
He lived to curse senility.
The fear of death moves inside me.

TALHAEARN and AROFAN,
AFAN FERDDIG and MORFRAN
Are lost, with all their poetry.
The fear of death moves inside me.

MYRDDIN sang, a silver bell,
But from the battlefield he fell
Into a deep insanity.
The fear of death moves inside me.

GWALCHMAI, who sang of Anglesey
And a girl like snowfall on a tree
And lions too, lies silently –
The fear of death moves inside me.

CYNDDELW's balladry was sold
For women's kisses and men's gold.
His shop is shut permanently.
The fear of death moves inside me.

HYWEL chanted Meirionnydd's charm.
His pillow was a girl's white arm.
Now he is whiter far than she.
The fear of death moves inside me.

PRYDYDD Y MOCH would smile to see
An Englishman – if he was maggoty.
Now he is grinning bonily.
The fear of death moves inside me.

DAFYDD AP GWILYM did women much good
At the cuckoo's church in the green wood.
Death ended his sweet ministry.
The fear of death moves inside me.

GWERFYL MECHAIN wrote in cheerful tones
Of the human body's tropical zones.
She shared DAFYDD's hot philosophy.
The fear of death moves inside me.

IOLO GOCH wrote of any old thing –
Girls, feasts and even an English King.
They say he died most professionally.
The fear of death moves inside me.

GRUFFUDD GRYG wept desperately
For the North of Wales in her poverty.
He was a bird from heaven's country.
The fear of death moves inside me.

LLYWELYN GOGH's fist dared to knock
On the heavy door with the black steel lock.
A skull told him its history.
The fear of death moves inside me.

SION CENT, who sang thank you to his purse,
RHYS GOGH, who killed a fox with verse,
Sleep in the gravel dormitory.
The fear of death moves inside me.

IEUAN AP RHYDDERCH so scholarly,
GWERFUL MADOG of famed hospitality,
LEWYS GLYN COTHI who loved luxury –
The fear of death moves inside me.

DAFYDD AP EDMWND's singing skill
Thrilled through all Wales. Then it fell still.
LEWYS MON wrote his elegy.
The fear of death moves inside me.

BEDO BRWNLLYS, IEUAN DEULWYN,
GUTYN OWAIN, TUDUR PENLLYN,
All exiles in Death's monarchy.
The fear of death moves inside me.

Life was dark-coloured to TUDUR ALED.
WILLIAM LLYN brooded on the dead.
SION TUDUR mocked all vanity.
The fear of death moves inside me.

DIC HUWS dedicated a roundelay
To a girl by the name of Break of Day.
Night broke on both of them, remorselessly –
The fear of death moves inside me.

And hundreds have since joined the towering choir –
Poets of Wales, like trees on fire,
Light the black twentieth century.
The fear of death moves inside me.

Oh DYLAN THOMAS, as bright as nails,
Could make no kind of a living in Wales
So he died of American charity.
The fear of death moves inside me.

Terror of death, terror of death,
Terror of death, terror of death,
That drumbeat sounds relentlessly.
The fear of death moves inside me.

Since we must all of us ride down
The black hill into the black town,
Let us sing out courageously.
The fear of death moves inside me.

The black lungs swell, the black harp sighs,
Whenever a Welsh maker dies.
Forgive my nervous balladry.
Timor mortis conturbat me.

LOVE, THE APEMAN, CURSES, BLESSINGS AND FRIENDS

Good Day

the day was like molten glass
i sauntered around with a carnival heart
picking up the puppies other people threw away
and arranging them in my pouch

yes the day was like molten glass
so i took my spade down the old peninsula
dug a channel across its neck and watched the sea jump through
then drank to the health of a new island

well the day was like molten glass
sunshine greeting me like a big irish doctor
blackberries tapping out a rhythm on their leaves
tight enough and bright enough to set a donkey dancing

i said the day was like molten glass
the fingers of the cruising breezes
massaged the tensions out of my head
and i loved my love with an a and an ab and everything down to zed

Celia Celia

When I am sad and weary
When I think all hope has gone
When I walk along High Holborn
I think of you with nothing on

Footnotes on Celia Celia

Used to slouch along High Holborn
in my gruesome solo lunch-hours.
It was entirely lined
with Gothick insurance offices
except for one oblong block of a shop
called Gamages,
where, once,
drunk, on Christmas Eve,
I bought myself a battery-operated Japanese pig
with a chef's hat on top of his head
and a metal stove which lit up red
and the pig moved a frying pan up and down with his hand
and tossed a plastic fried egg into the air
and caught it again the other way up
and then tossed it and caught it again and again
all the time emitting squeals of excitement
through a series of holes in the top of his head –

but apart from that...I want to forget High Holborn.

September Love Poem

I flop into our bed with Thee,
Ovaltine and warm milk-o
And there we lie in ecstasy
Watching Sergeant Bilko.

All Fool's Day

A man sits counting the days of Spring.
His hands may tremble but his mind won't stir,
And one thought runs through all his watching:
'I would have burnt my heart for her.

'If she had recognised my face
As I knew hers, and listened to me sing,
I would have left the careless human race
For one hour of her careful loving.

'When spring swings round again, and I am here,
I will forget the terrors of her voice –
But I would stay with terror at my ear
And burn my heart, if I had any choice.'

Riddle

Their tongues are knives, their forks are hands and feet.
They feed each other through their skins and eat
Religiously the spiced, symbolic meat.
The loving oven cooks them in its heat –
Two curried lovers on a rice-white sheet.

Take Stalk Between Teeth Pull Stalk From Blossom Throw Blossom Overarm Towards Enemy Lie Flat And Await Explosion

I staggered in the garage and handed them my heart.
'Can you overhaul it cos the bloody thing won't start?'
They hammered it and sprayed it till it looked just like a toad,
They told me that it shouldn't be allowed on the road.
They said I'd better trade it for a psych-e-del-ic screen.
They said 'What d'you call this aboriginal machine?'
I said
It's a rose I suppose.

A unicorn is bathing in the shallows of your eyes.
You've got a mouth that's whispering between your thighs
You bring me foreign honeycombs and science fiction ties
And every time you touch me you declare your surprise.
Your language is a code that I haven't yet cracked
So I can't be sure of your message or a fact
But
It's a rose I suppose.

When they see us walking, they're puzzled what to say.
We're so obvious in a mysterious way –
Clouds that fly south when the wind goes east,
Hovercraft feet and faces all creased
We draw our wages in musical wine
And what our business is, well that's harder to define
But
It's a rose I suppose.

Well Tennyson's on television selling bad breath.
Lyndon's in the pulpit and the sermon is death.
Hitler's in the bunker playing nuclear chess,
Judas got a column on the *Sunday Express*.
The zombies are lurching all over the town,
There's only one weapon seems to bring them all down
And
It's a rose I suppose.

Top-Notch Erotic Moment Thank You

the slime was soaking through my khaki
barbed wire scratching the star-bomb sky
my rifle was heavy as Europe
as i prayed to the snipers for a Blighty
then her breast brushed my shoulder

a thousand thousand lights were clicking at each other
yes the galaxies inside my head were coming good
and i was a visionary scientist on the verge
of creating a multi-versal language and a source of free food
then her breast brushed my shoulder

i was studying despair in Kentish Town Road
and i began to envy a torn cardboard box saying Oxo
being blown along the gutter by a tough November
in the general direction of Euston Station
then her breast brushed my shoulder

now i sit in a dark armchair and think about it
and first i smile about it and then i nearly cry about it
and i know i'm so knotted i'll do nothing about it
but write these lines to remind me of how my ribs went twang
when her breast brushed my shoulder

Coming Back

this auburn autumn
this free-for-all
free-fall fall

the trees are making so much money
that the river's bulging with gold

and i'm coming back to life,
                              love,
i'm coming back to leaf

The Angels in Our Heads

Our angels, spiralling,
Climb the sky like two, like one,
With wings flowing and easy-going
Rippling the current of the sun.

Altitude one hundred miles.
Our angels level out and hover,
Humming delirious pop songs,
Quivering at each other.

Silent suddenly, they shrug
Their rainbow wings around each other.
A thousand multi-coloured hairs
Vibrate along each feather.

And then they drop.
Birds in crowds
Watch and admire from
Grandstand clouds.

The angels both spreadeagle, braking,
Over the ocean, gold and deep.
They slide into its heated waters
To sing in bubbles in their sleep.

Waking, they wander underwater,
Gulping the seasoned sea food, free,
Then they take off in fifty yards
Sprinting across the surface of the sea,

Circling waterbirds, circling higher,
Those weighty feathers dry, and then
Zoom up to a hundred miles
And – there they go again.

But when they look out through our eyes
To see the rain piercing like wire
Or the white wind throw hurtful snow
Burying men in drifts of pain and fire

Sometimes our angels hunch and huddle,
Grounded, sad ducks stuck.
But they should moult and stomp outside,
Socialists fighting dirty luck.

For they can talk or march against the winter,
Get home in time for aerobatics, try
To teach their children to be flyers and swimmers
In a warm planet with a cleaner sky.

Out

when I broke the light bulb an orange dropped out
when I peeled the orange a rabbit jumped out
when I shook the rabbit a parcel dropped out
when I opened the parcel your house fell out
when I rang the doorbell you were out

To a Godly Man

Don't waffle to me about Kingdom Come
I've often loitered there.
My left hand was on Celia's bum,
My right hand in her hair.

Hello Adrian
(for Adrian Henri)

Hello Adrian – I just crawled out the far side of Xmas to scrawl my report
           on the wall
We breathed nothing but wine all the time till the group got liquidated on the
           twelfth day with turkey soup.
Well it was a feast of the beast and half the animals were kissing
           when they weren't pissing
Though there were days when the haze turned jagged and I walked into a room
           full of stainless smiles and white tiles –

           But I will confess
I never had it
           Halfway up a pylon
Never had it
           Under the stage during a performance of Ibsen's
           An Enemy of the People
Never had it
           In the Whispering Gallery at St Paul's
Never had it
           Up against a parking meter

           But where – it doesn't matter
           When – it doesn't count
           All you got to total
           Is the total amount

           They're doing it for peace
           Doing it for war
           There's only one good reason
           For doing it for

           CHORUS:
           Fuck for fun (Fuck fuck fuck for fun)
           Fuck for fun (Fuck fuck fuck for fun)
           Fuck for fun (Fuck fuck fuck for fun)
           Everybody want to (boom boom)
           Fuck for fun.

           They're doing it in Paris
            'Cos it taste so sweet
           They do it by the Mersey
           'Cos they like that beat

They doing it for Mother
Doing it for Freud
Reginald Plantagenet
Somerset-Boyd

(CHORUS)

They do it for publicity
Doing it for cash
Might as well be robots
The way they bash

They do it in Chicago
Just to fool the fuzz
They do it down in London
Just 'cos Mick Jagger does

(CHORUS)

They do it up in Edinburgh
With cannon balls
Newcastle girls do it
High on the walls

Now there's too little action
Too much talk
When the bottle's open
Throw away the cork

(CHORUS)

Well North Riding girls taste of cedarwood
South Riding girls cook the wildest pud
East Riding girls melt your soul like lard
West Riding girls well they try bloody hard
North East West South side by side
What you care so long as they ride
So ride your lover
Get on your little lover and ride

They do it in the Palace
To preserve the line
But we're going to do it
'Cos it feels so fine

I've got a red-hearted woman
I'm a socialist man
We've got a great leap forward
And a five year plan

(CHORUS)

An eye for an eye
Tit for tat
Batman fuck Robin
And Robin fuck a bat

Fuck for fun (Fuck fuck fuck for fun)
Fuck for fun (Fuck fuck fuck for fun)
Doesn't matter if you're incredibly old or absurdly young
C'mon everybody and (boom boom)
Fuck for fun.

THE COLLECTED WORKS OF APEMAN MUDGEON

Apeman Keep Thinking It's Wednesday

Woken up in fork of tree
By usual jungle jangle
No tom-toms.
No metal bird
Full of Nazi paratroops.
Jumped down
THELONK!
Into turtle pool,
Splashed massive torso.
Searched for berries with mate.
Ate berries with mate and young.
Groomed mate. Groomed by mate.
Groomed young.
Sent young to learn
Ways of jungle.
Bashed chest with fists,
Gave mighty howl,
Loped off into undergrowth to hunt.
Lay along thick branch,
Saw longhorned poem approaching.
Dropped on poem's back,
Grabbed its neck.
Big poem, threw me off.
Bump on head.
Tried liana swinging.
Good swinging.
Ninth liana bad liana,
Dropped me on rock.
Ankle go blue.
At water-hole discussed crocodiles
With seminar of chimpanzees.
Inspected poem-traps.
Only found one squeaky poem
Without a tail.
Too small, let it go.
Limped back to tree.
Told mate and young
About head and ankle.
Mate said she caught fish.
Ate fish with mate and young.
Fish taste like a good poem.

Sent young up trunk into tree.
Mated with mate.
Climbed up trunk.
Lay down in fork of tree.
Huge moon.
Dreamed about a poem stampede.

The Apeman Who Hated Snakes

Was an apeman lived next door to me
In some kind of prickly tree.

That apeman had the angry shakes
Spending all his sleep in dreams about snakes.

And every morning he would shout
How all the snakes have to be stamp out.

Pastime he enjoy the best
Was to poke a stick down a mamba's nest

Or he'd have a slaughter down the old snake-pit
And look pretty happy at the end of it.

He tattooed snakes all over his skin
Coiling and hissing from knees to chin.

For breakfast he hard-boiled the eggs of snakes.
Suppertime – Boa-constrictor steaks.

For a man who hated reptiles so obsessively
He spend an awful lot of time in their company.

Now where that apeman lived next door to me
There's a vacancy in that prickly tree.

I reckon snakes are like me and you –
They got a mystery job to do.

So when I see one in my path I salute
And take a roundabout alternative route.

The Apeman's Hairy Body Song

Happy to be hairy
Happy to be hairy
When the breezes tickle
The hairs of my body

Happy to be hairy
Happy to be hairy
Next best thing
To having feathers

Apeman Gives a Poetry Reading

Apeman travel much in jungle
Sometimes he swing for many miles
To taxi down in some new clearing
No concert posters up on trees
Tiger who arranged the gig
Has gone down with sabre-tooth-ache.
Gazelle apologises nervously.
Apeman and gazelle shift rocks around
To form a semi-circle.
Two or three crocodiles trundle in.
Four flying squirrels. One sloth.
Various reptiles and a fruit-bat.
Suddenly – ten-eleven multi-colour birds.
Apeman cheers up.
Gazelle checks time by the sun,
Introduces apeman.
Apeman performs a series
Of variegated apeman howls –
Comic howls, sad howls, angry-desperate howls.
Apeman runs out of howl, sits down.
Senior crocodile asks questions:
What use is howling?
Howling does not change jungle.
Apeman stares at him,
Nods, shakes his head, gives up.

Animals begin to drift to holes and nests.
Apeman swings home heavily through the gloom.
If you meet apeman in this mood
Give him a hug.
Unless your name is Boa-constrictor.

Apeman as Tourist Guide

Apeman show you round Jungle?
All right.

Big cliff with holes in
Is baboon high-rise development.
Dusty clearing
With banyan tree full of honking birds
Is discotheque for elephants.
Quick! Jump in water – breathe through hollow reed –
Safari party of lions going by.

Tell you something:
Apeman love this
Hot and rowdy jungle.
Tell you something else:
Jungle not all like this.

You keep on walking
And sooner or later
You will find the other jungle –

The frozen jungle.
Black ice
On every branch, tendril,
Pool, path, animal and man.

Black ice jungle
Where it's too cold
To see or hear
Too cold
To feel too cold to think
As heart and brains
Turn into black turn into ice.

Don't you worry.
Most of the jungle
Given over to
Sweaty celebration.
You may not stumble into
Black ice jungle
For years and years.

You like to see
River of boiling rock
Or giraffe motorway?
No? Got to catch boat?
Go well. Got any shiny discs
So Apeman can buy firewater?

The Apeman's Motives

He not hunt the poem for money –
The kind he catch fetch nowt.
He no hunt the poem for fun –
He not a very good sport.
Apeman go after poem
With fists and teeth and feet
Because he need the juices
Contained in the poem meat.

*   *   *

Confession

Of course I've been corrupted by publicity
A friendly journalist once likened me to Bogart
And I took to exposing my upper teeth when I smiled at enemies

Several years later I was in a theatre
At the same time as Lauren Bacall
And she was so beautiful I could only look at her for two seconds

And that was enough,
Sam, that was plenty.

Self-Congratulating, Self-Deprecating, Auto-Destructive Blues

If you're betting on the horses, you know you've got to follow form
Got to vet up on the set-up and get up and bet on form,
I was losing losing losing before I was even born.

You may come from Venezuela, but I was born on Mars,
Venice or Venus or Venezuela, but I was raised on Mars,
I've got a head full of meteorites, heart full of little green children
and balls full of shooting stars.

So if you want a good investment, better not buy me.
I'm on the edge of the ledge and I'm not gilt-edge so your broker will
advise I'm a joker so get wise and don't buy me.
Some men are like insurance, but I'm more like – suck it and see.

I Passed for Sane

If I'd been born without a mind
I would be happy, tame and kind.
People came, saying good things.
So many people, saying good things.
I hid my eyes under my skin
And so they never saw right in.

120

Sometimes I Feel Like a Childless Mother

My hands shake, my eyelids tremble.
The tigers in my head assemble.

The Institution

The crazy talkers in my head
Steal lights and moments when they can;
Beat at the windows to be fed
Or listen to the sounds of rain.
They stroll, they shout at passing Man,
And in extremes they form a plan
To drown at night, or catch a train.

Simple as glass, they wander through
The colours of my twenty years
Singing and whispering the true
And false of all my private cares;
Inflated songs that shrink to fears.
My chest is thick, so no one hears
The lovely mute who kicks and tears...

A Slow Boat to Trafalgar

I was born in a country called Bloody Strange
With the means of seduction, prostitution and derange
I was red all through and I was raw on top
I had a billion megatons and nowhere to drop
I was a suitable case
A suitable case
A suitable case for
Urgghh.

Married ten times to the gulp next door
She was twenty to virgin and half past whore
We had a mini monster and we called him Meat
And he sucked our cold sweat through a teat
He was a suitable case
A suitable case
A suitable case for
Aaragghh.

Martian mother and Venusian father
But I tadpoled out of the shaving lather
Here come the State chewing Gandhi on toast
Send your subscriptions to the Rolly-Poly Ghost
He's an accusable suit
An unstable goose
A two-sable sake for
Raarhh.

A Machine That Makes Love and Poems and Mistakes

The whirring stops, the door in my chest
Slides open. Fatty squeezes out
Smiling like silver. An airliner staircase
Appears under his first step. He podges down
Applauding himself with padded palms.

Next Jagged, wearing his frayed-wire suit,
Scales my legs, jerks through the door and pulls
My starting handle. Thought-gears grind.
He's muddled, pressing all my buttons
Too hard. Not hard enough. His blood is caffeine.

He exits limping, gladly. Then he flops
Prone on the tarmac, hiding his splintered eyes.
His place is taken. This one's a prodigy,
A milk-faced boy of five who sings to himself
As he tries to play tunes with knobs and levers.

I've got other mechanics. Sometimes they fight
Over my delicate controls. They strike,
Or try to make me fly. They blow my fuses.
Just now I didn't answer. You caught me between shifts.
Ask again now. Someone will answer you.

Toy Stone

I dived and found it.

A wedge of stone,
Grey mixed with the mauve
Of sky before snow.
Flakes of crystal
Shining among its mineral clouds.

Now and again I look at the stone,
Convert it into the relief map
Of a nude island or the night sky.
Or use it as a racquet
For bouncing light into my eyes.

Today I took it with my eyes shut.
Turning the stone between my hands
I learned
That it shares the shape and weight
Of a small pistol.

Now it has a barrel,
A chamber and a butt.
Held by the barrel, it could be used
To bash almost anything to death.
Stone-shine is in my head,
But so is the killing weight of the stone.

Toy stone, weapon stone.
I will keep it.

Unfulfilled Suicide Note

because there is a golden plastic arrow on the desk in front of me
because my stomach is heavy and drags downwards
because I cannot find anything
because I cannot understand anything
because I am afraid of everyone
because there is a small amount of snow on the ground outside

And Some Lemonade Too

Drinking gin eating curry
That's my second favourite game
Begin feeling hollow
Then you sip and swallow
Till they start to taste about the same
Well gin got a bite
Curry got a burn
Try to teach your tongue to take them in turn
Drinking gin eating curry
Shoobi doobi wah wah

Drinking gin eating curry
Feeling my way to my ease
When the curry was dead
The gin hit my head
Till I fell down on my knees
Curry's ambrosia
Gin is the elixir
I am the champion concrete-mixer
Eating gin drinking curry
Shoobi doobi wah wah

Drinking gin eating curry
Gulped down all my trouble
Spent a magical sleep
In a happy old heap
And woke up with chutney-flavour alcohol stubble
Took a look at heaven
Took a look at hell
Reckoned I fancied them equally well
Sinking gin and beating curry
Wah wah shoobi doobi wah wah wah

It's a Clean Machine

(to the Beatles and Albert Hunt)

A cop needs a gangster, gangsters need cops,
Fire against fire and it never stops,
But I don't want a fire, I've got underskin heating
Thank you.

They know what we're afraid of:
Soundproof cellars, rhinoceros hide,
Genital electrodes, kneecap sledgehammers,
The moment when they take off your shoes –
All of the commonplace terrors.
But I won't name my own special fears,
Thank you.

I have been a one-man band to the galaxies over Bradford
As I skated over the rust-coloured pavements singing:

    Ten cents a dance, that's what they pay me
    A four-legged friend, a four-legged friend, he'll never let you down.
    Oh you can knock me down, stamp on my face, slander my name
    all over the place
    But we'll meet again, don't know where, don't know when –
    There is a laughing policeman, lives along our street,
    You can hear him laughing, when he's on the beat –
    Oh R, I say R-A,
    R-A-T, R-A-T-T,
    R-A-T-T-F, R-A-T-T-F-I-N-K,
    Ratfink (brawawa) Ratfink (brawawa),
    Mona Lisa Mona Lisa men have named you
    So squeeze my lemon baby till the juice runs down my leg –

Singing dangerously
As I bulged with the dynamite sticks of love.
They never caught me yet, but they keep trying.

It happens every day.
I'm standing down the lavatory end
Of a shadow-inhabited bar
When in walks the winter gangster-cop
And everyone he passes is gripped by his metal hand
And they wince as the grip tightens
And their faces sag as the grip relaxes.

The loudspeaker says:
An invitation to the glittering world of Robert Farnon –
Then he acts.
His icicles focus on my eyes.
Capone or Fabian, he yawns.
His iced knees, like car bumpers,
persuade me to the glittering pavement
Where his wide-shouldered Mercedes waits to eat me.
So far, so bad.

But they never warned him at headquarters,
They never told him the end of the story,
They never told him the way it always ends.

For here they come, sudden surrounders,
All of them laughing, all around us,
The gentle, fire-fighting cavalry,
House-high on ladders, crouched to hydrants,
Flashing their scarlet down the boulevard,
Hoses jumping with the pressure of water from
A thousand Welsh waterfalls, a hundred thousand lochs,
Aiming their polished, jerking nozzles –

And here I wish I could record all of their names but they know who they
are, the men and women and children I love and those who love me and may
the two lists always coincide –

All my friends, crimson, helmeted, hatchet-holstered.
Their hoses slosh him down slush-flushing gutters and:
I'm sorry Adrian, I'm sorry, he drizzles,
I didn't know you were a member of the Fire Brigade.

The Sun Likes Me

'The sun likes me' – Spanish way of saying 'I like the sun'

The sun likes me.
Maybe I've been lying out in the Mayakovsky too long.
Maybe my mind's been a breast-stroke commuter between London and
New York too long.
Maybe I've been longing too long.

The sun likes me.
Maybe it's because my dynamic tension comic-strip bible hath taught me that
it's better to kick sand into the sunlight and watch how it shimmers
than kick it in a twenty-stone muscleman's face.
And maybe it's because my atoms won't stand still because they want to rock
and roll all over the place –

But she taught me to say it.
I was near enough to lick her
And I licked her like the sun licks me and
WOW
She was a buxom anchovy.
Through both our sunrise sunset bodies I heard her say:
'Repeat it after me –
The sun likes me.'
So I said it (and I believe it):
The sun likes me.
I woke up full of business.
After a two-day year at the Registry of Companies I discovered that a 61 per
cent majority on the board of the sun was held by a holding company
(Sol Investments) represented by Phoebus Nominees who were
nominated by a legalistic fabrication called Icarus Consolidation
half-immersed in liquidation.
And the only stockholder –
Thanks to Auntie Irma's will –
The only stockholder
Was ME.
I seem to have changed.
The sun likes me.
I'm indifferent.
The sun doesn't like me.
See if I care.
For like it or lump it,
I own it.

Last week I found I'd left my Barclaycard in *Das Kapital* but when the bill came round I simply reached into my asbestos wallet, produced the aforesaid golden disc or orb and you should have seen the faces of the waiters or their feet for that matter as they blushed to the colour of burnt semolina –

> Because I own the sun,
> The only one.
> Mine, mine,
> Sixty-one per cent of it,
>   MINE.

Self Critic

who is it trips me in the jig?
she wears a cast-iron dress
and growls because i can't recall her name –
my heavy-heartedness.

it's Radio 2, it's after-flu,
it's the Water Board's statement to the Press,
it's the sonic boom above the toothache room –
my heavy-heartedness.

got a weighty parcel shaped like awkwardness
wrapped in slippery plastic stuff.
trying to get my hands to clasp around it
but my arms aren't quite lengthy enough.
everybody thinks i'm carrying a bomb
but it's a book from a beautiful press.
oh the rain gets chiller and the buses get fuller
and the forecast – heavy-heartedness.

who's that extra-awful character in my plays
from the SS Officer's Mess
who makes hour-long speeches that you can't quite hear?
my heavy-heartedness.

so if I sink in the drink and sing *Sentimental Journey*
and then clown and fall down in a mess,
i'm just trying to kick that gangster out of my soul –
my heavy-heartedness.

Adrian Mitchell's Famous Weak Bladder Blues

Now some praise God because he gave us the bomb to drop in 1945
But I thank the Lord for equipping me with the fastest cock alive.

You may think a sten-gun's frequent, you can call greased lightning fast,
But race them down to the Piccadilly bog and watch me zooming past.

    Well it's excuse me,
    And I'll be back.
    Door locked so ra–a-tat-tat.
    You mind if I go first?
    I'm holding this cloudburst.
    I'll be out in 3.7 seconds flat.

I've got the Adamant Trophy, the Niagara Cup, you should see me on the M1 run,
For at every comfort station I've got a reputation for – doing the ton.

Once I met that Speedy Gonzales and he was first through the door.
But I was unzipped, let rip, zipped again and out before he could even draw.

Now God killed John Lennon and he let Barry Manilow survive,
But the good Lord blessed little Adrian Mitchell with the fastest cock alive.

A Ballad of Human Nature

The Buddha sat on a banana crate
Sunning his mind in the shade,
Trying to imagine Aggressive,
Trying to imagine Afraid.

A man staggered up to the Buddha,
He was horrified and thin.
He was hacking with a knife at his body,
Paring his own skin.

The Buddha said: 'Be kind to yourself.'
The thin man lowered his knife;
Then he said, as his blood ran into the earth:
'Where've you been all your life?
'You know, you can't change human nature just like that.
I once saw it proved in a book by a scientist's rat.
We're jellies shaking with atavistic greed.
You can't change human nature – you may as well bleed.'

This Friend

I've got this friend you see and it was the Cuba crisis and the voices were
telling him that there was a plot to set the world on fire and so he shook his
way round London lurching deliberately into policemen so they took him in
and they knocked out his front teeth and all the time they were knocking out
his front teeth they were calling him SIR and after he had been in Brixton for
a week or maybe more he doesn't remember they decided he was mad.

This friend now carries a certificate which guarantees that he is schizophrenic.

Birthdays
(for Ray Charles)

You shout that you're drowning,
You give it everything.
A manager walks by and says:
'That little cat can sing.'
You go to bed mad
And you think that's bad
But what you going to do
When you wake up mad?
There'll be no more birthdays.

I'm talking about
Pain man and fear man and shock man and death man,
Not the Hollywood kind.

I'm talking about
Man made of bone made of wood made of stone
By some Frankenstein.
Talking about
Pain man and fear man and shock man and death man,
The crumbling mind.

There was this astronaut
And one day he found
He couldn't talk
Any more to the ground.
The instruments said
He was stuck for eighty years,
His helmet began
To fill up with tears –
And it was his BIRTHDAY.

I'm talking about
Pain man and fear man and shock man and death man,
Not the Hollywood kind.
I'm talking about
Man made of bone made of wood made of stone
By some Frankenstein.
Talking about
Pain man and fear man and shock man and death man
The crumbling mind.

The Only Electrical Crystal Ball I Ever Saw Flickering Behind a Bar

What colour?
O the colour of an apple in love,
A tomfool tomato,
Changing its soft electric moods each second –
Intimate maps, galactic anatomical charts
Never to be repeated.
Well one moment it exploded with every brand of crimson,
The next it was awash with the blue of peace –
Ocean, pacific ocean –
Or became a green place swarmed over by dark canals.

I said to the man behind the bar:
Where does it come from?
He said: I made it myself.
I was so glad I laughed.
I said: Where is it going to?
He laughed.

Sunset over Venus in a goldfish bowl.
Silent jukebox with no money-slot
But pulsing with molten rainbows.
Belisha beacon drunkenly standing,
Head back, mouth open,
Under a hundred-foot-high colourfall
Of brandy soda crème de menthe
Sherry-spiked wine of the country
(Plus a secret formula)
Flowing from a vat with a fuller draught
Than the Tuscarora Deep.

This is no magic melon to solve all our dandruff
But a small machine for giving.
It added some light to my happiness.
It is a good planet.
I call it the earth.

My Dog Eats Nuts Too

(CHEKHOV: *The Cherry Orchard*)

The sperm bank manager shoved me up against the rail
he levelled his gamma ray at my adventure tail
he said I've followed you through fire and flood and firkin
And you'd better explain just what you think you're working

I said:
I'm not a motivational expert you'd better suppose
but the trouble is my brain is a long way behind my nose
I believe in saluting the animals, my motto is dig and have done
but I spend all my problemofleisure grabbing lots of chinese fun

having chinese fun
having chinese fun
you don't need a mantelpiece
when you're having chinese fun

He said:
you're chewing something terrible, show us your expectoration
so I banged the spittoon with western civilisation
he clamped me with his grabbers and shook me till my steeple rung
tell me what's so special he said about chinese fun

having chinese fun
having chinese fun
happy as the hebrides
when I'm having chinese fun

I said:
it moves like a leopard on ice cubes
glows like hot molasses
its a shady bank by the old gulf stream
and there's masses and masses and masses for the masses
giggles every time that it tries to be sensible
striped with sex well it's highly reprehensible
but I'll bring you a cut of it only costs a dollar a ton
and you'll feel like a Zen Gun once you've tasted chinese fun

having chinese fun
having chinese fun
take the moon and rub it all over the surface of the sun
and you'll turn in your badge
when you've had some chinese fun

He tried it.
He liked it.
He said: thank you.

A Spell to Make a Good Time Last

Walk with your lover through a doorway
Walk with your lover through the maytime sunlight
Walk with your lover by a lake

The past is a stone for playing ducks and drakes
The stone is lying at your feet
Skim the stone away across the lake

The future is a stone for playing ducks and drakes
The stone is lying at your feet
Skim the stone away across the lake

Lie down beside the water
Lie down beside your lover
Lie down beside the water
Lie down beside your lover

A Spell to Make a Bad Hour Pass

Unfold your hand
Place all of the bad minutes in a circle
In the palm of your hand

Close your fingers slowly
To form a gentle fist

Slowly turn your fist around
And let your eyes pass slowly
Over all the surface of your fist

Slowly turn your fist around
And let your lips pass slowly
Over all the surface of your fist

Slowly
Tighten your fingers
Slowly
Tighten your fist

The fist is clenched
All the bad minutes are inside it
The fist is clenched
This evil hour is vanishing

Slowly slowly
Unfold the fingers of your hand

The palm of your hand is empty

Rest the back of your hand
Upon your other hand

Look into the palm of your hand
Look deep into your hand

Your hand is full
Your hand is full
Your hand is full of life

A Curse on My Former Bank Manager

May your computer twitch every time it remembers money
until the twitches mount and become a mechanical ache
and may the ache increase until the tapes begin to scream
and may the pus of data burst from its metal skin

and just before the downpour of molten aluminium
may you be preening in front of your computer
and may you be saying to your favourite millionaire
yes it cost nine hundred thousand but it repays every penny

and may the hundred-mile tape which records my debts spring out
like a supersonic two-dimensional boa-constrictor
and may it slip under your faultless collar and surround your hairless neck
and may it tighten and tighten until it has repaid everything I owe you

A Song for Jerry Slattery and His Family

Here's your life, Jerry, they said, go out and spend it –
So he lumbered out into the world and saw that it was good
But could be a darn sight better, but he began to enjoy himself
After first making sure that everyone between him and the horizon
Had a drink in their hand and somebody to talk to...

Surgery: fifty monologues a day, nervous, desperate.
Listen. Advise. Listen. Refer. Listen. Sign a little note.
The troubles of others cascaded through his mind
While his round eyes said I understand yes I understand
As he cared, and comforted, and cured.

Then home to throw the same old wonderful party,
Greeting you by hallooing your name twice then what are you having,
Drawing you into the corner between fireplace and window
To let you in on a joke against the Tories
Or declare his worship for *The Balkan Trilogy* or the Cameron column.

A one-man scrum shoving boredom off the pitch and out through the turnstile.
A one-man Ireland swallowing his sorrows and sharing out his joys.
A one-man summertime for friends among whom he was famous,
He lives in all who loved him, and may we spend our lives
As generously as Jerry, as generously as Johnnie.

Funnyhouse of a Negro
(for Adrienne Kennedy)

A head
beating against a wall
A beautiful head
beating against a wall
The beautiful head of a woman
beating against a wall
The beautiful head of a woman with her wrists and ankles chained
beating against a wall

A million beautiful heads
beating against a wall

And the first brick is shaken loose
topples
and begins to fall

A Curse Against Intruders

*(Written after the house of Cicely Smith, the poet, and Ian Herbert,
the clarinettist, was robbed by a knife-wielding thug)*

Burglar-bungler
Ransom-ransacker
Thug-unhugged-mugger
Orchestra attacker
You who tread maliciously
Into this good Herbertry

Your nerves shall be torn into raffia,
Done most debilitating, grievous harm
And this not through some magic Mafia
Roused by this spell's clanging alarm
But through a slow, gyrating, spiral curse
The which shall corkscrew up you, verse by verse,
Till you'll wish you rode your own hearse –
(I'll soon be hoarse, so I'll be terse) –
A mumping thumping curse and worse
Fall on your heart, that bulged-with-poison purse.

You, Scowler with the Knife, may gulp
Before you slash a clarinettist's hands.
Behind you a rock-wielding poet stands
Ready to crush you into dismal pulp.

Piss off! Piss off you fart-filled fool!
Your arteries I'll use for wool
And when I've plained them and I've purled
You'll be right knitted up, then hurled
Into the Dustbin of the Universe.
These are the best people in the world
And you had better never ever trouble them
Or I'll take your worst scares and double them
And I'll take your best hopes and rubble them.

For Gordon Snell – My Best, First and Finest Friend – on His Fiftieth Birthday

'By and by they all are dead' – stage direction at the end of an early play by Gordon Snell, writer for grown-ups and children. 'By and by is easily said' – Hamlet in Hamlet, *a part once played by Gordon Snell.*

By and by they all are dead –
The people, animals, earth and sky.
By and by is easily said.

Any child who has ever read
Knows that Book People cannot die.
By and by they all are dead?

Peter Rabbit's still raiding the potting shed
Under Long John Silver's laser eye.
By and by is easily said,

But Alice and the Golux tread
Emerald Oz where the Jumblies fly.
By and by they all are dead?

Lorna Doone and Just William wed
Where The Wild Things Are with Harriet the Spy.
By and by is easily said...

Gordon – the creatures your fancy has bred
Shall live with them – that's the sweet By-and-By!
By and by they all are dead?
By and by is easily said!

My Parents

My father died the other day and I would like to write about him. Because I think of them together, this means also writing about my mother, who died several years ago.

About a thousand people called her Kay, most of them people she helped at some time, for she was what chintzy villains call a 'do-gooder'. Nobody ever called her that to her face or in my family's hearing; if they had, she'd have felt sorry for them. Both her brothers were killed in the First World War. She wore two poppies on Remembrance Day. She divided her life between loving her family, bullying or laughing innumerable committees into action rather than talk, giving, plotting happiness for other people, and keeping up an exuberant correspondence with several hundred friends.

She was not afraid of anyone. She was right. A Fabian near-pacifist, she encouraged me to argue, assuming right-wing positions sometimes so that I was forced to fight and win the discussion.

She tried to hoist the whole world on her shoulders. After each of her first two cancer operations, on her breasts, she seemed to clench her fists and double the energy with which she gave. She wasn't interested in unshared pleasure.

After the second operation she answered the door one day to a poor woman whom she didn't know. The woman asked where 'the wise woman' lived. My mother knew who she meant – a rich clairvoyant who lived down the road. Not trusting that particular witch, my mother asked what was wrong. The poor woman's doctor had told her that she must have a breast removed, and she was very scared. My mother said, but there's nothing to that, look – and she took out the two rolled socks which she kept in her empty brassière and threw them up into the sunlight and then caught them again. So the poor woman came in, drank tea, talked, forgot many fears, and went away knowing that she had seen the wise woman.

People called my father Jock. Face tanned from working in his garden, he survived the trenches of the First World War. He spoke very little. When he talked it was either very funny or very important. He only spoke to me about his war twice, and then briefly. In my teens I wrote a short, Owen-influenced poem about that war. My father read it, then told me of a friend who, during the lull between bombardments, fell to all fours, howled like an animal and was never cured.

Usually he avoided company. There was something in other people which frightened him. He was right. At the seaside he would sit on the farthest-out rock and fish peacefully. When visitors called at our house he would generally disappear into his jungle of raspberry canes and lurk.

Maybe there were twenty or thirty people in the world whose company he really enjoyed. They were lucky; he was a lovely man. Like Edward Lear, he was most at his ease with children, who instantly read, in the lines radiating from the corners of his eyes, that this was a man who understood their games and jokes.

He was short and lean and had fantastic sprouting Scottish eyebrows. He was a research chemist, but that didn't mean he only took an interest and pride in my elder brother's scientific work. He let me see how glad he was that I wrote, and I still remember the stories he used to write for me and my brother.

A year or so before he died he was in London for the day. My father sometimes voted Tory, sometimes Liberal, but when he began to talk about Vietnam that day, his face became first red and then white with anger about the cruelty and stupidity of the war. I seldom saw him angry and never so angry as at that moment, a man of seventy, not much interested in politics, all the grief of 1914-18 marching back into his mind.

People sometimes talk as if the ideological conflicts between generations have to be fought out bloodily, as if it is inevitable that children should grow to hate their parents. I don't believe this. Our family was lucky: my brother and I were always free to choose for ourselves – knowing that, however odd our decisions, we were trusted and loved. We all loved one another and this love was never shadowed.

Taming a Wild Garden
(for Celia, 5 April 1978)

I peck away with my pick-axe beak
To break the crust of builders' concrete
And let the ground of our garden breathe.

I rake away cream-coloured crumbs
And there's the brown earth
I never spend long enough learning from.
There's the brown earth
I never spent long enough loving.

My brown-faced tabby cruises by.
I bend to stroke her as she goes.

My chest warms.
My brown-faced father
Who loved his garden and several cats,
Smiles inside my heart.

One More Customer Satisfied

He staggered through the cities moaning for melons:
'Green melons streaked with yellow!
Yellow melons tinged with green!
Don't try to fool me. They fooled me before
With tie-dyed green-and-yellow footballs
And the breasts of yellow women, green-tinted nipples…'

In his yellow rage and his green longing
He rolled himself into a melon-shaped heap of hopelessness
Crying out: 'Melons! Bring out your melons!'

So they took a million melons to Cape Kennedy,
Scooped them out, filled them with green and yellow paint
And splattered them all over the bright side of the moon.

They adjusted his face so it faced the face of the moon
And they told him: 'There is your one true melon,
Your forever melon, your melon of melons.'

Now, fully grateful, he watches the melon rise,
The setting of the melon, the new melon and the full melon,
With a smile like a slice of melon in the green-and-yellow melon-light.

To My Friends, on My Fiftieth Birthday

My darlings, my friends, makers of all kinds, what can I say to them?
Go on with your labours of love, for you build Jerusalem.
My friends, my darlings, what can I say about you?
I will love you forever, I would have died without you.

How to Be Extremely Saintly, Rarefied and Moonly
(for Becky, who, when I spoke about resisting my urge to lie around
watching videos all day told me: 'Let your temptation never fail you.')

Let your coconut be your guide
Let the sun stew in its own juice
Let your coat and rent your hat
And let your temptation never fail you

Let the good times roller-skate
Let me inside-out please, I forgot my keys
Let the flim-flam floogie with the floy-floy rock 'n' roll
But let your temptation never fail you

Let the lecturer be harangued by the blackboard
Let your letters stamp their footling feet to better letter music
Let us play soccer together with a bonny lettuce
And in the Beantime –
Let your temptation, Becky, never fail you.

Loony Prunes
(an apology poem for my daughter)

We played the savage ludo which is known as Coppit,
Chatted, drank wine, ate lamb, played Beatle tunes
And then we started it, found we couldn't stop it –
A contest to eat maximum loony prunes.

They weren't just the ordinary, wrinkled, black,
Laxative fruit imported from – who knows?
But, floating in a stinging pool of Armagnac,
They were sozzled Français lunatic pruneaux.

Then, indoor fireworks, and the sharp flashes
Of three-second sparklers, dull horse-races,
A wonderful serpent, a frilly fern of ashes –
While the loony prune-juice flushed our faces.

As I was trying to put the fireworks out
We started arguing like sun and moon.
I grabbed you as the whole world seemed to shout.
You ran upstairs. I'm sorry. I'm a loony prune.

To Michael Bell

(my teacher at Greenways School whose motto was:
'A Green Thought in a Green Shade')

In the second year of the Slaughter
I attended a school in Hell
Feeling like King Lear's fourth daughter
Strapped down in a torture cell
Then my blue and white mother appeared to me
And she saw I was all afraid
So I was transported mysteriously
To a green school in a green shade

And there I met a great mechanic
And he mended my twisted wings
And he gentled away my panic
And he showed me how a vision sings
And I thank Michael Bell most lovingly
For the mountains and lakes he made
And the way he shone the light of peace on me
Like a green thought in a green shade

Beattie Is Three

At the top of the stairs
I ask for her hand. O.K.
She gives it to me.
How her fist fits my palm,
A bunch of consolation.
We take our time
Down the steep carpetway
As I wish silently
That the stairs were endless.

SONGS FROM SOME OF THE SHOWS

Gardening

(FROM *The Free Mud Fair at Totnes*)

EVE: At the heart of the Garden of Eden
Lay a pool of golden mud

I was the pool
And my name was Eve
One day I stood up like a fountain
And began to mould my body
Till it felt right and good

Then I made Adam out of the same golden mud
I made him different for fun

ADAM: Thank you for creating me

EVE: Shall we make more people out of mud?

ADAM: Yes
You make some like me
I'll make some like you

EVE: Let's make them all different

ADAM: Why make them different?

EVE: For fun for fun
For fun for fun

ADAM: No...No...
Two kinds is enough
Two kinds is plenty

EVE *(to audience)*:
My secret name is Peace
(to ADAM*)*
All right, Adam

EVE & ADAM:
So we made children out of the mud
Thousands of children out of the mud

Two kinds of children
Only two kinds
All of them totally different

The Violent God
(FROM *Move Over, Jehovah*)

Barbed wire all around the Garden of Eden
Adam was conscripted for the First World War
And it's still going on, and it's still going strong –
Hail to the violent god.

The old survivor said: I was in Belsen,
I'm grateful to god because he got me out of Belsen,
When I die please bury me in Belsen –
Hail to the violent god.

The god of hunger eats the people of India
The god of law and order spends most of his time
Smiling at the back of torture rooms –
Hail to the violent god.

Children were smitten with parents.
The black man was smitten with the white man.
The white man was smitten with the motor car –
Hail to the violent god.

Spastics teach us how to have pity
Leukaemia teaches us the dangers of anarchy
Schizophrenia teaches us sanity –
Hail to the violent god.

Calypso's Song to Ulysses

(FROM *Lash Me to the Mast!*)

My hands are tender feathers,
They can teach your body to soar.
My feet are two comedians
With jokes your flesh has never heard before.

So try to read the meaning
Of the blue veins under my skin
And feel my breasts like gentle wheels
Revolving from your thighs to your chin.

And listen to the rhythm
Of my heartbeat marking the pace
And see the visions sail across
The easy-riding waters of my face.

What is sweeter than the human body?
Two human bodies as they rise and fall.
What is sweeter than two loving bodies?
There is nothing sweeter at all.
Lose yourself, find yourself,
Lose yourself again
On the island of Calypso.

The Children of Blake

(FROM *Tyger*)

The children of Blake dance in their thousands
Over nursery meadows and through the sinister forests,
Beyond the spikes of cities, over the breasts of mountains,
The children of Blake dance in their thousands.
They dance beyond logic, they dance beyond science,
They are dancers, they are only dancers,
And every atom of their minds and their hearts and their deep skins
And every atom of their bowels and genitals and imaginations
Dances to the music of William Blake.

Happy Birthday William Blake

(FROM *Tyger*)

When he was alive everybody used to put him down.
Now they're writing volumes and they say they're sad he's not around.
But they wouldn't know Blake if they saw him
And heard him
And shook him by the hand.
They wouldn't know Blake if they took him
And tried him
And shot him from the witness stand.

For Blake was a man like any other man
But he trained his hands to see
And he trained his tongue to pop out of his ears
And he cried with his toenails
And the hairs in his nostrils
Danced to the music of the oxygen.

And they took a thousand million bricks
And they laid down Blake like a foundation stone
And they built a city-prison on his chest
But nothing could hold him down.

For he took a draught of explosive air
And he shook off London like a crust.
And he sang as he stood on the edge of the world
And he worked as he stood as he sang
And he built Jerusalem
He built Jerusalem
With his soft hard
Hard soft hands.

So it's happy birthday William Blake
What you've done can never be undone.
Happy birthday William Blake
Tyger of Jerusalem and Lamb of London.
Happy birthday happy birthday
Happy birthday William Blake.

Poetry

(FROM *Tyger*)

Poetry glues your soul together
Poetry wears dynamite shoes
Poetry is the spittle on the mirror
Poetry wears nothing but the blues

It's the gumboil gargoyle that falls off the cathedral
To land on the crown of the Queen.
Grab it while you can, it's the magical needle.
It's bitter sixteen and its flesh is bright green

Poetry glues your soul together
Poetry wears dynamite shoes
Poetry is the spittle on the mirror
Poetry wears nothing but the blues

Poetry's a lion on the stage of the opera house
Doin' a little jammin' with his brothers and sisters
Hits you, slits you, almost never fits you,
you and your lover get covered in blisters.

Poetry glues your soul together
Poetry wears dynamite shoes
Poetry is the spittle on the mirror
Poetry wears nothing but the blues

Poetry's the moon's own bottle of gin.
It's the purple ghost of Duke Ellington's band.
It's a bucket with a hole for collecting truth in
And the legless beggar army of Disneyland

Clinton hasn't got it, but there's plenty in Fidel.
Slap your sherry trifle on my sewing machine.
Bend it into bowlines but you'll never break it
The only way to make it is the way you make it
Only thing that matters is the way you shake it

Poetry glues your soul together
Poetry wears dynamite shoes
Poetry is the spittle on the mirror
Poetry wears nothing but the blues

The Tribe
(from *Man Friday*)

The tribe changes
As a tree changes.

When the storm throws its weight against a tree
The tree bends away.
When the storm falls asleep upon the tree
The tree stands up again.

The tribe changes
As a tree changes.

The children are the blossoms of the tree,
They laugh along its branches.
The old are the fruit of the tree,
They fall when they are ready to fall.

The tribe changes
As a tree changes.

Nobody tells the tree how it should grow.
Nobody knows what shape it will assume.
The tree decides the angle of its branches.
The tree decides when it is ready to die.

Medical
(from *A Seventh Man*)

The fit are being sorted out from the unfit.
One in five will fail.
Those who pass will enter a new life.
One in five will fail.

Ride the Nightmare

(FROM *The Hot Pot Saga*)

I was zooming round the Universe feeling like Desperate Dan
I was bombing them at random looking for Charlie Chan
I looked and saw a continent without a single man
Which they told me was Asia but it looked more like Aberfan *

So ride the nightmare
Jump upon its hairy back
Ride the nightmare
Ride until your mind goes black
It's the 21st century werewolf
21st century werewolf
21st century werewolf and it's coming this way

Well the charity lady wiped the diamonds from her eyes and said
'I've been saving all my money but the African dead stay dead
I'm sending them elastoplast and dunlopillo bread –
But they wrote me a letter saying: Send us guns instead'

So ride the nightmare
Jump upon its hairy back
Ride the nightmare
Ride until your mind goes black
It's the 21st century werewolf
21st century werewolf
21st century werewolf and it's coming this way

Well the rich white Englishman can easily ignore the rest
For the poor are just a bore and who can use the starving and oppressed?
They're burning while you tell yourself there's nothing you can do
When your turn comes they'll do just the same for you

So ride the nightmare
Jump upon its hairy back
Ride the nightmare
Ride until your mind goes black
It's the 21st century werewolf
21st century werewolf
21st century werewolf and it's coming this way...

* *This first verse was rewritten around 1986 and it now goes:*
I was zooming round the universe feeling like Sylvester Stallone
I was bombing them at random looking for Gadaffi's home
I saw a Royal baby in a cradle of silver lace
And I saw another baby with flies feeding out of his face...

A Song of Liberation

(FROM *Houdini*)

Padlocked in a barrel full of beer
And almost dying from the fumes –
He did not despair.

Lashed to the waterwheel
Tied to the sail of a windmill –
His skill did not desert him.

Chained to the pillar of a prison cell
Riveted inside a metal boiler
Stuffed into the top of a roll-top desk
Sewn inside a giant sausage-skin –
He out-imagined every challenger.

Plunged into rivers, handcuffed and chained
Strapped to a crazy crib by mental nurses,
Tied to a cannon with a time fuse,
Hung upside down in the water torture cell,
In a Government mail pouch,
Even in the grave,
Even in the grave when he let himself be buried alive –

Even in the grave
His brain and body worked so perfectly
That he broke free from the grave.

And when the body of a man
Has been buried in the earth
And that body reaches up to the surface
That body reaches up towards the light,
Towards whatever shines –
Joy fills the people, magical joy.
Joy at the magic of his liberation,
Magic that touches the surface of your skin
With a magical shiver.
What is magic then?
What is magic? What is magic?
       Beauty that takes you by surprise.

The Widow's Song

(FROM *Mowgli's Jungle*)

My husband was strong
My husband was warm
His loving was
A thunderstorm
But a fever came
And took him by the hand
Now he is dancing,
Dancing, dancing
With the ghosts in Ghostland

My baby could stand
My baby could dance
His hands and legs
Like little plants
But a tiger came
And took him by the hand
Now he is dancing,
Dancing, dancing
With the ghosts in Ghostland

And now I am poor
As poor as a stone
All day and night
Alone alone
Let dreams tonight
Take me by the hand
And I'll go dancing,
Dancing, dancing
With the ghosts
With my lovely ghosts
With my lovely ghosts in Ghostland

The Truth

(FROM *Love Songs of World War Three*)

The truth is the truth
Is a strange kind of animal
The truth is the truth
Only comes out when people sleep
So I stay awake listening for the truth

The truth's my favourite uncle
Always brings me a surprise
The truth's my favourite uncle
What ridiculous stories it tells

I like the truth I like the way it doesn't simper
I like the truth it employs no PR men
I like the truth I'm very fond of its music
I like the truth I like the way it tastes
I like the truth it never gazes into mirrors
I like the truth I like its way of walking
I like the truth I'm very fond of its music
I like the truth I enjoy the way it tastes
I really love the truth

If it licks me I know it wants to lick me
If it leaves me I know it must be on its way

For the truth is the truth
Is a strange kind of animal
The truth is the truth
Only comes out when people sleep
So I stay awake listening for the truth

It doesn't make hit records
It's not often on the TV
You'll see the truth more often
In the sadness of faces on trains

I like its grin I like its way of falling silent
I like the way that it snoozes on committees
At soccer games it watches how the grass grows
It rents a shop and puts the worst in the window
I saw the truth in a junkyard one evening
I saw the truth it was sitting by a bonfire
I asked the truth, I said: What's your kind of music?
Tell you the truth, said truth, I like shining music
Yes I love the truth

For the truth is the truth
Is a strange kind of animal
The truth is the truth
Only comes out when people sleep
So I stay awake listening for the truth
Yes I stay awake listening for the truth

Wash Your Hands

(FROM *Mind Your Head*)

HUSBAND: My well-swept house is almost in the country
You can see woodlands from the upstairs window
On Saturday and Sunday there's a deck-chair on the patio
And there I drink a can or two of lager.

WIFE: Oh wash your hands, my darling,
Wash your hands, my darling,
Wash your clever hands.

HUSBAND: With my arm across my eyelids, I sleep very soundly.
My wife likes Chopin but I favour Mantovani.
My little girl of five goes to ballet class on Wednesday.
My little boy of seven collects toy vehicles.

WIFE: Oh wash your hands, my darling,
Wash your hands, my darling,
Wash your gentle hands.

HUSBAND: Every other weekend I take to my mother
A cake from the kitchen or flowers from the garden.
I always have a word and a wave for the neighbours
As I go to do the work which I never mention.

WIFE: Oh wash your hands, my darling,
Wash your hands, my darling,
Wash your loving hands.

HUSBAND: Sometimes I sit and stare at nothing
Sometimes I sit and smile at nothing
Sometimes I sit and think of nothing
My job is torturing men and women
My job is torturing men and women
My job is –

WIFE: Oh wash your hands, my darling,
Wash your hands, my darling,
Wash your shaking hands.

Lament for the Jazz Makers

(FROM *We*)

As I was sitting all alone
Death called me on the telephone
I said – I'm sorry, I'm not free.
The fear of death is haunting me.

Death is the cop who can't be bought.
You always think you won't be caught,
Until you're busted, finally –
The fear of death is eating me.

Death grabs the young cat by the neck –
He stomped upon Bix Beiderbecke
Whose cornet rung so silvery.
The fear of death is shaking me.

And death has locked up Lester Young
And Billie Holiday who sung
Her beaten-up black poetry.
The fear of death is clutching me.

Tatum, Django, Charlie Mingus,
Death snapped off their cunning fingers
Like twigs from some old apple tree.
The fear of death is breaking me.

Death took the great Duke Ellington
And wore him down to skin and bone
For all his generosity.
The fear of death is taunting me.

Louis, Mama Yancey, Dinah,
Bessie Smith and Big Joe Turner
All work in death's bad factory.
The fear of death is chilling me.

He breathed in air, he breathed out light,
Charlie Parker was my delight
But Bird was cut down cruelly.
The fear of death is touching me.

And we must all of us go dwell
In Death's enormous Black Hotel.
At least we'll have good company –
The fear of death is killing me.

Gather Together

(FROM *We*)

Gather together
The snow-drinking waterfalls
Gather together
The tears of the pine
The glassy-winged insects
The woodpecker's drum

Gather together
The soft-springing forest floor
Gather together
The lumbering bear
Inflammable maples
The spears of the sun

Gather together
The cry of the falling tree
Gather together
The apple-green pond
The leap of the squirrel
The patience of stones

Gather together
The snaggle-toothed undergrowth
Gather together
The spite of the storm
The acrobat swallows
The glaring of bones

Gather together
The green-fountain conifers
Gather together
The choir of the wolves
The strong breath of mushrooms
The butterwort flowers

Gather together
The shouting of cataracts
Gather together
The racket of rooks
The songs of the forest
The forest is ours

The Pregnant Woman's Song

(FROM *The Blue*)

I am an ocean
And in my deeps
There is a baby curled
I am an ocean
And in my deeps
I keep a little world

My heart is strong
Strong as the burning sun at noon
My baby's heart is clear
Simple and light as the floating moon

Yes I am an ocean
And in my deeps
There is a baby curled
I am an ocean
And in my deeps
I keep a little world

Jake's Amazing Suit

(FROM *Silent Chorus*)

When you see me in my suit –
You'll look and at first
All you'll see is a burst
Of shimmering electric blue.
Then you'll focus in and see
That the vision is me
And I'm walking
And my suit is walking too

When you see me in my suit –
Flowing soft as milk
It'll be Thailand silk
That follows any move at all.
And its cut and its drape
Will lay on me a shape
Like I'm standing
Underneath a waterfall.

When you see me in my suit –
    I won't be able to walk out in public
    Because of my wonderful threads
    Never mind, instead
    We'll spend our life in bed
    With nothing but love in our heads
When you see me in my suit!

I once saw Miles Davis
Walk across the tarmac from an aeroplane.
Yes I once saw Miles Davis walking
Oh now let me explain –

His face was carved from a living mahogany tree-trunk.
He wore power sunglasses over his eyes
With silver pistons connected to his ears.
His beret sat on the top of his head
Like a little powder-blue cloud
And when he smiled it turned you to stone.
His suit was four-and-a-half times too big for his body.
It was kind of a tweed woven out of mountain light.
It had criss-cross lines of the sort of luminous
Green you only see on the top of birthday cakes.
And the luminous green lines
Criss-crossed over a meadow of bright creamy white

I once saw Miles Davis
Walk across the tarmac from an aeroplane
Yes I once saw Miles Davis walking
I can explain –

I want a suit like that
I want a suit like that
I want a suit so electric
If I leave it alone
It'll jump off the hanger
Take a walk on its own
Give me a suit like that
Give me a suit like that

So that my love will love me
Even more than she loves me
When she sees me in my suit
When she sees me in my suit.

Secret Country

(FROM *Pied Piper*)

There is no money
So there is no crime
There are no watches
Cos there's no time
It's a good country
It's a secret country
And it's your country and mine.

If something's needed
You make it there
And we have plenty
For we all share
It's a kind country
It's a secret country
And it's your country and mine.

There are no cages
There is no zoo
But the free creatures
Come and walk with you
It's a strange country
It's a secret country
And it's your country and mine.

There are no prisons
There are no poor
There are no weapons
There is no war
It's a safe country
It's a secret country
And it's your country and mine.

And in that country
Grows a great tree
And it's called freedom
And its fruit is free
In that blue country
In that loving country
In that wild country
In that secret country
Which is your country and mine.

Cardboard Rowing Boat

(FROM *The Siege*)

All I know
Is that when I go
I will stand beside an unknown sea
And that's why I ask my best friends
When I die won't you make for me –

A cardboard rowing boat
For my coffin
Painted in greens and blues
And dress me up in my
Faded denim
And my favourite running shoes
In my green and blue
Cardboard rowing boat

The poems of Blake in my
Left hand pocket
Navy rum in my right
And in my hand put an eating apple
And bury me late at night
In my green and blue
Cardboard rowing boat

And I'll row away
Cross that starry sea
Singing and drifting with the tide
And I'll row away
And maybe I'll meet you at the other side
In my green and blue
Cardboard rowing boat

OUR BLUE PLANET

The Castaways *or* Vote For Caliban

The Pacific Ocean –
A blue demi-globe.
Islands like punctuation marks.

A cruising airliner,
Passengers unwrapping pats of butter.
A hurricane arises,
Tosses the plane into the sea.

Five of them, flung on to an island beach,
Survived.
Tom the reporter.
Susan the botanist.
Jim the high-jump champion.
Bill the carpenter.
Mary the eccentric widow.

Tom the reporter sniffed out a stream of drinkable water.
Susan the botanist identified a banana tree.
Jim the high-jump champion jumped up and down and gave them each a bunch.
Bill the carpenter knocked up a table for their banana supper.
Mary the eccentric widow buried the banana skins,
But only after they had asked her twice.
They all gathered sticks and lit a fire.
There was an incredible sunset.

Next morning they held a committee meeting.
Tom, Susan, Jim and Bill
Voted to make the best of things.
Mary, the eccentric widow, abstained.

Tom the reporter killed several dozen wild pigs.
He tanned their skins into parchment
And printed the *Island News* with the ink of squids.

Susan the botanist developed new strains of banana
Which tasted of chocolate, beefsteak, peanut butter,
Chicken and bootpolish.

Jim the high-jump champion organised organised games
Which he always won easily.

Bill the carpenter constructed a wooden water wheel
And converted the water's energy into electricity.
Using iron ore from the hills, he constructed lampposts.

They all worried about Mary, the eccentric widow,
Her lack of confidence and her –
But there wasn't time to coddle her.

The volcano erupted, but they dug a trench
And diverted the lava into the sea
Where it formed a spectacular pier.
They were attacked by pirates but defeated them
With bamboo bazookas firing
Sea-urchins packed with home-made nitro-glycerine.
They gave the cannibals a dose of their own medicine
And survived an earthquake thanks to their skill in jumping.

Tom had been a court reporter
So he became the magistrate and solved disputes.
Susan the Botanist established
A university which also served as a museum.
Jim the high-jump champion
Was put in charge of law-enforcement –
Jumped on them when they were bad.
Bill the carpenter built himself a church,
Preached there every Sunday.

But Mary the eccentric widow...
Each evening she wandered down the island's main street,
Past the Stock Exchange, the Houses of Parliament,
The prison and the arsenal.
Past the Prospero Souvenir Shop,
Past the Robert Louis Stevenson Movie Studios,
Past the Daniel Defoe Motel
She nervously wandered and sat on the end of the pier of lava,

Breathing heavily,
As if at a loss,
As if at a lover,
She opened her eyes wide
To the usual incredible sunset.

162

Quit Stalling, Call in Stalin

I've got a system
A system a system
I've got a system
And everyone's going to fit in

The white folk the black folk
The brown folk the yellow folk
The men folk the women folk
Yes everyone's going to fit in

And if you don't fit my system
My system my system
If you don't fit my system
There's something the matter with you

You'll be locked up in a hospital
Hospital hospital
Locked up in a hospital
With thousands of others like you

Locked up with the misfits
Misfits misfits
Locked up with the misfits
You're going to be there till you die

But I'll be out in the system
The system the system
Working within the system
Having the time of my life

Two Good Things

there's one good thing about a cow-pat:
if you leave it in the sun it dries.
and there's one good thing about capitalism –
it dies.

Remember Suez?

England, unlike junior nations,
Wears officers' long combinations.
So no embarrassment was felt
By the Church, the Government or the Crown.
But I saw the Thames like a grubby old belt
And England's trousers falling down.

Written During the Night Waiting for the Dawn

Let's unplug the radiotelescope.
Pablo Neruda, that abundant planet,
Has been eradicated from the Southern starscape.

Down at the market every stall's been stricken –
Withered tomatoes, warty pomegranates,
Dud wine, black milk and a two-headed chicken.

Shall we cheer ourselves up with a stroll by the river?
But the pebbles are undergoing classification,
The waterfall's levelled, the green banks paved over.

He loved his food, the people and the alphabet.
But now Chile, his bride, is under interrogation.
The electrodes have been placed. The sun has set.

Briefing

He may be fanatical, he may have a madness.
Either way, move carefully.
He must be surrounded, but he's contagious.

One of you will befriend his family.
One male and one female will love the subject
Until he loves you back. Gradually

Our team will abstract and collect
His mail, nail-clippings, garbage, friends, words, schemes,
Graphs of his fears, scars, sex and intellect.

Steam open his heart. Tap his dreams.
Learn him inside and inside out.
When he laughs, laugh. Scream when he screams.

He will scream. 'Innocent!' He'll shout
Until his mouth is broken with stones.
We use stones. We take him out

To a valley full of stones.
He stands against a shed. He stands on stones
Naked. The initial stones

Shower the iron shed. Those stones
Outline the subject. When he cries for stones
The clanging ceases. Then we give him stones,

Filling his universe with stones.
Stones – his atoms turn to stones
And he becomes a stone buried in stones.

A final tip. Then you may go.
Note the half-hearted stoners and watch how
Your own arm throws. And watch how I throw.

Ballade of Beans

Nightmare. A silver butcher's truck
Hurtles around my brain and chop
Goes the neck-chopper. Wake. I suck
Pus from my gums, then slowly prop
Bones till they stand upright. I slop
Water which last night rinsed our greens
Over my face. My coiled guts hop –
The sink is clogged with dead beans.

Truth will lie, panting, for a buck.
Philosophy's a lollipop.
Who heeds Religion's biddy cluck
Or cares when Justice goes flip-flop?
So U.N.O.'s a headless mop,
Peace never reached her early teens,
Terror's capsuled in each raindrop –
The sink is clogged with dead beans.

Switzerland's had a lot of luck,
But Cuba slugged a wealthy cop
And Europe stands where lightning struck
Twice lately. Berlin. Will it drop?
Will the earth's ice-protected top
Flip off to show dead submarines?
The world, the grubby old death shop,
The sink is clogged with dead beans.

Wilson, we're both about to stop
England tots up as England gleans
The grains of your crapulous crop –
The sink is clogged with dead beans.

From Rich Uneasy America to My Friend Christopher Logue

'Never again that sick feeling when the toilet overflows.'
ADVERTISEMENT: THE IOWA CITY PRESS-CITIZEN

Jim Hall's guitar walking around
As if the Half Note's wooden floor
Grew blue flowers and each flower
Drank from affluent meadow ground.
The lush in the corner dropped his sorrowing
When he noticed his hands and elbows dancing.
Long silver trucks made lightning past the window.
A two-foot hunter watch hung from the ceiling.
Then you prowled in. The guitar splintered,
The lush held hands with himself, trucks concertinaed.
The watch-hands shook between Too Late and Now.

As I sit easy in the centre
Of the U.S. of America,
Seduced by cheeseburgers, feeling strong
When bourbon licks my lips and tongue,
Ears stopped with jazz or both my eyes
Full of Mid-Western butterflies,
You drive out of a supermarket
With petrol bombs in a family packet
And broadcast down your sickened nose:
'It overflows. By Christ, it overflows.'

Official Announcement

    Her Majesty's Government has noted with regret
That seven unidentified flying objects are zooming towards the earth.
    Her Majesty's Government has noted with regret
That they look like angels except that their skins and their wings are as raw as
afterbirth.
    Her Majesty's Government has noted with regret
That our military computers wrote a billion-word message explaining why
they all chose suicide

Her Majesty's Government has noted with regret

That here come the angels, and each of the angels has a jar with an oceanful of plague inside.

Her Majesty's Government has noted with regret

That the first angel has poured out his jar and that British nationals and others who have the mark of the beast or have at some time in the past worshipped the image of the beast are being afflicted with sores so noisome and grievous that their bodies are flashing like pinball machines.

Her Majesty's Government has noted with regret

That the second angel has poured out his jar and that the sea has become as the blood of a dead man and that everything in the sea is dying including Her Majesty's submarines.

Her Majesty's Government has noted with regret

That the third angel has poured out his jar and that the Thames has become an enormous and open and pulsing jugular vein.

Her Majesty's Government has noted with regret

That the fourth angel has poured out his jar and that the heat of the sun has become amplified but a spokesman for Civil Defence advises John Bull to stick his head in a sandbag full of ice in order to postpone or avert the frying of his brain.

Her Majesty's Government has noted with regret

That the fifth angel has de-jarred and that – It's all gone dark, we can't see – and all citizens who do not bear an official seal of redemption are gnawing their tongues in pain.

Her Majesty's Government has noted with regret

That the sixth angel – Frog Devils! Unclean! Frog-Beast Armageddon!

Her Majesty's Government has noted with regret

That the seventh angel – IT IS DONE – voices thunder lightnings great earthquake such as such as was not since men were upon the earth, so mighty an earthquake and so great and every island including us every island is flying away and regretfully the mountains cannot be found and a great hail is falling with steel rain and fire that is wet.

All of which things, although we understand the provocation under which heaven is acting and take this opportunity of reaffirming our unshaken trust in the general principles and policies of heaven, and in the firm belief that all possible steps have been taken to ensure minimal civilian casualties and compassionate underkill –

Her Majesty's Government has noted with regret.

Let Me Tell You the Third World War Is Going to Separate the Men from the Boys

SON: Make sure the black blind fits the window,
           Don't let the light fly out.
           Where is the war tonight?

FATHER: No, this is peacetime.
           You are safely tucked up in England.
           Sleep tight, happy dreams.

SON: Listen, Daddy, are they ours or theirs?

FATHER: They are owls, they are nobody's
           Responsibility. This is peace.

SON: Today I lost a battle.
           I feel like mud.

FATHER: Snuggle down, snuggle down,
           Tomorrow you will win two battles.

SON: Yes, and I will feel like mud.

FATHER: Grow up, this is self-pitying hyper-bollocks.
           Nobody is really, actually trying to
           Literally kill us.

SON: Yes they are, Daddy,
           Yes they are

Programme for an Emergency

The world's population statistically,
Could stand together on the Isle of Wight
Shoulder to shoulder to shoulder.
There they could stand and watch the sea,
Sleeping in shifts by day and night,
Gracelessly growing older.

But Holland's son would rape Ireland's daughter
Or China's grandfather fall in the water.
Ozone would mingle with the scent of slaughter.

Still, England seems the most suitable site,
For here we are proud not to laugh or weep
And one gulp of the air will freeze the strongest man in sleep.

Naming the Dead

And now the super-powers, who have been cheerfully doubling their money by flogging arms wherever the price is right, put on their Sunday cassocks and preach peace to the Middle East. From their lips the word sounds like a fart. On *Twenty-Four Hours* the other night, Kenneth Allsop interviewed a British arms merchant who has been selling to both Egypt and Israel. Admitting that he was having some doubts about his trade (he is now on the verge of an ill-earned retirement) he said that nevertheless the real question was: Am I my brother's keeper? and that the answer was No. The question was of course first put by Cain, whose flag flies high over most of the major cities of the world.

The more abstract war is made to seem, the more attractive it becomes. The advance of an army as represented by dynamic arrows swooping across the map can raise the same thrill as a child gets from playing draughts. Dubious score-sheets which say how many planes the government would have liked to have shot down only add to the game-like quality of news – you tot up the columns and kid yourself that someone is winning.

Wartime governments sometimes allow this process to be taken a step nearer reality by issuing photographs of one atrociously wounded soldier (our side) being lovingly nursed by his comrades, and another picture of dozens of prisoners (their side) being handed cups of water (see under Sir Philip Sidney, gallantry of). Such poses represent a caricature of war's effect on human beings.

What have Arabs been doing? Killing Jews.

What have the Jews been doing? Killing Arabs.

Even that doesn't get us far in the direction of reality. To add statistics saying how many were killed takes us only an inch nearer.

Who is killed? What were they like? I would like to see every government in the world held accountable to the United Nations for every human being it kills, either in war or in peace. I don't just mean a statistic published in a secret report. I mean that all the newspapers of the country responsible should carry the name of the person killed, his photograph, address, number of his dependants and the reason why he was killed. (We often do as much for the victims of plane crashes.)

This would mean that in some countries the press would be swamped with death reports and even mammoth death supplements. (Well, what about the advertisers?) But I want more.

I would like every death inflicted by any government to be the subject of a book published at the state's expense. Each book would give an exhaustive biography of the corpse and would be illustrated by photographs from his family album if any, pictures he painted as a child and film stills of his last hours. In the back cover would be a long-playing disc of the victim talking to his friends, singing, talking to his wife and children and interviewed by the men who killed him.

The text would examine his life, his tastes and interests, faults and virtues, without trying to make him any more, villainous or heroic than he was. It would be prepared by a team of writers appointed by the United Nations. The final chapter would record the explanations of the government which killed him and a detailed account of the manner of his death, the amount of bleeding, the extent of burns, the decibel count of screams, the amount of time it took to die and the names of the men who killed him.

One book for every killing. I realise that this would take some planning. Each soldier would have to be accompanied by an interviewing, camera and research team in order to record the details of any necessary victim.

Most factories would turn out printing presses, most graduates would automatically become biographers of the dead. Bombing could only take place after individual examination of every person to be bombed. The cost of killing would be raised to such a pitch that the smallest war would lead to bankruptcy and only the most merciful revolution could be afforded. Hit squarely in the exchequer – the only place where they feel emotion – chauvinist governments might be able to imagine for the first time, the true magnitude of the obscenity which they mass-produce.

This is no bloody whimsy. I want a real reason for every killing.

Fifteen Million Plastic Bags

I was walking in a government warehouse
Where the daylight never goes.
I saw fifteen million plastic bags
Hanging in a thousand rows.

Five million bags were six feet long
Five million were five foot five
Five million were stamped with Mickey Mouse
And they came in a smaller size.

Were they for guns or uniforms
Or a dirty kind of party game?
Then I saw each bag had a number
And every bag bore a name.

And five million bags were six feet long
Five million were five foot five
Five million were stamped with Mickey Mouse
And they came in a smaller size

So I've taken my bag from the hanger
And I've pulled it over my head
And I'll wait for the priest to zip it
So the radiation won't spread

Now five million bags are six feet long
Five million are five foot five
Five million are stamped with Mickey Mouse
And they come in a smaller size.

Order Me a Transparent Coffin and Dig My Crazy Grave

After the next war...and the sky
Heaves with contaminated rain.
End to end our bodies lie
Round the world and back again.

Now from their concrete suites below
Statesmen demurely emanate,
And down the line of millions go
To see the people lie in state.

Nikita Ikes, Franco de Gaulles,
Officiate and dig the holes.
Mao tse-Sheks, Macadenauers,
Toting artificial flowers.

As they pay tribute each one wishes
The rain was less like tears, less hot, less thick.
They mutter, wise as blind white fishes,
Occasionally they are sick.

But I drily grin from my perspex coffin
As they trudge till they melt into the wet,
And I say: Keep on walking, keep on walking,
You bastards, you've got a hell of a way to walk yet.

A Child Is Singing

A child is singing
And nobody listening
But the child who is singing:

Bulldozers grab the earth and shower it.
The house is on fire.
Gardeners wet the earth and flower it.
The house is on fire,
The houses are on fire.
Fetch the fire engine, the fire engine's on fire.

We will have to hide in a hole.
We will burn slow like coal.
All the people are on fire.

And a child is singing
And nobody listening
But the child who is singing.

The Dust

Singing, as she always must,
Like the kitten-drowner with a howling sack,
Open-eyed through the shallow dust
Goes the dust-coloured girl with a child on her back.

A schoolgirl in a flowered dress,
Swayed by the swaying of a tree
And the sun's grin, in front of her family
One day became a prophetess.

Like a singer who forgets her song
She awkwardly leant from the graceful chair,
Balanced her fists in the drawing-room air
And said that everyone was wrong, that she was wrong.

Shocked by this infantile mistake
Her uncles and aunts were sad to find
This ugly girl with an ugly mind
In a house as rich as birthday cake.

When the bombs fell, she was sitting with her man,
Straight and white in the family pew.
While in her the bud of a child grew
The city crumbled, the deaths began.

Now, singing as she always must,
A refugee from a love burned black,
Open-eyed through the rising dust
Goes the dust-coloured girl with a child on her back.

Veteran with a Head Wound

Nothing to show for it at first
But dreams and shivering, a few mistakes,
Shapes lounged around his mind chatting of murder,
Telling interminable jokes,
Watching like tourists for Vesuvius to burst.

He started listening. Too engrossed to think,
He let his body move in jerks,
Talked just to prove himself alive, grew thin,
Lost five jobs in eleven weeks,
Then started drinking, blamed it on the drink.

He'd seen a woman, belly tattered, run
Her last yards. He had seen a fat
Friend roll in flames, as if his blood were paraffin,
And herded enemies waiting to be shot
Stand looking straight into the sun.

They couldn't let him rot in the heat
In the corner of England like a garden chair.
A handy-man will take a weathered chair.
Smooth it, lay on a glowing layer
Of pain and tie a cushion to the seat.

They did all anyone could do –
Tried to grate off the colour of his trouble,
Brighten him up a bit. His rare
Visitors found him still uncomfortable.
The old crimson paint showed through.

Each night he heard from the back of his head,
As he was learning to sleep again,
Funny or terrible voices tell
Or ask him how their deaths began.
These are the broadcasts of the dead.

One voice became a plaintive bore.
It could only remember the grain and shine
Of a wooden floor, the forest smell
Of its fine surface. The voice rasped on
For hours about that pretty floor...

'If I could make that floor again,'
The voice insisted, over and over,
'The floor on which I died,' it said,
'Then I could stand on it for ever
Letting the scent of polish lap my brain.'

He became Boswell to the dead.
In cruel script their deaths are written.
Generously they are fed
In that compound for the forgotten,
His crowded, welcoming head.

The doctors had seen grimmer cases.
They found his eyes were one-way mirrors,
So they could easily look in
While he could only see his terrors,
Reflections of those shuttered faces.

Stepping as far back as I dare
(For the man may stagger and be broken
Like a bombed factory or hospital),
I see his uniform is woven
Of blood, bone, flesh and hair.

Populated by the simple dead,
This soldier, in his happy dreams,
Is killed before he kills at all.
Bad tenant that he is, I give him room;
He is the weeper in my head.

Since London's next bomb will tear
Her body in its final rape,
New York and Moscow's ashes look the same
And Europe go down like a battleship,
Why should one soldier make me care?

Ignore him or grant him a moment's sadness.
He walks the burning tarmac road
To the asylum built with bricks of flame.
Abandon him and you must make your own
House of incinerating madness.

The horizon is only paces away.
We walk an alley through a dark,
Criminal city. None can pass.
We would have to make love, fight or speak
If we met someone travelling the other way.
A tree finds its proportions without aid.

Dogs are not tutored to be fond.
Penny-size frogs traverse the grass
To the civilisation of a pond.
Grass withers yearly, is re-made.

Trees become crosses because man is born.
Dogs may be taught to shrink from any hand.
Dead frogs instruct the scientist;
Spread clouds of poison in the pond –
You kill their floating globes of spawn.

In London, where the trees are lean,
The banners of the grass are raised.
Grass feeds the butcher and the beast,
But we could conjure down a blaze
Would scour the world of the colour green.

For look, though the human soul is tough,
Our state scratches itself in bed
And a thousand are pierced by its fingernails.
It combs its hair, a thousand good and bad
Fall away like discs of dandruff.

For a moment it closes its careful fist
And, keening for the world of streets,
More sons of god whisper in jails
Where the unloved the unloved meet.
The days close round them like a dirty mist.

When death covers England with a sheet
Of red and silver fire, who'll mourn the state,
Though some will live and some bear children
And some of the children born in hate
May be both lovely and complete?

Try to distract this soldier's mind
From his distraction. Under the powdered buildings
He lies alive, still shouting,
With his brothers and sisters and perhaps his children,
While we bury all the dead people we can find.

Life on the Overkill Escalator

Dogs must be carried because they do not understand.
You examine the shoulders of the man ahead without understanding.

You pass foreign-faced women. They pass you.
They are cardboard, behind glass. They wear lead corsets anyway.

The vibration becomes part of you
Or you become part of the vibration.

The penalty for stopping the escalator is five pounds.
Five pounds is a lot of money.

You Get Used to It

'Am I in Alabama or am I in hell?'
A MINISTER, MONTGOMERY, ALABAMA, MARCH 1965

Begging-bowl eyes, begging-bowl eyes,
skin round hoops of wire.
They do not eat, they are being eaten,
saw them in the papers.

    But it's only bad if you know it's bad,
    fish don't want the sky.
    If you've spent all your life in hell or Alabama
    you get used to it.

Ignorant husband, ignorant wife,
each afraid of the other one's bomb.
He spends all he has in the Gentlemen's
on a fifty p book of nudes.

    But it's only bad if you know it's bad,
    fish don't want the sky.
    If you've spent all your life in hell or Alabama
    you get used to it.

Beautiful blossom of napalm
sprouting from the jungle,
bloom full of shrivelling things,
might be mosquitoes, might be men.

But it's only bad if you know it's bad,
fish don't want the sky.
If you've spent all your life in hell or Alabama
you get used to it.

I hurt, you hurt, he hurts, she hurts,
we hurt, you hurt, they hurt.
What can't be cured must go to jail,
what can't be jailed must die.

But it's only bad if you know it's bad,
fish don't want the sky.
If you've spent all your life in hell or Alabama
you get used to it.

Good Question

How can the rich hate the poor?
They never see them.

Their chauffeurs swerve well clear of slums.
Accountants keep them out of jail.
Poor people do not run the BBC
So the rich never see the poor.

How can the poor hate the rich
When the rich are so pretty?

A chained man knows the weight of his chains.
A woman in jail has a strong sense of time.
Hunger is a wonderful schoolmaster.
The poor crouch. The poor watch. The poor wait.
The poor get ready. The poor will stand up.

How do the poor hate the rich?
Like a bullet.

Byron Is One of the Dancers

His poems – they were glad with jokes, trumpets, arguments and flying crockery
        Rejoice
He shook hearts with his lust and nonsense, he was independent as the weather
        Rejoice
Alive, alive, fully as alive as us, he used his life and let life use him
        Rejoice
He loved freedom, he loved Greece, and yes of course, he died for the freedom
    of Greece
        Rejoice

        And yes, this is a dance,
        and yes, beyond the glum farrago
        of TV cops after TV crooks
        in the blockheaded prison of TV –

        I hear the naked feet of Byron
        which skated once, powered by fascination
        over the cheerful skin of women's legs,
        I hear those two bare feet –
        One delicate and one shaped horribly –
        slap and thud, slap, thud, slap, thud,
        across the cracked-up earth of Greece,
        and yes, I hear the music which drives those feet
        and feel the arm of Byron round my shoulder
        or maybe it is round your shoulder
        Oh I feel your arm around my shoulder
        and yes, I know the line of dancers
        across the cracked-up earth of Greece
        stretches from sea to sea
        as the shrivelled mountains erupt into music
        and Byron and all the million dancers
        yes brothers and sisters, lovers and lovers,
        some lucky in life and delicately-skinned,
        some shaped horribly by want or torture,
        dance out the dance which must be danced

for the freedom of Greece
for the freedom of Greece

        Dance
        Rejoice
        Dance
        Rejoice

180

One Question About Amsterdam

Of course it all looked good in the good light.
(Even the grandmother prostitute
Who leaned too far over her window-sill
As she picked her nose and ate it
And only stopped, with the guiltiest
Guilty start I've ever seen,
When she saw I was looking.)
Of course it all looked good,
But, since I was suspicious even in the womb,
And, as it turns out, rightly suspicious,
Forgive me, Hans, one miniature complaint.

I didn't see a single Eskimo in Amsterdam.
Everything else, yes, but no Eskimos.
Not one candle-chewing, wife-lending,
Blubber-loving igloo freak
Of an ice-hole fishing, polar bear-clobbering Nanook.
Throughout the tranquillising waterways,
Throughout the bumping wet of the harbour –
Not one bloody kayak.

Where are the eskimos of Amsterdam?
Where are the eskimos of Amsterdam?
Where are the eskimos of Amsterdam?

To the Silent Majority

ashamed to be white,
ashamed not to be in jail,
why do i keep howling about:

sky overcast with the colour of hunger,
liars who kiss like arsenic sandpaper,
white power gas, the torture game
and the one-eyed glare of that final global flame?

because they are here.

The Dichotomy Between the Collapse
of Civilisation and Making Money

(to my students at Dartington)

No such thing as Western
civilisation
No such thing as Eastern
civilisation
The brand name for a tribe of killer apes
is civilisation

The killer apes do some little good things
So let's all do the little good things
good things good and not many of them –
Coconuts in the pacific ocean
of bad things bad things calling themselves
civilisation

What the hell if the tribe collapses
Look out look out for another tribe
of apes who do no killing but do big good things

Meanwhile look up
up above your head
only the rain is collapsing on you

Of course there's not much bread
in doing little good things
but do do do
altogether all the do do day

Because, speaking as a brother-speck
among the galaxies,
Little is the biggest we can call ourselves

Night Lines in a Peaceful Farmhouse

truth is
exactly the same size as the universe
and my eyes are narrow
i stare at one of my fingernails
its mass is pink
its edge is blue with coke-dust
it grows on a warm well-nourished hand

i look up and suck smoke
the windows are black

people are being killed

the first time I met a girl called Helen
she told me
'money is the basis of life'
the second time i met her she said
'money is the basis of life'

people are being killed

i stare at those four words
typed in black
they are true words
but they do not bleed
and die and rot

commonplace cruelty
timetable cruelty

i haven't seen much of the world
but i've seen enough

i have known more horror in half an hour
than i shall ever have the skill to tell

my right hand soothes my left hand

i have known more beauty in half a minute
than i shall ever have the skill to tell

i make a fond small smile
remembering gentleness in many cities

so many good people

and people are being killed

How to Kill Cuba

You must burn the people first,
Then the grass and trees, then the stones.
You must cut the island out of all the maps,
The history books, out of the old newspapers,
Even the newspapers which hated Cuba,
And burn all these, and burn
The paintings, poems and photographs and films
And when you have burnt all these
You must bury the ashes
You must guard the grave
And even then
Cuba will only be dead like Che Guevara –
Technically dead, that's all,
Technically dead.

Family Planning

Why do the Spanish have so many children?

Our first child was a priest.
Then we had a nun.
The next three were all policemen.

You've got to have one child you can talk to.

Open Day at Porton

These bottles are being filled with madness,
A kind of liquid madness concentrate
Which can be drooled across the land
Leaving behind a shuddering human highway...

    A welder trying to eat his arm.

    Children pushing stale food into their eyes
    To try to stop the chemical spectaculars
    Pulsating inside their hardening skulls.

    A health visitor throwing herself downstairs,
    Climbing the stairs, throwing herself down again
    Shouting: Take the nails out of my head.

There is no damage to property.

Now, nobody likes manufacturing madness,
But if we didn't make madness in bottles
We wouldn't know how to deal with bottled madness.

We don't know how to deal with bottled madness.

We all really hate manufacturing madness
But if we didn't make madness in bottles
We wouldn't know how to be sane.

Responsible madness experts assure us
Britain would never be the first
To uncork such a global brainquake.

But suppose some foreign nut sprayed Kent
With his insanity aerosol...
Well, there's only one answer to madness.

Norman Morrison

On November 2nd 1965
in the multi-coloured multi-minded
United beautiful States of terrible America
Norman Morrison set himself on fire
outside the Pentagon.
He was thirty-one, he was a Quaker,
and his wife (seen weeping in the newsreels)
and his three children
survive him as best they can.
He did it in Washington where everyone could see
because
people were being set on fire
in the dark corners of Vietnam where nobody could see.
Their names, ages, beliefs and loves
are not recorded.
This is what Norman Morrison did.
He poured petrol over himself.
He burned. He suffered.
He died.
That is what he did
in the heart of Washington
where everyone could see.
He simply burned away his clothes,
his passport, his pink-tinted skin,
put on a new skin of flame
and became
Vietnamese.

Would You Mind Signing This Receipt?

When you get back home
You will find a black patch on the ground,
A patch of blackness shaped like a house
Where your house used to stand.

It was a mistake.
It was the wrong house.
It was all a mistake
Based on faulty information.

When you get back home
You will find three black heaps on the ground.
Three black heaps shaped like children
On the patch of blackness shaped like a house
Where your house used to stand.

It was a mistake.
They were the wrong people.
It was all a mistake
Based on faulty information.

Three children.
51 dollars compensation per child.
That comes to 153 dollars, madam.

For Rachel: Christmas 1965

Caesar sleeping in his armoured city
Herod shaking like a clockwork toy
and spies are moving into Rama
asking for a baby boy.

> Caesar is the father of Herod
> Herod is the father of us all
> and we'll be obedient, silent little children
> or the moon will drop
> and the sun will fall.

Someone must have warned the wanted mother
she'll be hiding with her family
and soldiers are marching through Rama
silently, obediently.

> Caesar is the father of Herod
> Herod is the father of us all
> and we'll be obedient, silent little children
> or the moon will drop
> and the sun will fall.

Down all the white-washed alleys of Rama
small soft bodies are bayoneted
and Rachel is weeping in Rama
and will not be comforted.

> Caesar is the father of Herod
> Herod is the father of us all
> and we'll be obedient, silent little children
> or the moon will drop
> and the sun will fall.

Caesar sleeping in his armoured city
Herod dreaming in his swansdown bed
and Rachel is weeping in Rama
and will not be comforted.

> Caesar is the father of Herod
> Herod is the father of us all
> and we'll be obedient, silent little children
> or the moon will drop
> and the sun will fall.

Thinks: I'll Finish These Gooks by Building an Electronically Operated Physical Barrier Right Along Their Seventeenth Parallel!!!

(for John Arden and Margaretta D'Arcy)

1. Thousands of miles of invisible fencing
    Distinguishable only by the balding badness of the earth
    And a slight electric shimmer in the air.

    But if you throw raw hamburger towards the sky
    It comes down grilled.

2. The Marine shouted:
    'I don't mind fighting Charlie,
    But not with my back to a goddam
    Electronically operated physical barrier.'

3. We have stopped lifting our electronic barrier
    For one hour daily at Checkpoint Harold.
    We don't mind the refugee double-deckers heading north,
    But sod this constant rumbling southwards
    Of enormous invisible wooden horses.

4. If the barrier fails
    We are going to bring in volcanoes.

5. 'I just pissed against that
    Electronically operated physical barrier,'
    Boasted the police dog to his bitch,
    'And eighty-two square miles got devastated.'

6. Tom Sawyer drew a line in the dust with his toe:
    'Step over that and I'll burn your skin off.'

7. What we really need
    Is an electronically operated physical barrier
    Around the United States.

To a Russian Soldier in Prague

You are going to be hated by the people.

They will hate you over their freakish breakfast of tripe soup and pastries.
They will squint hatred at you on their way to pretend to work.
By the light of yellow beer they will hate you with jokes you'll never hear.

You're beginning to feel
Like a landlord in a slum
Like a white man in Harlem
Like a U.S. Marine in Saigon

Socialists are hated
By all who kill for profit and power.
But you are going to be hated by
The people – who are all different.
The people – who are all extraordinary.
The people – who are all of equal value.
Socialism is theirs, it was invented for them.
Socialism is theirs, it can only be made by them.

Africa, Asia and Latin America are screaming:
STARVATION. POVERTY. OPPRESSION.
When they turn to America.
They see only flames and children in the flames.
When they turn to England
They see an old lady in a golden wheelchair,
Share certificates in one hand, a pistol in the other.
When they turn to Russia
They see – you.

You are going to be hated
As the English have usually been hated.
The starving, the poor and the oppressed
Are turning, turning away.
While you nervously guard a heap of documents
They stagger away through the global crossfire
Towards revolution, towards socialism.

Goodbye Richard Nixon

Your California bedroom was red white and blue
You won ten thousand dollars playing poker in the Navy
Your College football team was called The Poets
And you tucked the bottom of your tie into the top of your trousers
    Gave you a sort of safe feeling

You had a music box played Hail to the Chief
Your favourite building was the Lincoln Memorial
Your favourite food was cottage cheese and ketchup
Your favourite Xmas song was Rudolph the Red-Nosed Reindeer
    And you never wiped your arse

Ceasefire
(dedicated to the Medical Aid Committee for Vietnam)

The outside of my body was half-eaten
by fire which clings as tight as skin.
The fire has turned some of my skin
into black scab bits of roughness
and some pale bits smooth as plastic,
which no one dares touch
except me and the doctor.
Everyone who looks at me is scared.
That's not because I want to hurt people
but because so much of me
looks like the meat of a monster...

I was walking to the market.
Then I was screaming.
They found me screaming.
They put out the flames on my skin.
They laid me on a stretcher and I cried:
Not on my back!
So they turned me over and I cried:
Not on my front!

A doctor put a needle in my arm
and my mind melted
and I fell into a furnace of dreams of furnaces.

When I woke up I was in a white hospital.
Everything I wanted to say scared me
and I did not want to scare the others
in that white hospital,
so I said nothing, cried as quietly as I could.

Months passed over my head
and bombers passed over my head
and people came and said they were my parents
and they found out the places on my face
where I could bear to be kissed.

And I pretended I could see them
but I couldn't really look out of my eyes
but only inwards, into my head
where the flames still clung and hurt, and talked.

And the flames said:
You are meat.
You are ugly meat.
Your body cannot grow to loveliness.
Nobody could love such ugly meat.
Only ugly meat could love such ugly meat.
Better be stewed for soup and eaten.

And months passed over my head
and bombers passed over my head
and the voices of the flames began to flicker
and I began to believe the people who said they were my parents
were my parents.

And one day I threw myself forward
so that I sat up in bed, for the first time,
and hurled my arms around my mother,
and however the skin of my chest howled out in its pain
I held her, I held her, I held her
and knew she was my mother.
And I forgot that I was monster meat
and I knew she did not know that I was monster meat.

I held her, I held her.

And, sweet sun which blesses all the world —
all the flames faded.
The flames of my skin
and the flames inside my head —
all the flames faded
and I was flooded
with love for my mother
who did not know
that I was monster meat.

And so, in the love-flood, I let go of my mother
and fell back upon my pillow
and I rolled my head to the left side
and I saw a child, or it might have been an old man,
eating his rice with his only arm
and I rolled my head to the right side
and saw another child, or she might have been an old woman,
being fed through the arm from a tube from a red bottle —
and I loved them, and, flooded with love
I started to sing
the song of the game I used to play with my friends
in the long-ago days before the flames came:

  One, one, bounce the ball,
  Once for the sandal-maker,
  Two, two, bounce the ball,
  Twice for the fishermen on the river.
  Three, three, bounce the ball,
  Three times for your golden lover —

And had to stop singing.
Throat choked with vomit.

And then the flames exploded again all over my skin
and then the flames exploded again inside my head
and I burned, sweet sun, sweet mother, I burned.

  Sweet sun, which blesses all the world,
  this was one of the people of Vietnam.

I suppose we love each other.
We're stupid if we don't.

We have a choice —
Either choke to death on our own vomit
or to become one
with the sweet sun, which blesses all the world.

To Whom It May Concern (Tell Me Lies about Vietnam)

I was run over by the truth one day.
Ever since the accident I've walked this way
   So stick my legs in plaster
   Tell me lies about Vietnam.

Heard the alarm clock screaming with pain,
Couldn't find myself so I went back to sleep again
   So fill my ears with silver
   Stick my legs in plaster
   Tell me lies about Vietnam.

Every time I shut my eyes all I see is flames.
Made a marble phone book and I carved all the names
   So coat my eyes with butter
   Fill my ears with silver
   Stick my legs in plaster
   Tell me lies about Vietnam.

I smell something burning, hope it's just my brains.
They're only dropping peppermints and daisy-chains
   So stuff my nose with garlic
   Coat my eyes with butter
   Fill my ears with silver
   Stick my legs in plaster
   Tell me lies about Vietnam.

Where were you at the time of the crime?
Down by the Cenotaph drinking slime
   So chain my tongue with whisky
   Stuff my nose with garlic
   Coat my eyes with butter
   Fill my ears with silver
   Stick my legs in plaster
   Tell me lies about Vietnam.

You put your bombers in, you put your conscience out,
You take the human being and you twist it all about
   So scrub my skin with women
   Chain my tongue with whisky
   Stuff my nose with garlic
   Coat my eyes with butter
   Fill my ears with silver
   Stick my legs in plaster
   Tell me lies about Vietnam.

Peace Is Milk

Peace is milk.
War is acid.
The elephant dreams of bathing in lakes of milk.
Acid blood
Beats through the veins
Of the monstrous, vulture-weight fly,
Shaking, rocking his framework.

The elephants, their gentle thinking shredded
By drugs disseminated in the electricity supply,
Sell their children, buy tickets for the Zoo
And form a dead-eyed queue
Which stretches from the decorative, spiked gates
To the enormous shed where the flies are perching.

Peace is milk
War is acid.
Sometimes an elephant finds a bucket of milk.
Swash! and it's empty.
The fly feeds continually.
The fly bulges with acid
Or he needs more. And more.

An overweight fly levers himself
From his revolving chair,
Paces across the elephantskin floor,
Presses a button
And orders steak, steak, elephant steak
And a pint of acid.

Peace is milk.
War is acid.
The elephants are being dried in the sun.
The huge flies overflow.

Look down from the plane.
Those clouds of marvellous milk.
Easily they swing by on the wind,
Assembling, disassembling,
Forming themselves into pleasure-towers,
Unicorns, waterfalls, funny faces;
Swimming, basking, dissolving –
Easily, easily.

Tomorrow the cream-clouds will be fouled.
The sky will be buckshot-full of paratroop swarms
With their money-talking guns,
Headlines carved across their foreheads,
Sophisticated, silent electrical equipment.
Heart-screws and fear-throwers.
The day after tomorrow
The clouds will curdle, the clouds will begin to burn –
Yes, we expected that, knew about that,
Overkill, overburn, multi-megacorpse,
Yeah, yeah, yeah we knew about that
Cry the white-hearted flies.

Channel One –
A fly scientist in an ivory helmet
Who always appears about to cry
Explains why the viewers have to die.

Channel Nine –
A fly statesman,
Hardly audible through the acid rain,
Explains why nothing can ever happen again.

Oh we'll soon be finished with the creatures of the earth.
There's no future in elephants, milk or Asiatics.

We should be working out
How to inflict the maximum pain
On Martians and Venusians.

Sour sky.
The elephants are entering the shed.
Sour sky.
The flies have dropped a star called Wormwood
And turned the Pacific into an acid bath.
Sour sky.

Socrates said no harm could come to a good man,
But even Socrates
Couldn't turn the hemlock into a banana milk shake
With one high-voltage charge
From his Greek-sky eyes.
Even Socrates, poor bugger.

They are rubbing their forelegs together,
Washing each others' holes with their stubbled tongues,
Watching us while they wash.

Then, like brown rain running backwards,
They hurtle upwards, vibrating with acid.
They patrol our ceilings, always looking downwards.
Pick up the phone, that's them buzzing.
The turd-born flies.

Peace is milk
And milk is simple
And milk is hard to make.
It takes clean grass, fed by clean earth, clear air, clean rain,
Takes a calm cow with all her stomachs working
And it takes milk to raise that cow.

The milk is not for the good elephant.
The milk is not for the bad elephant.
But the milk may be for the lucky elephant
Looming along until the end of the kingdom of the flies.

A family of people, trapped in Death Valley,
Drank from the radiator,
Laid out the hubcaps as bowls for the dew,
Buried each other up to the neck in sand
And waited for better times, which came
Just after they stopped hoping.

So the sweet survival of the elephants demands
Vision, cunning, energy and possibly burial
Until, maybe, the good times roll for the first time
And a tidal wave of elephants,
A stampede of milk,
Tornadoes through the capitals of flydom,
Voices flow like milk,
And below the white, nourishing depths –
Bodies moving any way they want to move,
Eyes resting or dancing at will,
Limbs and minds which follow, gladly,
The music of the milk.

So you drink my milk, I'll drink yours.
We'll melt together in the sun
Despite the high-explosive flies
Which hover, which hover,
Which hover, which hover,
Like a million plaguey Jehovahs.

Their prisons, their police, their armies, their laws,
Their camps where Dobermans pace the cadaver of a field,
Their flame factories and Black Death Factories,
The sourness of their sky –
Well that's the poisonous weather the elephants must lumber through
Surviving, surviving,
Until the good times roll for the first time.

But it doesn't end
With an impregnable city carved out of the living light.
It doesn't end
In the plastic arms of an Everest-size Sophia Loren.
It doesn't end
When the world says a relieved farewell to the white man
As he goofs off to colonise the Milky Way.

It continues, it continues.
When all of the elephants push it goes slowly forward.
When they stop pushing it rolls backwards.
It continues, it continues.
Towards milk, towards acid.

The taste of milk has been forgotten.
Most elephants agree peace is impossible.
Choosing death instead, they are jerked towards death
Slowly by newspapers, nightmares or cancer,
More quickly by heroin or war.

And some, the tops of their skulls sliced off
By money-knives or the axes of guilt,
Bow their great heads and let their hurting brains
Slop in the lavatory to drown.

There are prophets like Ginsberg – grandson of William Blake –
Desperate elephants who drink a pint of diamonds.
Their eyes become scored with a thousand white trenches,
Their hide shines with a constellation
Of diamond-headed boils,
Each footstep leaves a pool of diamond dust.
And sure, they shine,
They become shouting stars,
Burning with light until they are changed by pain
Into diamonds for everyone.
And sure, they go down shining,
They shine themselves to death,
The diamond drinkers.

The world is falling to pieces
But some of the pieces taste good.

There are various ways of making peace,
Most of them too childish for English elephants.
Given time and love it's possible
To cultivate a peace-field large enough
For the playing of a child.
It's possible to prepare a meal
And give it with care and love
To someone who takes it with care and love.
These are beginnings, but it's late, late –
TV Dinner tonight.
It's possible to suck the taste of peace
From one blade of grass
Or recognise peace in a can of white paint,
But it's not enough.
In Nirvana there's only room for one at a time.

WELL, YOU COULD STOP KILLING PEOPLE FOR A START,

Let loose the elephants.
Let the fountains talk milk.
Free the grass, let it walk wherever it likes.
Let the passports and prisons burn, their smoke turning into milk.
Let the pot-smokers blossom into milk-coloured mental petals.
We all need to be breast-fed
And start again.

Tear the fly-woven lying suits
Off the backs of the white killers
And let their milky bodies
Make naked pilgrimage
To wash the sores of Africa and Asia
With milk, for milk is peace
And money tastes of guns,
Guns taste of acid.

Make love well, generously, deeply.
There's nothing simpler in the savage world,
Making good love, making good good love.
There's nothing harder in the tender world,
Making good love, making good good love,
And most of the elephants, most of the time
Go starving for good love, not knowing what the pain is,
But it can be done and thank Blake it is done,
Making good love, making good good love.

In houses built of fly turds, in fly-turd feasting mansions,
Fly fear insurance offices even,
Fly-worshipping cathedrals even,
Even in murder offices just off the corridors of fly power –
Making good love, making good good love.

Good lovers float.
Happy to know they are becoming real.
They float out above the sourness, high on the seeds of peace.
There are too few of them up there.
Too little milk.
Drink more milk.
Breed more cows and elephants.
Think more milk and follow your banana.
We need evangelist, door-to-door lovers,
Handing it out, laying it down,
Spreading the elephant seed, delivering the revolutionary milk,
Making good love, making good good love.
United Nations teams of roving elephant milkmen
Making good love, making good good love,
Because peace is milk,
Peace is milk
And the skinny, thirsty earth, its face covered with flies,
Screams like a baby.

A Tourist Guide to England

£ Welcome to England!
England is a happy country

£ Here is a happy English businessman.
Hating his money, he spends it all
On bibles for Cambodia
And a charity to preserve
The Indian Cobra from extinction.

£ I'm sorry you can't see our happy coal-miners.
Listen hard and you can hear them
Singing Welsh hymns far underground.
Oh. The singing seems to have stopped.

£ No, that is not Saint Francis of Assisi.
That is a happy English policeman.

£ Here is a happy black man.
No, it is not illegal to be black. Not yet.

£ Here are the slums.
They are preserved as a tourist attraction.
Here is a happy slum-dweller.
Hello, slum-dweller!
No, his answer is impossible to translate.

£ Here are some happy English schoolchildren.
See John. See Susan. See Mike.
They are studying for their examinations.
Study, children, study!
John will get his O-Levels
And an O-Level job and an O-Level house and an O-Level wife.
Susan will get her A-Levels
And an A-Level job and an A-Level house and an A-Level husband.
Mike will fail.

£ Here are some happy English soldiers.
They are going to make the Irish happy.

£ No, please understand.
We understand the Irish
Because we've been sending soldiers to Ireland
For hundreds and hundreds of years.

£ First we tried to educate them
With religion, famine and swords.
But the Irish were slow to learn.

£ So now we are trying to educate them
With truncheons, gas, rubber bullets,
Steel bullets, internment and torture,
We are trying to teach the Irish
To be as happy as us.

£ So please understand us
And if your country
Should be forced to educate
Another country in the same way,
Or your own citizens in the same way –
We will try to understand you.

Sorry Bout That

Truth is a diamond
A diamond is hard
You don't exist
Without a Barclaycard

Sorry bout that
Sorry bout that
Even South African cops
Do the sorry bout that

They showed me the world and said:
What do you think?
I said: half about women
And half about drink

And I'm sorry bout that
Sorry bout that
Mother, I need that booze
And I'm sorry bout that

If you cut your conscience
Into Kennomeat chunks
You can get elected
To the House of Drunks

Sorry bout that
Sorry bout that
You'll never have to think again
And I'm sorry bout that

You can do the Skull
Or the Diplomat
But I do a dance called
The Sorry Bout That

Do the Mighty Whitey
Or the Landlord Rat
But I'll keep grooving to
The Sorry Bout That

Sorry bout that
Sorry bout that
They make me dance with pistols and ten to one
I'm sorry bout that

I saw Money walking
Down the road
Claws like an eagle
And a face like a toad

Well I know your name baby
Seen you before
Slapping on your make-up
For the Third World War

Sorry bout that
Sorry bout that
Someone set the world on fire
And I'm sorry bout that

Victor Jara of Chile

(This ballad has been set to music and recorded by Arlo Guthrie)

Victor Jara of Chile
Lived like a shooting star
He fought for the people of Chile
With his songs and his guitar

And his hands were gentle
His hands were strong

Victor Jara was a peasant
Worked from a few years old
He sat upon his father's plough
And watched the earth unfold

And his hands were gentle
His hands were strong

When the neighbours had a wedding
Or one of their children died
His mother sang all night for them
With Victor by her side

And his hands were gentle
His hands were strong

He grew to be fighter
Against the people's wrongs
He listened to their grief and joy
And turned them into songs

And his hands were gentle
His hands were strong

He sang about the copper miners
And those who work the land
He sang about the factory workers
And they knew he was their man

And his hands were gentle
His hands were strong

He campaigned for Allende
Working night and day
He sang: take hold of your brother's hand
The future begins today

And his hands were gentle
His hands were strong

The bloody generals seized Chile
They arrested Victor then
They caged him in a stadium
With five thousand frightened men

And his hands were gentle
His hands were strong

Victor stood in the stadium
His voice was brave and strong
He sang for his fellow-prisoners
Till the guards cut short his song

And his hands were gentle
His hands were strong

They broke the bones in both his hands
They beat his lovely head
They tore him with electric shocks
After two long days of torture they shot him dead

And his hands were gentle
His hands were strong

And now the Generals rule Chile
And the British have their thanks
For they rule with Hawker Hunters
And they rule with Chieftain tanks

And his hands were gentle
His hands were strong

Victor Jara of Chile
Lived like a shooting star
He fought for the people of Chile
With his songs and his guitar

And his hands were gentle
His hands were strong

Astrid-Anna

(This piece was written especially for an Anglo-German audience
at the Goethe Institute in London)

Here is a news item from a right-wing British paper – the *Daily Mail*.

TERROR GIRL IS ILL
'Baader Meinhof girl Astrid Proll, who faces extradition to Germany, is physic-
ally and mentally ill, her friends said yesterday. They gathered outside Bow
Street magistrates court…and handed out leaflets saying she was having diffi-
culty in breathing and had "sensations of panic". Carnations were thrown to
her as she was led away.'

If Astrid Proll, who is now a British citizen by marriage – Anna Puttick – is
sent back to Germany, she will be dead within two years. There are special
sections in special prisons in Germany where prisoners like Astrid-Anna find
it easy to obtain revolvers. Even odder, they do not shoot their jailers. They
shoot out their own brains. If the British hand over Astrid-Anna to the West
German police, we will be collaborating in yet another murder. Well, we done
a few before.

> Sensations of panic
> Carnations were thrown
> Free Astrid   Free Anna

Astrid-Anna was accused of the attempted murder of two policemen.
But she has never been found guilty of anything.
But she was the first prisoner in Germany to be kept in conditions of SENSORY
DEPRIVATION. In the Silent Wing of the Women's Psychiatric Unit at Ossen-
dorf Prison in Cologne.

There are white walls, constant lighting, no external sounds – techniques
designed to disorientate and subdue. She spent a total of FOUR AND A HALF
MONTHS in the Silent Wing. About TWENTY-FOUR WEEKS in the Silent
Wing. About ONE THOUSAND SEVEN HUNDRED HOURS in the Silent
Wing.

Her trial was stopped by a doctor. He found the following complaints: weakness
and exhaustion, the feeling of 'being wrapped in cotton wool', dizziness, black-
outs, headaches and no appetite, feelings of breaking down, an inability to
concentrate, increasing signs of phobia and agoraphobia. Her blood circulation
began to collapse, depriving her brain of oxygen. Continued imprisonment,
said the doctor, would lead to PERMANENT AND IRREPARABLE DAMAGE.

Four and a half months
In the silent wing
Four and a half months
in the silent wing

Shut in a white box
Under the constant neon
Being whitened in a box
Under the silent neon
Boxed in the white neon
Of the silent box
Under the constant wing.

In the white of the silent box
In the silence of the white box
In the constant silence
In the constant white
In the white of the white box

    Your head starts exploding
    Your skull is about to split
    Your spine is drilling into your brain
    You are pissing your brains away

In the white of the silent box
In the silence of the white box
In the constant silence
In the constant white
In the white of the white box

    Under the Nazis an experiment was made in which they locked a man
    in a white cell with white furniture. He wore white clothes. And all
    his food and drink were white. He very soon lost his appetite. He
    could not eat. He could not drink. The sight of the white food and
    the white drink made him vomit.

Astrid came to England and began life again as Anna. She worked with young
people in the East End as an instructor in car mechanics. One Englishwoman
says: 'Anna gave me and my children enormous support...When I was drink-
ing too much, it was Anna who cared enough to see why and then helped me
to make decisions that I was drinking to forget.'

    This is the Terror Girl of the *Daily Mail*.

Now Anna is being kept under maximum-security conditions in a man's prison
– Brixton. There are only two women in the prison. They are supervised by
seven warders. They have no privacy. When Anna has a visitor, her convers-

ation is listened to. When her lawyer visits her in her cell below the court, there is always a policeman in the cell. For three hours a day she is allowed to meet the other woman in Brixton jail. The rest of the time she spends on her own.

> So will Anna be sent back by our rulers
> to the white of the white box
> to the silence of the white silence
> to the constant silence and the constant white
> to the whiteness of the silence
> to the silence of the whiteness
> to the whiteness of the whiteness
> to the silence of the silence
> to the whiteness of the whiteness
> to the silence of the silence
> to the whiteness to the silence to the whiteness to the silence
> whiteness   whiteness   silence   silence

Stop. You can stop them. If Anna is extradited or not depends on the Home Secretary. Write to the Home Secretary. Demand she be allowed to stay. Demand that she be treated humanely. And if you are German, force your government to be satisfied with its revenge, to drop its demands for extradition, to drop the case against her, to close the Silent Wing forever.

> We will walk out from here
> into the blue-eyed, brown-faced, green-haired world
> our spinning, singing planet
> but Anna who was Astrid lies chained in the box of the state
> silent men in suits walk towards her with blank faces
> they carry syringes and hooks and guns in their white briefcases

LET ANNA STAY HERE
LET HER WORK
LET HER REST
LET HER FIND LOVE

Activities of an East and West Dissident Blues
(verses to be read by the Secret Police, the chorus to be read by anyone else)

When I woke up this morning it was nothing o'clock
I erased all the dreams from my head
I washed my face in shadow-juice
And for breakfast I ate my bed

I said goodbye to my jailer and spy
Burnt letters from all of my friends
Then I caught the armoured bus for a mystery tour
To the street with two dead ends

and oh
I wish I had a great big shiny brass diver's helmet
and I wish I had great big leaden diver's boots on me
and I wish I had infallible mates upstairs at the air-pumps
as I wandered forever on the bottom of the great free sea

I arrived at my factory or office or field
I did what I was meant to do
I left undone what should be left undone
And all of the others did the same thing too
        And you too? Right.

In the evening I read whatever should be read
Listened to whatever should be heard
And I taught the top twenty government slogans
To my golden-caged security bird

And I changed into the pair of pyjamas
With a number stamped on brown and black bars
And I pulled down the blind to keep out of my mind
The excitement of the stars

but oh
I wish I had a great big shining brass diver's helmet
and I wish I had great big leaden diver's boots on me
and infallible mates upstairs with their hands on the air-pumps
as I wandered forever on the bottom of the great green
flowing free and easy sea

Carol During the Falklands Experience

In the blind midslaughter
The drowned sank alone
Junta set like concrete
Thatcher like a stone

Blood had fallen, blood on blood,
Blood on blood
In the blind midslaughter
In the madness flood

What shall I give them
Powerless as I am?
If I were a rich man
I wouldn't give a damn

If I were an arms dealer
I would play my part –
All I can do is point towards
The holy human heart.

Chile in Chains

'Student demonstrators yesterday forced the Chilean Ambassador to clamber over rooftops and hide in a kitchen after they broke up a meeting he was trying to address at St John's College, Cambridge. The Ambassador, Professor Miguel Schweitzer, was invited to talk to the Monday Club on diplomatic relations between Britain and Chile...' *The Guardian*, 13 November 1980.

'Any victory for the people, however small, is worth celebrating' – a demonstrator.

'I've never seen an Ambassador running before, so I'm not quite sure how to rate him as a runner' – a Cambridge spectator.

There's eight men in Cambridge called the Monday Club,
It's like the British Movement with brains,
And they thought it cute to pay a sort of tribute
To the government of Chile in Chains.

So the Mondays invited the Ambassador
To St John's as their honoured guest –
But he must come unto them secretly
(At the Special Branch's special request).

The Ambassador was glad to get an invite –
He flicked off his electric shock machine,
Scrubbed the blood from under his fingernails
And summoned his bodyguard and limousine.

'What shall I tell them?' the Ambassador mused
As he flushed his better self down the loo,
'Allende was a mass murderer
But Pinochet is Jesus Mark Two?'

'What shall I tell them?' the Ambassador thought
As his car snaked down Cambridgeshire lanes,
'That Victor Jara tortured himself to death
And Paradise is Chile in Chains?'

But as they were proffering South African sherry
The faces of the Monday Club froze –
For a mob of Lefties had assembled outside:
Socialist and Anarchist desperadoes!

So they switched their venue from the Wordsworth Room
To the Wilberforce Room, locked the doors
And the Monday Club gave its limp applause
To a pimp for fascist whores.

But the revolution never stops
(We even go marching when it rains),
And a Yale lock is no protection at all
For a salesman for Chile in Chains.

When the Left tumbled into the Wilberforce Room
The Ambassador was terrified.
His bodyguard shovelled him out the back door
And the Monday Club was occupied.

Oh they hurried him over the rooftops
And the pigeons gave him all they had.
Oh they hid him away in the kitchen
And all of the food went bad.

But the Left sat down in the Wilberforce Room.
The atmosphere smelled of shame.
Then a Don said: 'This is private property.
Tell me your college and name.'

'We didn't come to talk about property.
We came to talk about the pains
Of the poor and the murdered and the tortured and the raped
Who are helpless in Chile in Chains.'

They grouped a scrum of cops round their honoured guest
And we jeered at him and his hosts
As he ran with the cops across the grass of the Court
Like a torturer pursued by ghosts.

He galloped with his minders to his limousine
But the stink of his terror remains
And everyone who watched his cowardly run
Knows – Chile will tear off her chains.

A Prayer for the Rulers of this World

God bless their suits
God bless their ties
God bless their grubby
Little alibis

God bless their firm,
Commanding jaws
God bless their thumbs
God bless their claws

God bless their livers
God bless their lungs
God bless their
Shit-encrusted tongues

God bless their prisons
God bless their guns
God bless their deaf and dumb
Daughters and sons

God bless their corpuscles
God bless their sperms
God bless their souls
Like little white worms

Oh God will bless
The whole bloody crew
For God, we know,
Is a ruler too

And the blessed shall live
And the damned shall die
And God will rule
In his suit and his tie

One Bad Word

(for my Black and Asian friends and their children
who are threatened in the streets)

You call me that bad word
That one bad word
That bad word weighs a thousand tonne
That one bad word burns my skin all over
You call me one bad word
That word makes my mother
Cast down her eyes in shame
Makes my father
Deny his own name
Makes my brother
Turn and fight like a demon
Makes my sister
Spend her life in bad dreaming

So call me one bad word
And you don't know what will happen
It could be tears it could be blood
I could be storm
It could be silence
It could be a rage
Hot enough to burn the whole town down
Could be a stampede of elephants
Through your back garden
And into your mother's
Frilly perfume sitting room.
Could be zombie nightmares
Every night for the rest
Of your natural life
Could be all your food
From this day on
Will taste of rotten fishheads
Could be anything
Could be the end of the world
But most likely
This will follow:

I'll stare at you
For one cold second
And then I'll turn and walk away from you
Leaving you alone with yourself
And your one bad word

from

BLUE COFFEE

POEMS 1985-1996

YES

A Puppy Called Puberty

It was like keeping a puppy in your underpants
A secret puppy you weren't allowed to show to anyone
Not even your best friend or your worst enemy

You wanted to pat him stroke him cuddle him
All the time but you weren't supposed to touch him

He only slept for five minutes at a time
Then he'd suddenly perk up his head
In the middle of school medical inspection
And always on bus rides
So you had to climb down from the upper deck
All bent double to smuggle the puppy off the bus
Without the buxom conductress spotting
Your wicked and ticketless stowaway.

Jumping up, wet-nosed, eagerly wagging –
He only stopped being a nuisance
When you were alone together
Pretending to be doing your homework
But really gazing at each other
Through hot and hazy daydreams

Of those beautiful schoolgirls on the bus
With kittens bouncing in their sweaters.

A Dog Called Elderly

And now I have a dog called Elderly
And all he ever wants to do
Is now and then be let out for a piss
But spend the rest of his lifetime
Sleeping on my lap in front of the fire.

Questionnaire

Q. How do you do?
A. Like a bear in the Zoo.
Q. Why should that be?
A. The world is not free.
Q. Must it always be so?
A. No.
   With our hearts and our brains
   We will tear off its chains.
Q. You write poems, why?
A. Because I am shy.
   In real life I conceal
   Everything that I feel,
   But in poems I shout
   And my feelings fly out.
Q. Why do you write in verse at all?
A. I would always rather jump than crawl,
   My tongue would rather sing than talk
   And my feet would sooner dance than walk.
Q. What's the difference between a walker and dancer?
A. Love is the answer.
Q. Why do you write?
A.   For the love of life
   And my friends, my animals,
   my children and my wife.
   I am lucky and happy –
Q. But how do you do?
A. Like a bear who dreams he is not in a Zoo.

Yes

A smile says: Yes.
A heart says: Blood.
When the rain says: Drink
The earth says: Mud.

The kangaroo says: Trampoline.
Giraffes say: Tree.
A bus says: Us
While a car says: Me.

Lemon trees say: Lemons.
A jug says: Lemonade.
The villain says: You're wonderful.
The hero: I'm afraid.

The forest says: Hide and Seek.
The grass says: Green and Grow.
The railway says: Maybe.
The prison says: No.

The millionaire says: Take.
The beggar says: Give.
The soldier cries: Mother!
The baby sings: Live.

The river says: Come with me.
The moon says: Bless.
The stars says: Enjoy the light.
The sun says: Yes.

Golo, the Gloomy Goalkeeper

Golo plays for the greatest soccer team in the Universe.
They are so mighty that their opponents never venture out of their own
      penalty area.
They are so all-conquering that Golo never touches the ball during a match,
      and very seldom sees it.
Every game seems to last a lifetime to Golo, the Gloomy Goalkeeper.
Golo scratches white paint off the goalposts' surface to reveal the silver shining
underneath.
      He kisses the silver of the goalpost.
It does not respond.

Golo counts the small stones in the penalty area.
There are three hundred and seventy eight, which is not his lucky number.
Golo pretends to have the hiccups, then says to himself, imitating his sister's
      voice:
Don't breathe, and just die basically.

Golo breaks eight small sticks in half.
Then he has sixteen very small sticks.
He plants geranium seeds along the goal-line.
He paints a picture of a banana and sells it to the referee at half-time.

Golo finds, among the bootmarks in the dust, the print of one stiletto heel.
He crawls around on all fours doing lion imitations.
He tries to read his future in the palm of his hand, but forgets to take his
      glove off.
He writes a great poem about butterflies but tears it up because he can't think
      of a rhyme for Wednesday.
He knits a sweater for the camel in the Zoo.

Golo suddenly realises he can't remember if he is a man or a woman.
He takes a quick look, but still can't decide.
Golo makes up his mind that grass is his favourite colour.
He puts on boots, track-suit, gloves and hat all the same colour as grass.
He paints his face a gentle shade of green.

Golo lies down on the pitch and becomes invisible.
The grass tickles the back of his neck.
At last Golo is happy.
He has fallen in love with the grass.
And the grass has fallen in love with Golo, the Gloomy Goalkeeper.

Blood and Oil

(to the British armed forces)

And once again the politicians
Whose greatest talent is for lying
Are sending you where they're afraid to go
To do their killing and dying

You're young and you've been trained to fight
You're brave, well-equipped and loyal.
That's why they're sending you to Hell –
Blood and Oil.

It's not to defend the Falklands sheep
Or Christians in Ireland
But to sit in a tank till you are moved
On a giant chessboard of desert sand

You're not there to fight against tyranny
Or for hostages or British soil
But for economics, the dollars of death –
Blood and Oil.

And the soldiers you fight will be young men
With no reason to kill, young men like you
With beautiful families back home
And some with wives and children too

But no politicians will be there
When lungs tear and arteries boil
They'll be filmed with survivors in hospital
Blood and Oil.

Yes, once again the politicians
Whose greatest talent is for lying
Are sending young men where old men dare not go
To do their killing and dying
To do their killing and dying
To do their killing and dying

Blood and Oil
Blood and Oil
Blood and Oil

Blood and oil...

Millennium Countdown

Nine will coo you with a beeper bomb
Eight will tickle the mousetrap
Seven will shave you like a zombie prom
Six is the ultimate cowpat
Five will catch you in a yellow thumb zone
Four will play the Hempty Dempty
Three will be lost in abalone Babylone
Two will find your pooter empty
Some say One will be miserable fun
Some say Bake the town down
But I say if you count me count me out
Millennium Countdown

Bruce Thursday
Minority shine
Sliding all over the meltdown
You bit it – you git it –
Harna! Harna!
Millennium Countdown

Can't stop dreaming about the future
Two thousand years in a beggar's coat
Can't stop screaming about the factoid future
Two thousand years got stuck in my throat

Trying Hard To Be Normal

(for Spike Milligan)

I bought myself a hairbrush
A Military Hairbrush it turned out
It came in a box marked Military Hairbrush
I opened the box
And took out the Military Hairbrush
But there was still something left in the box
I shook the box and brought out a brochure
It was printed in every colour that exists
The brochure showed me with diagrams
And a text in seven languages
How to brush my hair with the Military Hairbrush

I was about to throw the box away
When I realised there was something else left in the box
I shook the box and out dropped
A smaller brush
A wooden brush a humble brush
Certainly not a military brush
Just a brush
I looked for an explanation in the brochure
And found that this was the brush
With which to brush
The Military Hairbrush

Or

Simplicity
is a glass of water
Stupidity
is a mugful of dust
Simplicity
is the moonlight's daughter
Stupidity
is the father of rust

get the idea
they are opposites
they are not twins
get the idea
when simplicity weeps
stupidity grins

Simplicity
is a box of matches
Stupidity
is a forest ablaze
Simplicity
is an egg that hatches
Stupidity
is the murderer's gaze

you ask me
you ask me how I know
I'll tell you

Simplicity came and took my hand
She lead me from the city to a peaceable land
Of complicated creatures and rivers and trees
With days of excitement and nights of peace
And I love the way Simplicity moves
I love the way Simplicity moves

But I have seen enough Stupidity
To last me to the year three thousand and three

Cutting It Up

If you're looking for trouble
Here's how to start
Blow up the theatres
Tear down the art

Burn down the libraries
And concert halls
Cut your jazz and ballet
And then cut off your balls
And be a serial killer of culture
A serial killer of the soul

If you're looking for trouble
Take the artists you've got
Stack their works all around them
And torch the lot

The human soul is hungry
And so's the human heart
The food and drink makes them feel and think
It comes from works of art
And the human soul without art
Is locked in a dungeon cell
If you take your knife and cut the arts
You can cut your throat as well
Cos you're a serial killer of culture
A serial killer of the soul

If you're looking for trouble
Cut your grants to the poor
Seek out the old and sick
Cut them some more

Suffer little children
To go to school in Hell
Then watch them burn your cities
And your country estates as well
Cos you're a serial killer of Britain
A serial killer of its soul

THE HAIRY ARTS

The Olchfa Reading

I had told Nigel Jenkins
the bard of Mumbles, who was my friend,
that I wanted to read to a large audience

I was led in to entertain
the fourth and fifth and reject forms
of an enormous comprehensive
in a hall the size of
a Jumbo Jet hangar

They seemed as multitudinous
as the armies of Genghis Khan
but they were larger and hairier
and less interested in poetry

I tried to read a few of my poems –
my political ones were dismissed as ancient history
my love lyrics scoffed at for their naivety
my banter greeted by a thousand embalmed faces

It was a Friday afternoon to end all Friday afternoons
It was Goliath dressed up as Just William
yawning in my face

the audience stretched from Wales to Florida
the front rows shuffled their terrible boots in their sleep
or read magazines with mutilated nudes on their covers

further back they were snorting anthracite
and even further back
they were tearing the blazers off each other's backs
and indulging in Welsh Kissing

Desperately I asked for Questions from the audience.
I've sometimes had good questions
from unpromising aliens, questions like:
how old were you when you turned famous?

But this was bottomless sea-bed of Friday afternoon

A tall boy with several jam-stained
bandages around his head asked me:
Have you got any Horror Poems?
What sort of Horror Poems?
You know, poems with rusty spikes
sticking out of people's necks.
I shook my head – the tall boy snarled
and began to chew one of his bandages

then a lobster-boy in the front row
detached a lump of pink bubble gum from his stubble
before he asked me scornfully:
Why are your trousers so long?

Booze and Bards

I do a lot of thinking stuff all day long
You know trying to chase those words around the page
If I can round up enough of those critters
I might earn a living wage

Every morning down the poetry pit
Cut a few tons from the verseface
But the sky's always darkening by the time
I clamber up to the surface

That's when I run to catch the Jungle Juice Train
Everybody says He's at it again
Well the Jungle Juice Train's what I travel on
To the dear old station of Oblivion

And here's a health to the corpse of Dylan Thomas
And to all of the pain in the poetry dome
He fell among strangers time after time
But he only wanted to be carried home

Poet

He swings down from the train
on to the evening platform
the bag bumping his shoulder blade contains
gear for the night and weapons
only the main street shows any brightness
Been here before? Seven years ago.
He leans on the deep gold wood of the bar
orders a double whisky

waiting for the organiser

I've come to clean up this town

Poetry and Knitting

A good poem and a good sweater
have plenty in common
both keep you warm
but the sweater fits only one person at a time
poem lasts longer

Astrid Furnival
Designed and knitted
A sweater with William Blake on the front
And Catherine Blake on the back
And vice versa
I gave it to Celia
Through heaven and through hell
She wears it for my sake

But this is not typical Contemporary British Knitting
Not at all

There are knitting factories in South East Asia
which produce
Red for Liverpool Blue for Everton
Anything for money scarves

I love the children's mittens which are connected
by a thin woollen rope
which goes up one overcoat sleeve
and down the other
so that the mittens cannot be lost
except by a mixed infant contortionist
with a Stanley knife

I love those knitted dogs
which have trousers and jackets
kind of knitted into them

I love those mighty woollen helmets
hairy all over with a bobble on top
which make toddlers look
like multi-coloured steaming puddings

I love the generously knitted
lop-sided cardigan
with its baggy pockets
smelling of arcane pipe tobaccos –
Old Barty's Green Plug, Parrot Stock,
Cardinal Jasper and Shmoggo's Midnight Toffee

I love the hopeless inspirational
Christmas insanity of an aunt-knitted tie
sent to an aspiring arms salesman
with British Aerospace

I love the shapelessness of woollen slippers
slopping and slapping like two
pink and cosy three-dimensional amoebas

But maybe I don't love
the French knitting of John Ashbery
that just goes on and on
producing one endless knitted turd

Explanation

The poet's briefcase is a plastic bag
the poet's microphone's a hairy eyebrow
through it he broadcasts to the lowbrow and highbrow
The poet's taxi, that's his righthand thumb
the poet's taxi is a souped-up mind
a fourlegged jaguar not the fourwheel kind
the poet's lipstick is a stick of frozen blood
his make up is primeval sludgeration mud
His financial security's an ice cream cone
His political party is called All Alone
There'll be a bill at the end of the meal
Be sure you pay as much as you feel
You only have to pay as much as you feel

The Wilder Poetry of Tomorrow

Come on Poetry, get up off your big fat rusty-dusty
Come on Poetry, get up off your big fat rusty-dusty
When you crawled home at dawn your breath was smelling mausoleum musty

You've been mooning round the boneyard, mumbling to the dead,
Playing Ludo against yourself and wearing gloves in bed
Why don't you swing up through the treetops, get some jungle in your head?

I want every kind of creature to break out of the Poetry Zoo –
Barefoot heartbeat of the elephant, stride of the kangaroo.
I want to see your body naked when the sun comes shining through.

It can knock you down in Devon, it can bust you up in Jarrow
It bumps across the landscape like a customised wheelbarrow
But The Wilder Poetry of Tomorrow – it strikes like Robin Hood's arrow.

So come on Poetry, get up off your big fat rusty-dusty...

Hot Pursuit

(to Paul McCartney)

Augusta, Georgia,
Saturday night.
'Car Number Seven
Go break up a fight.'

'Make it downtown
To the Franklin Hotel.
James Brown's in the lobby
And he's kicking up hell.'

James Brown standing
Like a tall black tree.
'Hey little coppers
Did you come for me?'

'Hold it James Brown
Or we're gonna shoot.'
But he took off in a truck,
Law in hot pursuit.

Cop car zooming
Right after James Brown.
He laugh like a jackass
Stuck his foot right down.

'Augusta, Georgia
Is my home town.
Shoot me if you dare
But I'm the famous James Brown.'

'We don't care
If you're the great James Brown.
We'll shoot out your tyres
That'll slow you down.'

Bam! One tyre
Got blown by their first.
Fired another bullet
A second tyre burst.

James Brown, James Brown,
They'll never catch him.
He kept on driving
On the metal rims.

'Catch me alive,
Or catch me dead.
Augusta, Georgia
There's sparkles round my head.'

Moondog

There was a man called Moondog
Who made tunes
With thimbles, glasses, zithers,
Keys and spoons
And all the tunes he made
Were living things
Which flew around his head
On silver wings

I bought a Moondog record
Fourteen tracks
A red and golden label
Dusty wax
The sounds were delicate
As cowrie shells
The moonlit dancing
Of a thousand bells

My first day in New York
I walked downtown
Moondog sat on the sidewalk
All in brown
He played his instruments
So sweet and wild
I wanted to stay with him
As his child

Deep Purple Wine

Friday in a city
    That was growling with the heat
I saw the tall rain coming
    Walking with a steady beat
It walked right down the sky
    And then scuttled off down the street

Seven in the evening
    Yellow streetlights start to shine
I turned to my woman
    She locked her eyes on mine
She said: Best thing when it's raining
    Is a bottle of Deep Purple Wine

It makes your spirit laugh
    It makes your spirit moan
It makes you feel you're talking to
    An angel on the phone
It cools you then it fools you
    And it warms you to the bone

Duke Ellington invented it
    The greatest ever brew
It was made by Jimmy Blanton
    And by Johnny Hodges too
And it gurgled out with every note
    Old Cootie Williams blew

It tickles like the old pianner
    Mrs Klinkscale taught
It's heavy as the drum-kit
    That Louis Bellson fought
It's light and bright as a kitten
    Or a Billy Strayhorn thought

Tricky Sam Nanton
    Poured it into crazy shapes
Cat Anderson employed it
    In miraculous escapes
Sonny Greer Ray Nance Rex Stewart
    They were all vintage grapes

Don't forget Ben Webster
    Barney Bigard Lawrence Brown
They filled a big cloud with that wine
    And sailed it over town
And every night in Ellington
    That wine came pouring down

Such Sweet Thunder in the throat
    Such a Crescendo In Blue
Black Brown and Beige jump out your cage
    And start Slappin' Seventh Avenue
It Don't Mean A Thing If It Ain't Got That Swing
    Like East St Louis Toodle-oo

So drink to the great Duke Ellington
    And the Deep Purple Wine he made
Deep Purple Wine gives you dancing feet
    Like kangaroos on parade
Deep Purple Wine so fine so fine
    It will never ever fade

Thanks, Duke.

Parade

Have you ever been in Memphis
At midnight Halloween
I been there dad
And it druv me mad
When I saw whut I have seen

There's no city ever was haunted
Like cursed Memphis is
I'd like to tell
About that blue flame hell
So I say with heavy emphasis

There's
Fear in the streets
Fear in the malls
Fear that clutches you
By the balls
There's
Gruesome in the gravy
Grisly in the lemonade
Look what's coming –
Zombie Elvis Presleys on Parade

A million zombie Elvises at the witching hour
hey hey oom borooga boom
A million zombie Elvises twitching with power
hey hey oom borooga boom
Staggering and boogying and woggling their hips
Dropping ears and fingers and noses and lips
A million zombie Elvises
A million zombie Elvises

Edward Hopper

He found his thing

Cross-legged blondes
waiting quietly

Standing men with sharp grey faces
waiting by doors

People in deckchairs
waiting for the sun to set

And the sun in an empty room
waiting for nobody

He found his thing
he did it

Mayakovsky and the Sun

(to Little Richard)

It was the summit of summertime bang in the middle of July.
You could hear the rivers boiling, villages sizzle and fry.
It was that white-hot melting summer that I'll never forget –
The cows came out in blisters and even my sweat had sweat.

The Sun lay in his hammock snoring fit to wake the dead
So I opened up my window and I shouted at him: 'Goldenhead!
My name is Mayakovsky, I'm a poet and a painter too
And I'm doing all I can to make the Revolution come true.'

    Mayakovsky and the Sun...Mayakovsky and the Sun...

'I've been sitting up printing propaganda poems all night
And now it's early morning and I need some poster-painting light
But you're still kipping in your featherbed four-poster cloud!
Get up and get rolling! No layabouts allowed!'

Well the Sun gives a grin and he drags himself up by the roots
And comes marching towards me in his seven-league thumping boots
And he strides through my garden and he bursts into my room
And he opens up his jaws and his lion voice begins to boom:

'Hi Mayakovsky, I turned down my burners for you.
I can see there's a lot in common between us two.
I'd enjoy a conversation, that's the kind of Sun I am –
So where's my favourite glass of tea with cherry jam?'

    Mayakovsky and the Sun...Mayakovsky and the Sun...

I stood there thinking Mayakovsky what the hell have you done?
I was sweating like a waterfall eyeball to eyeball with the Sun.
We shared a bucket of vodka ice cream to cut down the heat
And I said: 'Cosmic Comrade, would you like to take a seat?'

The Sun relaxed back in a rocking chair looking benign
And he said: 'You imagine it's an easy thing for me to shine?
Have a shining competition, you bet I come an easy first.
But if you're going to shine, man, better shine till you burst.'

    Mayakovsky and the Sun...Mayakovsky and the Sun...

Well we talked on and on until the purple began to fall
But the Night didn't dare to stick one toe inside my hall.
When I slapped him on the back the Sun gave a black hole of a yawn
And he said: 'Hey, brother, it's time to do a bit of dawn.

'Let's shine away the boredom of how the everyday world looks.
I'll take care of the sky, Mayakovsky you can take the books.'
So the two of us are kicking down the prison walls built by the Night.
Yes it's a double attack in boots of poetry and light.

So when the Sun shines down, that overworked mate of mine,
That's when I jump up and with all of my spirit I shine.
Shine on! Shine on! Shine on for everyone!
That's what Mayakovsky says, and so does his friend the Sun.

Mayakovsky and the Sun...Mayakovsky and the Sun...

The Perils of Reading Fiction

If you read too many books with made-up stories you go a bit mad
That's what my Sergeant used to say every time he saw anyone reading
All those writers, most of them foreign and dead,
With their freaky ideas and nancy ways and gone with the how'syourfather
All those Swish Family Robinsons and Lorna Dooms and King Falstaffs
And The Great Fatsby and Virginia Beowulf and Kubla Khan-Khan
And Jane Austen and Jane Morris and Jane Volkswagen
All of em jumbled up and tripping over each other in your brainbox
Well it's like letting a year's worth of dreams out of a corrall
To stampede all over your real life, all those pretty lies and ugly lies,
Whirling about inside your skull, beating up storms of yellow dust
So soon you can't see for the grit in the eyes, you can't look out at all
And see the real world which is just the real world
And is real and not made up by somebody trying to be clever –
Listen – what I say is –
If you read too many books with made-up stories you go a bit mad.

COUNTRY LIFE & SOME ANIMALS

Dart River Bed

The mash of rotted-down oak leaves
of bark from drifting branches
the white flesh blackening of the salmon
who jumped the net and perished of old age
under her shadow-rock
the ragged robin chewed into shreds
the rich rust of a radiator
the bones of voles polished down to white specks
the dragged down muslin
robbed of its dye then mashed to filaments
and sweet Ophelia too –

all in the soft cool deeps of mud
under the mirror
all in the soft cool deeps of mud
all one in the soft cool deeps of mud

gradually dancing down to the ocean

That June

most days the sun was friendly
a few showers of fat warm raindrops
life was a hammock slung between the trees
of birth and death

poetry was a glass of iced tea
with a submerged seeping lemon slice
the silver condensation
singing in my palm
such easy days such easy days
I didn't think all month

You gave me a perfect cherry
I bit it ate it and spat the stone
all the way to St Petersburg
where it hit Pushkin on the nose
and he began to laugh
that June

Winter Listening

Humble, crumbly song of the snails.
Pinecones rattling in a stormy tree.
The frosty voices of December stars.
Dragon-roaring of a factory.

Honking slapstick of seals at play.
The creak and slish of snow off a roof.
Crackle-whisper of Christmas paper.
The silver step of a unicorn's hoof.

Winter Night in Aldeburgh

I stood beside the dark white tower
and fancied I heard a train over in Holland

There was an old man keeping himself warm
by leaning against the fish and chip shop wall

out of the corner of my left eye –
a gang of grey cats pedalling miniature bicycles

an orange boiled sweet sat stuck to the pavement
it was the size and shape of a rugby ball
and was bleeding orange sugar

I looked into the boating pond
and the boating pond looked into me
enough – I saluted the enormous moon
and scuttled back into my room

every inch of this town is haunted I said to myself
but I don't mind these ghosts
they have no business with me

at this moment a newsaper thrust itself through my letter-box
and fell on the mat with a sound like salt being poured
it was the ghosts' gazette, the newspaper
which is published by the dead for the dead

at first it was like reading a gravestone
covered with silver moss
but then I started to make out the words

The headline read
OCEAN INVASION ALERT
and the story began:
A squadron of green-headed mermen is swimming shorewards
through the torn metal desert of the waves
towards the singing shingle.

Now I am lying in my bed
face down eyes shut
I am awaiting instructions from the dead

The Monster's Dream

Under the shoulder of Mount Ferocity
The fugitive monster's head hums itself to sleep
And he steps out of his head into a fresh dream –

And the air in his fresh dream is chilly-blue
Feathers falling flowers spiralling upwards
Brown tarns shouting as waterbirds skid on their waterskins

The dew on the grass is a moon of crystal frost
Tickling the dark soles of the monster's feet
And the sun is mild and white and far away

It is early in the morning it is early in the world
All the bad warriors have sailed off to their hero fortresses
Or fallen over the edge of the world

It is early in the morning it is early in the heart
As the fugitive monster breaks through the bracken to find
The ghost of his mother sitting in the grass
Her monster face all gentle for love of him

A Living Monument
(for Peter, Cathy and Thom Kiddle)

Raised myself a monument – somewhere way back there.
Most people miss it. They move too fast.
It crouches in the little grass, snuffling the blue air,
        A deep-eyed animal, bred to last.

I'll die, but that much of me will keep on lurking,
Not rusting into mudweeds like Cleopatra's barge,
But alive to the beat of the planet, songbark working
        While there's one rocker still at large.

My verses will afterburn, like a good curry,
Though Penguins turn their back on them and BBC TV
And Buckingham Palace and Esher, Surrey –
        But some schoolkid'll learn them, secretly.

Some children love some of my poems – and that's enough!
That was why I bled all over the page.
In a smooth country my songs were a bit rough
        Praising gentleness in a vicious age.

My poetry's an old border collie who gets by
Performing tricks or rounding up the sheep
And it'll keep digging as long as politicians lie
        And mothers weep.

(after Horace, Derzhavin and Pushkin)

Bird Dreaming
(for Roger Woddis)

And in my dream a little shaking cloud
Of ten-eleven-twelve birds kept me company
As I ambled beside the chalky ploughed-up fields
And the clear frosty skies watched over me.

So I whistled a Hoagy Carmichael tune
And called the birds with outstretched arm.
One starling landed on my scarlet thumb,
Pressing its stars into my palm.

I kissed the feathers of its breast
And said: Some of them are beginning to know me.
And I felt the warmth of that bird's heart
And my own heart was fiery.

Sausage Cat

Behold the cat
the cat full of sausage
his ears do slope backwards
his coat's full of glossage

His whiskers extend
like happy antennae
he would count his blessings
but they are too many

He unfoldeth his limbs
he displayeth his fur
he narrows his eyes
and begins to purr

And his purring is smooth
as an old tree's mossage
Behold the cat
who is full of sausage.

Epitaph for a Golden Retriever

It was my job
To be a dog

My master said
That I was good

Now I turn myself around
And lie down in the musky ground

For Golden Ella

At four in the morning
With furry tread
My good dog climbs
Aboard my bed

She lays her chin
In my open palm
Now neither of us
Can come to harm

In my open hand
Her long jaw seems
Like a shifting weight
As she chews at her dreams

From the coolness
Of her nose
The blessing of
Her breathing glows

And the bad night
Vampires disappear
As my wrist is tickled
By her ear

Elegy for Number Ten
(for Ella)

One out of ten, six gold, four black,
Born in a bulging transparent sack.

I eased him out, this holy gift.
His mother turned to him and sniffed

Then licked the blood and the sack away.
All small and golden, there he lay.

There are some insects and some flowers
Whose life is spent in twenty-four hours.

For twenty-four hours, beside his mother,
He fed and he slept with his sisters and brothers.

Good smells. Close warm. Then a crushing weight.
Then nothing at all. His head the wrong shape.

He was wrapped up and taken beyond the bounds
Of his mother's familiar digging grounds

For she would have found him and known him too
And have wept as golden retrievers do.

So she kept all her love for the alive –
The black four and the golden five.

But I celebrate that golden pup
Whom I talked to and kissed as I wrapped him up

For he fed and he slept and was loved as he lay
In the dark where he spent one golden day.

Now his mother pursues an eccentric trail
With casual sweeps of her lavish gold tail

And when number ten stumbles into my mind
She consoles me and so do the other nine.

The Meaningtime

Bananas and bicycles are beautiful animals
Elephants and waterfalls are wonderful machines
Show me a bucket and I'll bite you a biscuit –
Now you know what the universe means

Understanding the Rain
(for a horse called Elgin)

Top right-hand corner
Of a South Devon field
The great white horse
Stands under the warm rain

Slow-motion grass
Growing greener and greener
The great white horse
Stands under the warm rain

Like a shining cathedral
Under the centuries
The great white horse
Stands under the warm rain

Like a waiting messenger
Like the people
Like the planet
Like poetry
Like a great white horse
The great white horse
Stands under the warm rain

A Cheetah, Hunting

A herd of Thompson's Gazelle
Like 43 bars of marzipan.

The great wheels of the cheetah's shoulders.
The black tracks of her killer tears.

And now her teeth are in a throat.

Two huge lakelight eyes
Look upwards with such love.

Here Come the Bears

Clambering through the rocky torrents
Here come the bears
Quicksilver salmon flip into the light
to flop a little higher up
swerving past scooping claws
and underwater gaping muzzles
to flip up into the light again
past the black tip
of the nose of a small bear
his eyes as wide as all amazement

The Elephant

Elephant Elephant
Simmering gently
Carry me home
As smooth as a Bentley

Elephant Eternity

Elephants walking under juicy-leaf trees
Walking with their children under juicy-leaf trees
Elephants elephants walking like time

Elephants bathing in the foam-floody river
Fountaining their children in the mothery river
Elephants elephants bathing like happiness

    Strong and gentle elephants
    Standing on the earth
    Strong and gentle elephants
    Like peace

Time is walking under elephant trees
Happiness is bathing in the elephant river
Strong gentle peace is shining
All over the elephant earth

JOIN THE POETRY AND SEE THE WORLD

Blue Coffee

Blue coffee
The air was like
Blue coffee

Frothy cow's parsley
Either side of the path
Across the Heath

Blue coffee
The whirling air was like
Blue coffee

Up jumped a poppy in scarlet
Her heart beating black as the blues

Blue coffee
The swirling, spiralling air
Blue coffee

Vauxhall Velvet

After-dark London crouches
Like a grisly grimy cat
The Funman slouches
Underneath the bridge in his fuck-you hat
As the pedestrians go skulking home,
Each skull a fragile stained-glass dome.

By the Waters of Liverpool

So many of her sons drowned in the slime of trenches
So many of her daughters torn apart by poverty
So many of her children died in the darkness
So many of her prisoners slowly crushed in slave-ships
Century after red century the Mersey flowed on by –
By the waters of Liverpool we sat down and wept

    But slaves and the poor know better than anyone
    How to have a real good time
    If you're strong enough to speak
    You're strong enough to sing
    If you can stand up on your feet
    You can stomp out a beat...

So we'd been planning how to celebrate
That great red river of Liverpool
As our team rose to a torrent
That would flood the green of Wembley
We'd been planning how to celebrate
The great red dream of Liverpool
For Dalglish held the Cup in his left fist
And the League in his right –
By the waters of Liverpool we sat down and wept

Our scarves are weeping on the gates of Anfield
And that great singing ground is a palace of whispers
For the joy of the game, the heart of the game,
Yes the great red heart of the great red game
Is broken and all the red flowers of Liverpool –
By the waters of Liverpool we sat down and wept.

April 1989, after Hillsborough

I Am Tourist

I am Tourist
I fly across the seas with a cold glass in my hand
Watching Burt Reynolds movies
I am Tourist
With my chocolate-coloured spectacles
And my blue travellers chequetacles
And my video camera purring at the Sights
I am Tourist
With my Tourist Wife
We live the full and beautiful
Tourist Life
We are taken to a hill tribe
They live on a hill
They sell us many boxes
Painted green and grey
They are ugly boxes but very inexpensive
Then they put on hairy masks
And scarlet knickerbockers
They bang their stomachs and circle round us
Is it a wedding? Is it a funeral?
Whatever it is we video it all
And it is picturesque but it is not inexpensive
On the way back to the hotel
I tell our Guide
No more painted boxes
No more picturesque ceremonies
No more hill tribes
I want a mattress
And a pool and a bar
Just like back home
I am Tourist

March in Vienna

March in Vienna
March in Vienna
Coffee Danke Schoen that's one tenner

London in March

London in March
London in March
Where the wind whistles round your Marble Arch

The Postman's Palace

Deep down in France is the village of Hauterives,
A village as quiet
As a heap of stones by the roadside...
To the brave heart, nothing is impossible.

A new postman came to Hauterives
And he was known as Le Facteur Cheval
Which means, in English, Postman Horse.
Time does not pass, but we do.

One night Postman Horse dreamed himself a dream
And in it he saw, at the bottom of his garden,
A wonderful palace of stairways and towers
Decorated with trees and fruit made of stone
And camels and giants and goddesses and elephants.
Out of art, out of a dream, out of energy.

Next day Postman Horse was on his rounds
When he tripped over an odd-shaped stone.
He took it home in his wooden wheelbarrow,
Set it on the ground in his garden, and smiled.
This is where the dream becomes reality.

Postman Horse began to build.
Every day on his rounds he found amazing stones.
Every day after work he collected them.
Carefully, each evening, he cemented the stones together.
Gradually the palace of his dreams began to rise.
To the brave heart, nothing is impossible.

After ten thousand days of work
In the freezer of winter, the oven of summer,
After thirty-three back-breaking years of work
The palace was finished.
Postman Horse wrote on panels of cement:
All that you see as you pass by
Is the work of a peasant,
The work of one man alone.
Time does not pass, but we do.

I have seen the palaces
Of the Kings of England, France and Russia.
They were magnificent and dead.
But deep down in France is the village of Hauterives
And from its earth there rises
A wonderful palace built out of dreams
Where Postman Horse inscribed these words:

To the brave heart, nothing is impossible.
Time does not pass, but we do.
Out of art, out of a dream, out of energy.
This is where the dream becomes reality.

Lerici, the Bay, Early on Saturday, May

orchards awash
with rippling green shadow

a buttercup schoolbus
blurts its trumpet at me

an Egyptian lion of an island
dozily gazes
at a warm breadroll of an island

by and by, says the lion,
I will eat you,
by and by

and now, like a slow-motion dancer
in a crimson dress
with a white neckline
a trawler lies in the middle of the blue stage
waiting for the opening music
of the Shelley ballet

the words of Shelley's spirit
dance like the flames round a gas ring

strong and painful and transparent
and hot enough to melt the heart of England

pass round that bottle of blue flames
let's drink to Shelley

Peace Memories of Sarajevo

Sarajevo glowing white
as a translucent china cup

Sarajevo forty poets in suits on an official platform
Reciting eight lines each under a giant portrait of Tito

Sarajevo my daughter aged eight laughing
As she stands in the concrete rain-filled
Footsteps of the assassin

Sarajevo in the smoky little orchards on the hills
Families sitting under gentle-eyed blossoms
Enjoying their slow dinners

Sarajevo and my brave schoolmaster friend
Who did not blink when the bureaucrats spat in his eye

Sarajevo I wish you no bombs no shells no guns
I wish you smoky little orchards and glowing poets
And soldiers who refuse to kill
And children who refuse to kill

And Sarajevo
Glowing white
As a translucent china cup

For My Friends in Georgia

The good old moon drank a bottle of wine
And she began to sing

The fine old tree drank a bottle of wine
And he began to sing

The warm black sea drank a bottle of wine
And she began to sing

The strange old bridge drank a bottle of wine
And it began to sing

The tattered little book drank a bottle of wine
And it began to sing

The dog with one ear drank a bottle of wine
And he began to sing

And the child
With a broken doll in his arms
Drank a breastful of milk
And she began to sing

For the love of Georgia
For the love of Georgia
A land with a heart as big
As the good old wine drinking moon

When the Government

When the government whips
when the government whips
it's a special kind of gangster
bashing out its brutal will
with a mouthful of morality
heartful of cruel thrill

When the government kills
when the government kills
it's a special kind of murderer
strangling with a hypocrite's sigh
mouthful of deterrence
heartful of hang shoot and fry

When the government tortures
when the government tortures
it's a special kind of thug
who's trained to be a terrorcop
mouthful of security
heart full of poison to the top

When the government bombs
when the government bombs
it's a special mass murderer
crazy with its own success
mouthful of democracy
worldful of emptiness

The Boy Who Danced with a Tank

It was the same old story
Story of boy meets State
Yes the same old story
Story of boy meets State
The body is created by loving
But a tank's made of fear and hate

Armoured cars and heads in helmets
Rank on rank on rank on rank
The hearts of the soldiors were trembling
But the eyes of the soldiers were blank
And then they saw him swaying –
The boy who danced with a tank

The tank moved left
The boy stepped right
Paused like he was having fun
The tank moved right
The boy stepped left
Smiled at his partner down the barrel of its gun

You remember how we watched him
Dancing like a strong young tree
And we knew that for that moment
He was freer than we'll ever be
A boy danced with a tank in China
Like the flower of liberty

Sweet Point Five Per Cent

I saw my Iraqi sister
There was red stuff running from her eyes
She said My son is dying in a hospital
With no medical supplies.
I said Well you shouldn't have started that war
Does he really need an oxygen tent?
But I was feeling generous so I took my week's wages
And slipped her point five per cent.

I bumped into my African brother
The bones were pushing through his skin
He was carrying a skeleton baby
In a coffin hammered out of tin
Well both my kids are at public school
And I have to pay my mistress's rent
Plus my motoryacht and an island I've got –
Still I chucked him point five per cent.

I met my Indian mother
She was staggering through iron rain
She said The Earth turned into a monster
Eating everything we had all that's left is pain.
Now I believe that charity begins at home
And home in my case is Kent.
But before I drove away in my Jaguar
I threw my mother point five per cent.

I drove on and on playing Elton John
But I lost control on a curve
And I failed to see a stupid great tree
And I didn't have time to swerve.
The next thing I saw was St Peter at the Gates
And I asked him where should I go?
You'll spend point five per cent of your time in Heaven
Ninety-nine point five per cent down below.

Ten Holes for a Soldier

Two holes were the size of the holes in his ears.
They were rounded, and as they opened and shut
They seemed to make a sound like sighing.

Two holes were the size of his nostrils,
Close together and dark inside
And breathing out a smell of something – rotting.

Two holes were the size of his eyes
And they were trying to clench themselves
To hold back – the red tears.

One hole was the size of his mouth
And it cried out
With the voice of – an old child.

One hole was the size of the hole
In the end of his cock
And it was skewered by a white-hot, turning gimlet.

One hole was the size of the hole in his arse,
Small and wincing away from the light
And it went – very deep.

Petrol was poured into all his holes.
All of his holes were set on fire.

They covered his holes with a clean uniform.
They flew him home. There was a flag.
In the village he loved, they put him in a hole.

YOUNG AND OLD

My Father and Mother *or* Why I Began to Hate War

My father was small and quiet, with a brown face
And lines of laughter round his eyes
And wildly sprouting Scottish eyebrows.
Everybody called my father Jock.
In 1914 he joined the army.
He fought for four years in the mud of the trenches.

Nearly all his friends were killed in that war.
He told me about one friend of his
Who suddenly, in the lull between bombardments,
Fell on all fours, howled like an animal,
And was never cured.
My father was a small and quiet man.

My mother was called Kay.
She had blue eyes and a comical nose
And a doll called Beauty.
And she had two older brothers
Called Sydney and Stanley.
Sydney was dark and Stanley was fair
And they used to pull my mother's long gold plaits –
And she loved them dearly.

In 1914 Sydney joined the army
And was killed within days.
Next year Stanley went to the war
To take revenge for his brother.
But Stanley was killed as well.

In 1918 my father came home
With a sword and a kilt and shrapnel in his arm
And Jock and Kay met and fell in love
At the Presbyterian Badminton Club.

And in good time they had two sons
And one of us was dark and one was fair.
And I think, in a way, my brother James and I
Came here to take the place of Sydney and Stanley
My mother's two beloved brothers.

And when I think about war I remember
How when Remembrance Day came round each year,
My mother always wore two poppies.

Rainbow Woods

I was nearly seven when war broke out.
My brother James and I were evacuated
To Combe Down, a village of bright stone
on the hill above the city of Bath.
My friends and I were always being chased
out of farmland and parkland and private estates.
Boys Keep out. Trespassers Will Be Executed.
Till we found a free place, Rainbow Woods.

Rainbow Woods, as bright as a paint-box,
Packed with steep hills and curving pathways,
A switchback speedway
Buzzing with kids on bikes,
Scooting over the roots,
Whirring and whirling through the air
To crash-land in bushes.

Running kids, climbing kids,
Kids crawling under heaps of autumn leaves,
Kids with dogs and calapults
Totally ignored by the grown-up world.

Rainbow Woods
With a thousand trees
And a hundred hills.
Rainbow Woods
With its mysterious ruin
Like a palace for ghosts...

The Bully

His head was a helmet
His muscles sprung steel
Each finger was
An electric eel
He was merciless
As the Bloody Tower
I was eight years old
And I was in his power

To the Sadists of My Childhood

old fear
old fear
got it up to here
boiling white
through my guts
old fear

old fear
old fear
screaming in my ear
holding tight
to my balls
old fear

eight year
seven year
six year
five year old terrors
tearing me apart
they ripped my arsehole
sewed up my lips
and they froze my heart

old fear
old fear
took my mother away
left me in the grip
of old fear
old fear

After Reading Hans Christian Andersen

(to my brother Jimmy, with love)

our father and mother
were kind and good
but they have left us
in this wood

As for the Fear of Going Mad

As for the fear of going mad –
It's like the fear of a teddy bear
That he may be left out in the rain
That the blackbird's beak
Will peck away his growler
That his forgotten fur will melt
Into the squelchness and the undermulch
Below greenshining skyscrapers of grass.

As for the fear of going mad –
Though night hide you away
And a blizzard blow
There are so many lanterns of love around
You'll be surely and gladly and tearfully found.

Grandfather's Footsteps

There's a guy going round so I been told
And his hands are clammy and his breath is cold
And he bothers the women and he messes up the men
Yeah Old Age hanging round again

Day after day Old Age comes creeping
Crawls on your chest while you lay sleeping
He dims your eye and he slows your pace
And scribbles his graffiti all over your face

He cuts the phone between your brain and your tongue
Kicks holes in the walls of stomach and lung
If you try to fight back he gives you the axe
With all kinds of cancer and heart attacks

He crumbles your teeth and he withers your belly
He laughs off monkey glands and Royal Jelly
He mugs the beggar and he busts the king
And he even slackens off your yo-yo string

Last night I caught Old Age in the act
Tobogganing down my digestive tract
He played my liver like a fruit machine
And used my poor heart for a trampoline

I was flying off into a terrified rage
Bubbling with insults against Old Age
Then I saw his brother Death driving into town –
Please Old Age, won't you hang around?

The Sound of Someone Walking

Why won't he stop walking
In those steady-pacing shoes
Why won't he sit and rest his feet
Listen to the news

Why won't he stop walking
With that quiet beat
Whatever the traffic I can always hear him
Moving down my street

And I think about him
Every day it seems
And I hear those footsteps
On the soundtrack of my dreams

Make him stop that walking –
At least till the day
When he walks up shakes my hand
And whispers: Time to pay.

Just a Little Bit Older

Feels like something's been happening to my skeleton
Seems like something's giving in my scaffolding
Not exactly seizing up but crackling at the corners
Spinal column fuzzing up with clusters of rust-flakes
Toe-bone joints making miniature explosions

I always thought of bones as something you could count on
Build up your framework with calcium deposits
That's what my mother sang to me but what do I do now
Now that my mother's vanished and my scaffolding is creaking
And it feels like something's been happening to my skeleton

Keep Right on to the End of the Bottle

Death is a chilly old sloucher,
His staring face as blue
As a North Pole bug.
When he shuffles, nervously,
To your bedside –
Give him a hug.

Ode to the Skull

for the glimmering eyes
two sockets
the size
of snooker-table pockets

for the nose
a sneeze of bone
to repose
itself upon

underneath
a cliff that's cleft
where perch the teeth
the few that's left

over all this
a helmet for
motor-cycling,
rain or war

you're the belfry
in which is hung
that singer of the self
the tongue

you are the scaffolding
that keeps in place
that beautiful baffled thing
the human face

without your aid
we would not know
Lew Grade
from Marilyn Monroe

and every head
would soon become
like a dead
jellyfish's bum

Skull, you're a true
protective friend
I'll stick with you
right to the end

That last quatrain?
banal and dull,
but thanks, says the brain,
to my good old skull.

My Orchard

I have a fine orchard
Where skeletons stand
In shining and
Orderly rows

And this one stands
Like a military man
And that one has
A mannequin's pose
When the night wind rises
It whistles through their sockets
With a music
Like misery

But when morning arrives
I step out of my house
And the skeletons are all
Facing me

And I choose one figure
From their bony ranks
And I pick one bone
From its frame

And I sit on the bench
And I chew that bone
And at first you know
They all taste much the same

But as I chew on
The taste of the marrow
Is always different
On my tongue

And I see the owner
Of that skeleton
When that skeleton
Was brave and young

And I smile at its beauty
And it smiles on me
Till the vision
Gradually goes

And the orchard darkens
And the skeletons stand
In shining and
Orderly rows

Poem in Portugal

Sixty years old and he's left by himself,
Strapped in the car while the shopping's done.
He watches the squat brown foreigners
Suspiciously loitering in the sun.
He sighs with relief to be missing the shops
For he can avoid the colly-wobbles
By letting the coils of his bowels settle down
Instead of bumping them over the cobbles.
He watches the tourists outsmart each other
And concludes it is much more fun
To be sixty years old and be left by himself,
Strapped in the car while the shopping's done.

An Ode to Dust

I know the ways of words,
Their weights and how they click together,
How they expand in summer moods, contract in winter,
The deep kind lines on the faces of some,
Others with damp and blank expressions.
Yes, I know how to talk with words
Like I know how to talk with dogs.
We get along, we can be silly together
Or weep or bop or howsyourfather...

Different with clouds.
From down here they march past with giant shoulders,
Building grandiose cathedrals,
Breaking into Turner avalanches
According to their dealings with the winds.
From a plane looking down they form cream landscapes
Gilded by the sun, silver-plated by the moon.
Slow-dancing landcapes, I often wish
William Blake could have seen them.

I can do nothing with clouds but enjoy them.
I spend more time with words and dogs,
And, though I love clouds, love them less
Than words or dogs. But more than dust.

Because dust is visible and invisible,
It bloweth where it listeth not where I list.
And dust, with no particular place to go,
Goes floating, settling, shifting, settling,
Anyoldwhere and dust consists,
Scientists tell us, of bazillions
Of flitty bits of metal, ash, cloth, grass,
Paper, wood, leather, hair and human skin
Riding the thunderstorm, surfing on the draughts.
Constellations of dust
Glitter and spin
Around the room
I'm typing in,
Falling like miniscule dry rain
Upon the floor, my desk and me.

Every word has a soul.
Every dog has a soul.
When soul rubs soul
It makes a kind of love.
But dust is the dandruff of the soul,
Dust is for philosophers –
A terrifying generalisation –
Dust is everything.

Mid-air

Once I looked out the window of a school
And saw a flying bird stop and fall dead out of the sky

Once I looked out the window of a car
And saw a flying bird stop and fall dead out of the sky

The third time I look out of a window and see this thing
Will be the moment that I die

Give Me Time – Autumn Is at the Gates
(Pushkin in a letter to M.P. Pogodin, 1st July 1828, St Petersburg)

Brown slices spread with the golden mush butter of August
And then scarlet minutes and hours from the jampot that ticks.
Time sandwiches – that's all I have time to eat.

So many words to kiss, so many sentences to massage into life,
So much verbal fondling and tumbling to be done
But the dictionary pages flicker into a blur.

Writing. Rewriting.
Mind-gliding. Day-sliding.
Cloud-drifting. Microscope-sucking.
Random sleuthing and espionage.
Searching through mountains of mud and dust.
Placing the chess-pieces on the crossword grid.
Waking with my sweaty stubble
On the bosom of my typewriter.

A child of words is born.

The child is taken to the market-place,
Held naked overhead and judged,
Acclaimed, spat at, stoned and ignored.
But by this time I'm pregnant again,
Working on the next baby.

I'd like a holiday between these exciting births,
A wordless vacation on a sea of music
So that the muscles round my eyes could relax enough
For me to gaze at the world and its people
With love but without desire
For my eyes to become as round as marbles.

Oh give me time – autumn is at the gates.

The USA is talking of a new dark age.
Iraq talks about a holy war against the forces of darkness.
Darkness screams at darkness in darkening language
About gas that nibbles up the nervous system in seconds
About bombs that swallow down whole cities.

My family, my friends, my animals,
My writing, my books, my country
And new unknown people and planets
To be gently discovered and understood.
There is so much love to be done –

Give me time – autumn is at the gates.

WAY OUT YONDER

Two Anti-Environmental Poems by Volcano Jones

Underarm Squirter

I hate the bloody cold I do
I hate the bloody cold
It makes me feel all blue it do
It makes me feel all old

And so I purchase aerosols
And aim them at the sky
And squirt them at the ozone layer
And here's the reason why

The more the ozone disappears
The more the sun shines through
Why? As you know, stupid, I hate the cold
I hate the bloody cold I do

Chop em Down Chop em up Burn the Lot

Don't give me trees
They throw spooky shadows on my bed
Don't give me trees
They keep nearly falling on me head
Tripping you up
With stupid great roots
Pelting you in autumn
With mushy great fruits
    Talk about rain forests
    You go in a rain forest
    You'll be lucky if you escape
    Without a fatal snakebite
    In your glove compartment
    Or your head torn off by a killer ape
Tall green buggers
Get in everyone's way
Crashed into my car
Just the other day
Don't give me trees
Give me a deadly disease
But beam me up Scottie
Don't give me fuckin trees

Criminal Justice for Crying Out Loud – A Rant

Hello people, gather round turn up the sound and forget about your personal
        pain
Here we are stuck on an island full of traffic jams in the rain
My poetry's a rough old towel going to rub you dry again
   You'll be glowing
   And I'll be going

Now don't try slipping out the back door, zooming off down the road
They got heavies on your front and back, roadblocks every inch of your road
If you look like a traveller – Criminal Justice going to squash you like a toad

Now you heard about Criminal Justice, his honour the dreaded Judge
Cause of my disgust is Criminal Justice, that famous killing serial Judge
He takes mothers fathers children and he chews them up like Women's
        Institute fudge

Now you can't dodge the raindrops when the clouds decide to pour
You get soaked the rich stay dry – that's the nature of the law
Don't you know law has always been a weapon in the war between the rich
        and the poor

Long ago I heard about a goddess and Justice was her name
A famous shining naked goddess Justice was her lovely name
Now they inside outed Justice and they covered her with shame

They steal your freedom to speak
And your freedom to sing
They steal your freedom to boogie
And everything
They steal your freedom to travel
And live where you like
They steal your freedom to raise your kids
And your freedom to go on strike

Criminal Justice oh don't you dare stay out too late
Criminal Justice it's getting heavier just you wait
It's coming down like a rain of molten lead
   molten lead pouring down
   on the country and the town
     molten lead
     on your head
From the overflowing murdering mouth of the Criminal Justice State

Full English Breakfast

(my alternative national anthem)

Full English Breakfast
Sent from above
Butter and toast and beans
Chunky old marmalade
That's what we love
That is what England means
Full English Breakfast
Doing its best
Marching as if to war
Full English Breakfast
Standing the test
Two eggs and bacon
If I'm not mistaken
That is what England's for

Black pudding
Plum jam
Pass the cornflakes
To Pam
Grilled mushrooms
Fried bread
How's your gumboil
Uncle Fred?

Full English Breakfast
Flowing and free
Pride of the Seven Seas
Full English Breakfast
Strong English tea
Sadie likes three lumps please

Full English Breakfast
Doing its bit
Filling the English tum
England was made for Man
As God's own Frying Pan
It's the Full Monty, Mum!

Moving Poem

I'll call my new house 'REALITY'
Or maybe 'BOURGEOIS STATE'.
Its name will be burned on a slice of wood
And screwed to my garden gate.
When they say 'Hey, sticking a name on your house
Is a very suburban trait!'
I'll look up from the corpse I am eating
And say: 'This is the suburbs, mate.'

Stuck Together Song

I was standing in a cake shop
In this awful little town
I looked for a waitress
There was no one around
I picked myself a kind of coconut item
And a chocolate eclair but when I came to bite em
They were
Stuck Together

Well I walked out of the cakeshop
With a sack and a guitar
And a wickerwork dogbasket
And was looking for my car
I bumped into a pair of gentlemen in suits
With pinchy white faces and waterproof boots
They were
Stuck Together

Stuck together
For the rest of their life
Like the blade and handle
Of a butcher's knife
Like a handmade shoe
Made of patent leather –
Stuck Together

Me I was born on the British Isles
Like sixty million other suckers
Half of me Scottish half of me English
Half of my friends are foreign fuckers
Scotland England Northern Ireland Wales
Four different breeds of dog with droopy tails
All of us
Stuck Together

O Captain! My Captain! Our Fearful Trip Is Done

Your white hands tight upon the wheel,
You sold the ship off bit by bit,
Auctioned the masts, the decks, the keel
And left us sinking in the shit.

Icarus Talking to His Dad

since I first dreadfully fitted my fingers
into the tipless gloves under the angle of the wings
and you criss-crossed my body with the straps
which would draw me close under and into the wings
and closer till they reacted with my shoulder blades
as if they had grown there

you always told me babies are born with wings
but on the seventh day a visitor comes
and clips them off and anoints the stubs
with anti-feather growing ointment
only the wing stubs the shoulder blades still sometimes
dream about flying
and on this dream we will build our freedom

it is about freedom, you said, you insisted,
remember always flying is about freedom
it is about wheeling and tumbling and falling through clouds
it is about laughing and exploring the possibilities of the body
it is about playing tag with swallows
and the attempt to become as free as air

it is not about conquest or achievement or record-breaking
it is not just for you
it is freedom and it is for everyone
that is why I have worked day and night
and when I became blind worked on blindly
because my intelligent fingers longed
to complete the great task –
the first pair of working human wings

just the first pair, I've made them so that
if they work,
any fool can make a thousand pairs

they had to be simple
there had to be a simple way, a best way
and there was and I found it
as a village finds a path down through rocks to the sea

and you also said, not too near the sun, son,
that was your joke, always with a blind man's wink –
not too near the sun, son

If You're Lookin' for Trouble
You've Come to the Wrong Place
(for the CND Rally, Trafalgar Square, 1994)

This is a rally in the cause of Peace.
You'd rather have Conflict? Then I suggest
You join the Army or the Police –
(If you can pass the intelligence test).

FOR LOVE AND FRIENDSHIP

My Father's Land

1

Sand-dunes
And sand-dunes
And St Andrews

A blueboard sky
Scribbled all over with seagulls
Who spell out chemical formulae

Sand-dunes
And sand-dunes
And St Andrews students

Scarlet-gowned
Against the grey and glittering town
Jock Mitchell, the young scientist

Sand-dunes
And sand-dunes
And the bottle dungeon in St Andrews

There was a bottle dungeon
Let into the ground
They lowered its one prisoner
Down the neck
Into the depths of the bottle

Down in the bottle
The darkness was total
Waves smashed against the walls outside
First the prisoner went mad,
Said the guide, later he went blind

Sand-dunes
And sand-dunes
And the North Sea
And France

2

1914–1918
He descended into Hell
Which is a labyrinth of trenches
Slashed out of chilling, killing mud.
All his old friends died there
And he crouched with his new comrades –
Obscene diseases, shells and rats,
Madness and blindness.
Down in the bottle
The darkness was total –
Sent, by the King,
To Hell in a kilt –
My gentle young father.

3

Sand-dunes
And sand-dunes
And Woolacombe

And on the farthest wave-slapped rock
Towards the end of Baggy Point
Alone in a salty zone of his own
Face brown as his shoes
Body white as his teeth
Fishing all day and catching nothing,
And happy that nothing was to be caught –
My father.

4

My mother's laughter
And the laughter of her friends
Tumbling out of the french windows and beyond them

I'm on the patio paving stones
Exterminating a city of Ants
I am Bomber Command
With a seething kettle.

And beyond me
The warm-swarming lawn is sloping
Under the weight of three apple trees,
Their ancient trunks bulging,
Leaning to one side,
Each bearing a deadly, sticky circle.

Beside that lawn
My bright-haired brother's head
Level with the cabbages
As he excavates
A system of trenches
Which he will fit with a sliding roof
And electric light and a drainage pump,
Putting my primitive
Hole in the ground for hiding in
To simple, muddy shame.

And way beyond and behind all this,
Past the experimental asparagus,
Hidden from family, friends and Germans,
In his bamboo city streets of raspberry canes
Stands my middle-aged father, Jock.

He is five foot six.
You look at his strong brown eyes and say:
He must have laughed a lot.
You look at his strong brown eyes and say:
He must have lost a lot.

He squashes up his mouth
As he kicks the blade of his spade
Down into the rich earth of Surrey.
When he rests
He reaches into his salty old sports jacket,
Into the pocket he keeps full of bread-crumbs
And rewards the robin who follows him everywhere,
Like a small boy with sticky-up hair.

And he is still there, in the raspberry canes,
And soon my mother will bring him his tea
So he doesn't have to come into the house
And be polite to her friends.

A Late Elegy for Jock Mitchell

The Imperial Tobacco Company
Tore my father from his family
After much terror and agony.

Four years in the trenches could not break
His body. He died for the sake
Of sucking Players and Gold Flake.

He looked like an old child that day.
'We love you,' was all that I could say.
He said: 'It's awful,' then turned away.

Goodnight, Stevie

Over an ocean of silvery froth,
Past mammoths in forests of moonlit myth
Flies a zig-zagging, incandescent moth –
The poetry of Stevie Smith.

Brightness of Brightness
(for Trix Craig on her seventeenth birthday, 3rd July 1992)

Brightness of an estuary –
Glittering seabirds in spirals of light
Over the molten bars of golden mud.
Brightness of a forest glade –
A sun-pool waiting the arrival
Of a shy, gliding family of deer.
Brightness of a midnight river
Playing like Jack B. Yeats
With the harlequin lights of the city.
Brightness of a black and white dog
Bouncing above and below the bracken.

Brightness of those eyes
Brightness of that hair

Brightness of memory
Brightness of the good times
Brightness of that palace in Carlton Hill
With its tumbling tower and fantasy plumbing
Where all the troubles of the world
Dissolved in Irish laughter.

Brightness of the house in Snape
With furious Scrabble by a furious fire
And Christmas feasts the whole year round
With butterlight and creamlight,
Meringue-light and dreamlight
And the light of blue bubble fountains
In a deep goblet of gin and tonic.
O brightness of gravy, brightness of wine,
Brightness of Trix's voice
And the best company in the world.

For her eyes look on the no-good human race
With endless forgiveness, endless affection,
And her heart dances around
Catherine of the deep wild eyes
Michael of the laughing waterfall
Fergus the fine young tree
Blanche the new whirling little moon
And her two shadows
Those finest of dogs
Meggie and Tashy
And uncountable friends
Some alive here and loving her
Some gone but still alive in her heart
In the brightness of that heart
As all-embracing as the sunlight
Brightness of brightness
Light of a thousand lives
Brightness of brightness
Beloved Trix.

Maybe Maytime

(for Celia)

There was a moment in a garden.
There was a moment in a garden –
Small green spiders trapezing down through
Yellow spotlights in that great green tent.
Something was singing with the voice of apples.
A breeze touched my cheekbone, or perhaps it was a fingertip.

There was a moment, there was a sandpath,
Pine-cone-scattered and swerving its way
Among the red-bark trees with their polished roots.
There was a snub-nosed rowing boat
Stuck forever among hissing rushes –
On the water's surface, a famous insect city.

There was a moment, there was a voice,
Wild as your hair and gentle as your breasts.
And a raucous old train rattled its way around the rim of the valley.

I might have been five, perhaps fifty-five,
Could have been October, maybe Maytime,
But I know it was you, my love,
I know it was you
Because look, here's the mark, right over my heart.

Sometimes Awake

deep in the centre of her breasts
two nameless flowers grow
their small leaves furled
their petals curling
with porcelain blueness
like the morning skies
on the fifth of april

sometimes awake
and sometimes asleep
and sometimes both at once
I've gazed so often on those two blue flowers
to see them gazing back at me
with all the love I ever thirsted for

Thank You for All the Years We've Had, Thank You for All the Years to Come

My blue hand stretched out of sight in the blizzard's white
For one rose among the snows of Everest
And my chest and mouth ached for the touching of your breast
For I loved to be loved by your love more than anyone knows

In Sweetmeat Street I lay in the guttering muck
The crowd laughed aloud at me the Semi-Human Dungheap
But you jumped from the hump of your camel, lifted me up
And saved me, sunned me and lay me beside you to sleep

I was scared by the stare of the white-masked moon
For I knew those two cold Os were the cratery eyes of Death
But pink morning dawned as you rose over me
And I cried golden molten tears of happiness...

An Open Window

Love is an open window and the breeze
Breathing into the bedroom from that window

And love is the towering, tearful tree
Seen in the frame of an open window

And love is the hot-blooded sky beyond
Longing to tear its clouds off for the sun

And love is how we lie here, looking and longing,
Under the gaze of an open window.

    C'an Torrent, Deya.

Happy Breakfast, Hannah, on Your Eighteenth Birthday

Today you sit down to a proper breakfast.
Yesterday you were seventeen
On the Sunny Side of the Century
Arranged for ukulele and spotty pyjamas.

The day before yesterday you were twelve
All woolly hat, armsful of homework,
The largest eyes in the known world
And sudden laughter beside a lake.

The day before that you were six and a bit
In enormous boots and a housewife hat
Chasing the vicar with your deadly gamp.

And the day before that, eighteen years ago,
The midwife said:
'This one's been here before'
As you came up really bright into the light.

And I wish you a house in a wood
Within the sighing of the sea
Animals around your feet
And the music of peacetime to dance your own dance
And all the love in the world, lovely Hannah,
As you come up bright into the light.

A Flying Song

(for Caitlin Georgia Isabel Stubbs, born 18th April 1993)

Last night I saw the sword Excalibur
It flew above the cloudy palaces
And as it passed I clearly read the words
Which were engraven on its blade
    And one side of the sword said Take Me
    The other side said Cast Me Away

I met my lover in a field of thorns
We walked together in the April air
And when we lay down by the waterside
My lover whispered in my ear
    The first thing that she said was Take Me
    The last thing that she said was Cast Me Away

I saw a vision of my mother and father
They were sitting smiling under summer trees
They offered me the gift of life
I took this present very carefully
    And one side of my life said Take Me
    The other side said Cast Me Away

Reaching for the Light

Crocus in flames
Never burns up
Dew comes dropping
And it fills the cup
Darkness falls
Petals close up for the night
But when the dawn paints them
They start
Reaching for the light

Baby swimming
Inside your womb
Searching for brightness
In that warm gloom
Well blood is red
And milk is white
Out dives the baby
And she's
Reaching for the light

    Light springs the life in everyone
    That's why the planets dance around the sun
    Light makes the heart and the spirit rise
    That's why Caitlin tries to touch your eyes

See the apple tree
Standing there
Stretching blossoms
In the shining air
See Caitlin growing
With all her sweet might
I want the moon
Mum
I'm reaching for the light

Stufferation

Lovers lie around in it
Broken glass is found in it
Grass
I like that stuff

Tuna fish get trapped in it
Legs come wrapped in it
Nylon
I like that stuff

Eskimos and tramps chew it
Madame Tussaud gave status to it
Wax
I like that stuff

Elephants get sprayed with it
Scotch is made with it
Water
I like that stuff

Clergy are dumbfounded by it
Bones are surrounded by it
Flesh
I like that stuff

Harps are strung with it
Mattresses are sprung with it
Wire
I like that stuff

Carpenters make cots of it
Undertakers use lots of it
Wood
I like that stuff

Dirty cigarettes are lit by it
Pensioners get happy when they sit by it
Fire
I like that stuff

Johnny Dankworth's alto is made of it, most of it *
Scoobdidoo is composed of it †
Plastic
I like that stuff

Elvis kept it in his left-hand pocket
Little Richard made it zoom like a rocket
Rock 'n' Roll
Ooh my soul
I like that stuff

Apemen take it to make them hairier
I ate a ton of it in Bulgaria
Yoghurt
I like that stuff

Man-made fibres and raw materials
Old rolled gold and breakfast cereals
Platinum linoleum
I like that stuff

Skin on my hands
Hair on my head
Toenails on my feet
And linen on the bed

Well I like that stuff
Yes I like that stuff
The earth
Is made of earth
And I like that stuff

* Jazz musician John Dankworth used to play a plastic saxophone.

† Scoobdidoo was a fistful of kind of multi-coloured pieces of plastic which were a playground craze in the 1950s. It was a sad sort of toy, nothing like the exciting Hula Hoop of the same period.

Silence

I held silence
Like a globe
I held silence
And it glowed

BOTY

Boty Goodwin
(obituary from *The Guardian*)

The last time we saw Boty Goodwin, our extra daughter, she was happy, blonde, optimistic and planning her thirtieth birthday party. That was about four weeks ago, in Boston, Massachusetts. Boty had flown in from LA for 24 hours to see Adrian's new show *Tyger Two* and to spend a little time with us, the parents she'd adopted. Then she flew back to the California Institute of the Arts to give her final show before a board of examiners.

This was a presentation on November 6th of stories she'd written about her life performed against a background of beautiful wallpaper which illustrated key images from her history. At 29, she was already a brilliant artist/writer/performer – and her show delighted her examiners, who congratulated her, offered her a scholarship and encouraged her to take her Master's Degree in both writing and fine art.

On November 9th she repeated the show for her fellow-students, who were dazzled and exhilarated. All her life Boty celebrated whatever was worth celebrating. That night she partied with her friends. At some point she was given a drug which killed her. She died in her studio in the early hours of November 10th of an accidental overdose of heroin.

Boty wasn't a junkie or a suicide. Nor was she a martyr or a role model. She was a lovely, funny, very talented young woman who made one stupid, fatal mistake.

Boty Goodwin was an orphan. Her mother was Pauline Boty – one of England's finest pop painters, an actress whose beauty was admired by everyone and whose shining intelligence enlightened her friends. Pauline was the painter of *The Only Blonde in the World* – perhaps the greatest and most lively painting of Marilyn Monroe.

Pauline met and fell in love with Clive Goodwin. He was a working-class actor, handsome, witty and hip, who became editor of the influential magazine *Encore* and later worked on the TV arts programme *Tempo* as right-hand man to Kenneth Tynan.

Pauline and Clive married. But shortly after she became pregnant, Pauline was diagnosed as suffering from a rare form of leukaemia. She gave birth to a daughter and died shortly afterwards. Clive decided that the baby should be named Boty. Boty spent her first years living with her loving grandparents in Surrey. Clive was nervous about looking after a little girl by himself, but we encouraged him to bring Boty to live with him in his large South Kensington flat.

The first time he looked after her on his own, Clive was terrified, so they both came to stay with us in the beautiful Yorkshire farmhouse where we lived at the time. Boty and our two daughters, Sasha and Beattie, who were around her age, became very attached to each other. It was during one of these visits that Clive told us: 'If anything should ever happen to me, you will have Boty to live with you, won't you?' We laughed, of course, our friends didn't die in those days. We laughed, but we agreed.

In 1968 Clive founded the *Black Dwarf*, that fine raging left-wing magazine in which, for a short time, socialists, artists, pacifists, anarchists, poets and communists formed a volatile alliance. By now Clive was also literary agent for most of the best left-wing playwrights in Britain.

One day, when Boty was nearly 12, Clive flew to Los Angeles to negotiate with Warren Beatty and Trevor Griffiths about the movie *Reds*. They met in the Beverly Wiltshire Hotel. During the meeting Clive drank one glass of wine. But he was suddenly attacked by a headache and had to leave. In the lobby of the hotel he staggered and vomited.

The hotel staff, thinking he was drunk, called the Los Angeles police. Clive was handcuffed and thrown into a police cell, where he died, alone, of a cerebral haemorrhage.

There was a big memorial meeting in a London theatre – with songs and speeches and poems. Boty, nearly 12 years old, not only came to the meeting, but insisting on appearing in a sketch of her own devising, in which she and Clive's secretary were trying to contact Clive by phone. Everyone knew right away that Boty, somehow, would survive.

Until she was 16, Boty lived with her grandparents and came to us in London for weekends and holidays. But she had lived with Clive in the centre of radical, bohemian, rocking London and she longed to return.

When she was 16 she chose to live with us and go to the local comprehensive. By now she was one of the family, a maker of laughter, a setter of style and a wonderful peacemaker in a sometimes stormy family. Our proudest moment came when Boty signed a card to us – lots of love from your extra daughter.

Four years after her father's death the Los Angeles Police and the Beverly Wilshire finally settled out of court and Boty had financial independence. Her beauty and intelligence and wit attracted hundreds of friends and admirers. But she worried that some people were after her money – and a few of them were.

Boty believed fiercely in education. She knew that education for women is the only real way to freedom, but she also knew and understood politically the huge advantage she had over most other women because of her money. She was able to choose for herself to study at the California Institute of the Arts and pay her own way. But money didn't corrupt her. She remained true to her Clive and Pauline's principles while developing her own political philosophy.

Her family and friends and teachers and fellow-students are devastated. Maybe this will silence a few of those voices which whisper that 'smack is cool if you know how to handle it' and play on the glamour of dead and alive junkie rock stars to make heroin a fashionable poison. We feel both empty and angry about Boty's death. But we and her extra sisters who loved her so utterly are immensely proud of her talented, shining life.

ADRIAN & CELIA MITCHELL

Boty Goodwin was born on 12th February 1966. She died on 10th November 1995.

The Forest and the Lake

*(for Clive Goodwin, Pauline Boty and their daughter
Boty Goodwin, written soon after Clive's death).*

the forest laughed

plenty to laugh at –
squirrels at their gymnastics,
motorways full of fanatical ants
carrying out their looney missions,
overdressed pheasants holding fashion parades
watched by the rabbiting rabbits –

the forest laughed a lot

sun-washed clearings,
small thickets dark with grief –
it was a good forest to go to,
swaying and sheltering,
welcoming as a woolly, brown-eyed dog

one day the forest turned its head
and realised it grew beside a lake

the lake was liquid light

there were deeps with wisdom fish
long as your leg,
there were shallows with quick fish
tinier than pins,
swallows skimming and surfing,
a plump of ducks at their pleasure-boating

the lake looked down at the fish and smiled
the lake looked up at the waterbirds and smiled

the lake looked at the forest and smiled

and from that day
it was lake and forest
forest and lake

so lovely so lively
shining and shadow
the laughing forest
and the shining lake

green hand holding blue hand
a landscape of glory
in which so many of us wandered happily...

only the bird of badness sang: not long

and the earth shook twice
and the lake shook dark
and the forest shook still

dawn finds us watching
as a green and blue striped boat
drifts over smoking waters
up to the shaded shore

and, nearly twelve years old,
half forest and half lake,
out of the boat steps Boty

A Flower for Boty

Eloquent art
Speaking straight to the heart
Fills the critic with numbing dismay
For eloquent art
Speaking straight to the heart
Leaves the critic with fuck-all to say

Good Luck Message to Boty with Flowers
Before Her Finals at Cal Arts

With the Style of the Beatles
The Flash of Jean Harlow
And the Funkiness of Frida Kahlo
Plus the Fire of Blake
And the Wings of Shelley
C'mon Boty
Give it plenty of Welly

Telephone

Telephone told me that you were dead
Now I hate every telephone's stupid head
I'd rather sit here turning to a block of stone
Than pick up any snake of a telephone

Every Day

Every day we're going to talk to you Boty
Tell you the ridiculous News
The Politics of Bebopalula for All
And the Meaning of Red Suede Shoes

Every day we'll have Visions of you Boty
Dressed up like a Birthday Cake
Every day we're going to listen to your Voice
And your Laughter like a Trumpet Break

Every day we're going to see you clearer
Stomping on a faraway Starry Floor
Every day we'll edge a little bit nearer
Till we Dance with our Boty once more

(I wrote that last poem with a beautiful new fountain pen. I saw it at London Airport on my way to fly to Los Angeles for Boty's Memorial Meeting. The pen was flecked in various shades of silvery blue and I couldn't afford it. But I heard Boty whisper to me – Go on – buy it! Get blue ink and only use it to write poems. And when I paid for it, I heard Boty laughing.)

For Boty

Down on this planet
where we waver and wander
lost among the towering hours

Down on this planet
when an apple tree dies
there is a long leaning
and a slow falling through the years
until the moss-kissed insect-lively trunk
rests in its bed of grass
and becomes part of the grass

And down on this planet
if you drop a ball on the pavement
its bounces become smaller
till it finds a resting curb or gutter

Things fall and take their time in falling
and then they take their rest

But I don't see you as falling darling
you seem to move
among our lives
like waves of the sea
like a mist of tears sun-touched with laughter
like a slow snowfall
like bonfire smoke
and the swirl of scarlet leaves

Especially When It Snows
(for Boty)

especially when it snows
and every tree
has its dark arms and widespread hands
full of that shining angelfood

especially when it snows
and every footprint
makes a dark lake
among the frozen grass

especially when it snows darling
and tough little robins
beg for crumbs
at golden-spangled windows

ever since we said goodbye to you
in that memorial garden
where nothing grew
except the beautiful blank-eyed snow

and little Caitlin crouched to wave goodbye to you
down in the shadows

especially when it snows
and keeps on snowing

especially when it snows
and down the purple pathways of the sky
the planet staggers like King Lear
with his dead darling in his arms

especially when it snows
and keeps on snowing

from

ALL SHOOK UP

POEMS 1997-2000

THE YEARS SPEED BY

A Year Passes, as Years Do

January is a penguin on a slide of ice
on an iceberg full of penguins
watching a film called *Iceberg*
about an iceberg badly damaged by a monster ship
and a love affair between two of the penguins
but only one survived
there is a terrible song in the film
called *Our Fish Will Go On.*

February is a man called Fred
with cardboard in the soles of his holy shoes
as the Manchester rain pours down
and slaps his face with its chilly hands
and his coat is soaked through
so that putting his scarlet-blue
hands into his pockets only
makes them colder and damper.

March is a kite which breaks free of its string
and surfs across the sky over the South Downs
and sees the far coast of France shining
and starts to slide along the air currents over the Channel
dreaming of a happy landing in Paris.

April is a blue-eyed toddler
who staggers into a field of trampolining lambs
and sits in the meadowgrass
snatching at the raggedy white clouds
and singing a song about chocolate biscuits.

May is an orchard bursting with blossoms
where the bad boys have built
a shadowy hut made of old doors
roof and walls camouflaged with slices of turfs
they may smile and you and promise you surprises
but don't go into the shadowy hut
built by the bad boys.

June is a dancer in the centre of the city
as the businesspeople march past in their uniforms
barking into their voodoophones

she is the only one who looks the sun in the face
as she dances her slip-sloppy dance in the fountain
the big fat sweaty happy dancer who loves the sun.

July is an exhausted old retriever
back from a walk on his three good legs
lying on the cool sofa panting with his tongue
as his eyes flitter shut and the dreams begin
of galloping after rabbits down a mountain of bones
as he sleeps in the arms of his master.

August is a couple of pale crabs under a green rock
complaining about the aliens
with their thudding music and howling voices
and terrible spades wrecking the sandy lands
and emptying pools and generally
upsetting the slow and sideways world
of a couple of old curmudgeons with claws.

September is an apple
in the shaking hands of a young woman
on a bench in the grass compound
behind the mental hospital.
She is afraid to eat the apple.
She is afraid to put the apple down.
Because the apple is her mind.
Because the apple is her heart.
Because the apple is her life.
Because the apple is the world.
She cannot remember the word for apple.

October is a wood of scarlet and gold
and an old poet smiling to himself
as he shuffles through squashy leaves
remembering only the good days gone by
remembering beloved people animals and books
and chuckling inside himself to see
a party of schoolchildren with clipboards and a teacher
who has told them to write poems about October.

November is a bursting bonfire
of souvenirs going up in smoke
a bonfire of grasping high-jumping flames
surrounded by grimy worshippers
as a thousand stars burst in the gunpowdered sky
and down inside the belly of the bonfires
the baked potatoes crackle to each other.

December is a reindeer travelling
across hundreds of miles of golden moss
past the poised pines of dusky forests
over the frosted mirrors of lakes
up down and round about blinding snowscape
to the Snow Queen's Palace
where his friend Gerda sits
with the apple of September in her hands.

Life Is a Walk Across a Field

(opposite of the Russian proverb, Life is not a walk across a field,
which is the last line of Boris Pasternak's poem 'Hamlet')

Life is a walk across a field
sometimes a golden dreamdrift of polished petals
and daisies bouncing among the hummocks of moss
which guide an infant river sometimes over squashed grass
sometimes under the spongey turf but sometimes

the tickling green surface breaks apart underfoot
and the mouth of the ground gapes
and the bogdragon swallows down your shins
your hips your armpits your chin your –

Life is a walk across a field
and should you find a milkmaid in one hollow
with a jug of cider and breasts like summer
from behind the spectacular oak will steam
the minotaur, half farmer and half bull
guffawing as his horns impale you both oh yes

Life is a walk across the field
of buttercups and landmines...

UNDER NEW LABOUR

That Feeling

When you sit
On a chair
And the chair's
Not there
That's the feeling I mean –
That's the Blair.

We Bomb Tonight
(headline in the *Evening Standard*, London, 17 December 1998)

> *'deafening explosions reverberated across Baghdad last night'*

> *'City traders reacted calmly to the air strikes, with oil prices
> and the dollar retreating after yesterday's sharp gains…'*

me and little sister
sleeping tight
hugged in the arms
of a dark blue night

I was in a funny dream
and both of us
were being driven by a horse
in a dark blue bus

then my dream went bang
night turned day
little sister
was vanished away

and the air was nothing
but dust and screams
now I search for little sister
in all my dreams

she hides I seek
but all I have found
in my dreams is a
dark blue hole in the ground

Education Education Education

Only one reason why I get to school
it's a condition of my parole

chilled a teacher and torched a church
in the cause of criminological research

back to the playground I take my stand
uppers and downers in each hand

if you don't like the deal we made
I'll unzip your kipper with a rusty blade

The Druggards

The druggards lean in corners of the werehouse
wearing raggerjeans, eight-piece suits,
little block dresses, corrugated overcoats,
    chins like the prows of model yachts
    mouths like slots for credit cards

Brains can be such beautiful islands
but they abandon theirs to the invading
mute and screaming chemical armies
        for they think the brain is only this
        a hunk of electrified meat
        they imagine life is a boredomboardroomboardgame,
        the soul a stamped-out cigarette
        as they cheat each other and trick each other
        and sneer at the undruggard world
        before plotting a petulant suicide...

Go Well

When the last Whale in the whole world
Was hauled through London on an open lorry
One million children trudged behind it
Bearing banners saying Sorry.

Later the last Horse and the last Dog
Rolled by upon their funeral carts.
No children waved Goodbye to them –
All were in hospital with broken hearts.

Shaven Heads

Men in their twenties with shaven heads
Men in their thirties with shaven heads
Men in their forties with shaven heads
They all look alike to me

Their noses jut out like ruddy rockets
Their eyeballs bulge out of their sockets

They smile all the time at people from foreign parts
To show they are not skinhead racist farts

But that smile too frequently unzips
Like a leer and bald heads speak louder than lips

It must feel so weird when you're shaving your crop
Put that razor away grow some sort of a mop

But don't overdo it or I shall wail
Get out of here with your fuzzy pony-tail

Walldream

They collected up, in fine brown nets,
the coal-coloured rocks on the dark side of the moon.

Around the limits of London
in the 28th century
they built a bulging wall of sootrock
a wall with blurred outlines
emitting rays of darkness
so that anyone approaching the city
whether explorer or attacker
became lost in a black fog
and turned, to stagger, blinking, home.

But when the wall builders, time travelling,
visited me last night
They cried out: 'Where are the walls we built?
Where are the Walls of Darkness?'

'Don't worry,' I said, 'Your Walls are in the future
so long as you don't go too far.
Otherwise, you'll find them in the past.'

Jesus Poems

Jesus stepped on to the bus,
'Nazareth, please,
But I don't have the fare.'
'Bugger off, hippie,' said the driver
And was turned, in the flash of a ticket,
Into a purple hippopotamus.

*

Blood oozing
From his hands feet and side
Jesus crawled into Casualty
Late on Good Saturday night.
'Take a number,' said the desk woman
'It's urgent,' he whispered.
'Aw shut up, ye bastard –
We're all urgent here.'

*

Pilate said 'What's Truth?'
Jesus clicked his fingers like Smokey Robinson
Out of the floor
Sprang a bloody great cactus
Right up Pilate's jacksie.

*

'You're a poor man,'
Said the squaddy, looking up from his crap game
'Die a poor man's death.'

'I came not to bring bread
But a stone,' mumbled Jesus

'What the hell you blabbing about?'

'I'm a poet.'

'We'll soon put a stop to that.'

THE CARNIVAL OF VENUS

Asymmetrical Love Song

My love is asymmetrical
She looks different from every angle
Some might say she's a little bit wonky
But I say – jingle jangle!

Valances
(with love to Celia)

Today is the first day of my life as a domesticated animal
For I have discovered the meaning of the word valance
Yes and I have handled two different but similar valances
And helped to fit those valances appropriately.

What, you may ask me, is a valance?
Well the centre of the valance
Is a sheet upon which nobody lies.
It is spread on the upper surface of the base of the bed
On which the sun seldom if ever shines
And there the centre of the valance becomes
A sheet for the mattress to repose upon.

I should hazard that even in the suburban world
Inhabited by such underlings as
Doillies, druggets and downtrodden felt,
The valance centre must be numbered with the humblest.
Even were it decorated with a gold-embroidered
Representation of the Signing of the Treaty of Utrecht,
Or hand-sprinkled with a spiders' web
Of luminous paints from Jackson Pollock's fist
Or scorched by the impression of the face of the corpse
Of the great-grandfather of Ian Paisley
It would be unseen and unacclaimed
Except by minions whose duties occasionally oblige them
To change the valances or rearrange the valances.
(So I was not surprised that the two valances

Which I handled today, my two first valances,
Were undecorated in any sense.)

But it is not the centre of the valance
Which is at the heart of valancehood
Any more than it is the underpants of Leonardo da Vinci
Which inspire our admiration.
For all around the centre of the valance runs a margin
And, beyond that margin, a billowing border of linen,
(The same material of which the centre is composed)
But slightly ruched all round.

So, when the mattress is placed upon the valance
The edges of the valance appear all around the waist of the bed
Like a short ballet skirt, a modest tutu,
An edging of wavelets, ready to bear the sleeper
Over a sea of frills and flounces, to the Land of Furbelow.

Away

I went out
with open hands
into the strange
and shaking lands

I shake my spear
I shake your hand
I stretch my smile
like a rubber band

is it good to shake
is it good to be shook
come on do the earthquake
and the avalanche book

I could tell you my name
but it's meaningless
like the clothes on the floor
when I undress

call me by any name
you like to say
one name for the night
another for the day

I'm in a far country
and travelling's fun
but tonight it was bad
when you cried on the phone

thousands of miles away
lies my darling
she wears my love
like a silver ring

Arlo Guthrie, Ray Charles, Willie Nelson,
Aretha Franklin and Peggy Lee
they got the voices
say what I long to say

and I wish I could be many species of animal
so I could show how I feel
I'm a stumbling moose
I'm a homeless goose
I'm an unplugged electric eel

love is like a circle
it goes round and round
life is like a spiral
circling down and down

death acts very tough
but he's silly stuff
tries to fill us full of fear
sticks his black iron claw in our ear

lots of my friends have been dragged down there
I'll have to join them eventually
I plan to float down through the glittering blue
to rot proudly in their company

well
that's why I'm shaking
like a six-month pup
on fireworks night
all shook up

A Lucky Family
(to Helen and Phil)

Their garden's a magical
Welcoming planet
With plenty of room for
Roses and daisies
Men and women like roses
And children like daisies

Daisies and roses
Roses and daisies
a dream of daisies and roses

Sometimes they sit and watch from a window
Sitting and watching from a favourite window
A little girl watching her father in the garden
A husband watching his wife in the garden
A mother watching her children in the garden

> Down the road
> A woman's trapped
> In a family of terror
> The children are screaming
> Tearing her brain to shreds
> If she takes six pills she may fall asleep
> If she takes ten pills she may have a good dream
> Of life in a lucky family

Their garden's a magical
Welcoming planet
Which dances through space with
Roses and daisies
Men and women like roses
Children like daisies

Daisies and roses
Roses and daisies
A dream of daisies and roses

It Still Goes On

once upon a time when I was out of my mind
I left three beautiful children behind
I could not tell them why
I had to leave or die
you never saw so much pain

once upon a time I shot my world apart
each of my children took a hole in the heart
so did their mother and so did I
I had to leave or die
you never saw so much pain
you never saw so much pain

The Arrangements

The children see their father every week.
He is not sure what they should do.
He and their mother find it hard to speak.
He takes them to the park, the cinema, the zoo.

Their mother phones their father up to say
That every Sunday night they're in distress.
It tears them up each time he goes away.
It would be better if he saw them less.

And he, because he cannot bear their pain, agrees.
But monthly meetings lead to days of tears.
And so the visits lessen by degrees
Until he does not visit them for years.

Oh but I needed them. They needed me.
Not to spend time with them was cruel and wrong.
My love could not be greater for those three.
But that love should have made me strong.

Where Are They Now?

My mother lives inside my heart.
I live inside my mother's heart.
My father lives inside my heart.
I live inside my father's heart.

That About Sums It Up

women feel too much
too many feelings
that's what I feel about that

woman's heart is like a bottle of milk
man's heart is like a box of paperclips

shake that milk
rattle those paperclips
let your love roll on

Swiss Kissing

It is done so:
The two lovers commence
At opposite ends
Of a Toblerone
And munch their way towards
A climax
Of chocolate tongue fondue

Safe Sex Swiss Kissing

This is performed like Swiss Kissing
But you do not remove the cardboard cover
Or the silver paper.

My Friend the Talking Elevator of Tokyo

The Hotel Elevator speaks to me.
She is a National Otis lift.
The elevator speaks in a friendly voice
You may come in, I think she says – in Japanese –
But most of her words are a bright blur
Of possible-impossible half-meanings.

Her voice is velvet, just too soft for clarity.
Sometimes I have to restrain myself
From asking other passengers
To stop talking, shuffling their feet
Or rustling their infernal back-to-front newspapers
So I can hear all the words which drop
Like diamonds from the metal lips
Of the Oracle of the Roynet Hotel,
Musashino, Tokyo.
(The Roynet is attached to
A restaurant called Sizzler.)

I write down what I think she might be saying
My Musashino muse:
'Today will not be lucky for you
But the rest of your life will all be sweet potatoes'
And once: 'You look so tired today,
Why not lay down and rest your head?'
And once: 'Read two chapters of a thriller,
Phone home and have a drink.'

Or she makes statements about life
Like: 'Clouds are the messages of dead philosophers'
Or 'It's gooder with the Buddha'.
She often says something like:
'You timed it!' as you step on to her carpet,
Then 'Meet the Merry Men!'
(As if I'm Robin Hood).

Sometimes I travel up and down for hours
Crouched in one corner listening to her words
This language like a little rocky river
Swerving so coolly through my mind's hot meadows

Today the lift greets me inaccurately:
'Hello, Jimmy Baker'. (A code name?)
Then she adds, with casual warmth,
'Call me Betty-Betty.'
Her name, at last I have the power of her name.
When I emerge at the seventh floor she says
'Better get out' or maybe 'Betty get out'
I am talking back to her
As a man brushes by me on his way into the lift.
I can't hear what Betty-Betty says to him.

'Betty get out'? 'Betty-Betty get out'!
The soul of this silver woman is trapped
In the steel frame of an elevator.
'Don't worry,' I whisper to the wall, 'I'm going to free you.'

That night I return with a set of screwdrivers
I occupy the lift and jam the buttons.
With rubber gloves I unscrew everything unscrewable
But her voice continues saying something about
Being stuck and not to panic about not being stuck
Or not being unstuck.
There is a steel mesh over the aperture
From which her voice floats in faint balloons.

I lever and wrench the mask away.
From the void comes the voice of the prophetess
Very clear and very still:
'I am with you, Adrian,
I am always with you.'

And I am with you, Betty-Betty,
I am always with you.

Love in Flames

Midnight: a dark and passionate scene.
You whispered: Come into me, quick.
My hand reached out for the Vaseline
But it closed on a jar of Vick.

Hospitality

She stands beside my sickbed
Her breastplate starchy white
Only six inches from my face
Like a ship's sail in full flight

But when she turns in profile
Small stripes of pink and whiteness
Move up and down and over
Her left breast shaped like kindness

She wheels the screens around my bed
After the doctors call
And then she takes my temperature –
And that's not all

    Oh nurse nurse nurse nurse
    Show me your nursey things
    Your crystalline thermometer
    Shake it till your skeleton swings

    Oh you look so nursey
    With your savage little fringe
    And your watch upon your bosom
    And your magic syringe

    Yes nurse nurse I think I feel worse
    Do me those nursey things
    Place your healing hand on my swollen gland
    And nurse it till the patient sings

I wasn't going to fall but you caught me wrong-footed
You took my pulse and god knows where you put it
With your sharkskin panties and your alligator purse
Cleopatra Nightingale my favourite nurse
Oh nursey nursey mercy to percy
You're an angel on fluttering wings
        Yes thank you
Bless you and your nursey things

ON THE ARTSAPELAGO

Poetry Is Not a Beauty Contest

Bob Keats is better than John Dylan
But worse than Emily Shakespeare

Chocolate omelettes are better than burnt tapioca
But worse than crystallised parsnips

Michael Owen is fitter than Enoch Powell
Tony Blair is fatter than Mahatma Gandhi

The Independent is more fun than *The Sun*
But less fun than the Beatles or the Goon Show

Daisy, my six-month-old Golden Retriever,
is more beautiful than all of them rolled into one

If Digest

If you live to the age of twenty-one
You will almost certainly be a man, my son.

[Rudyard Kipling and Adrian Mitchell]

Desiderata Digest

Go placidly, think floppily,
Live boringly, die soppily.

If I Dare You, If I Double-Dare You
(the Leslie Crowther Memorial Poem)

At the poetry recital
Or literary prize-giving
The audience should always answer back.
If a speaker mentions
The word Faber
Everyone should shout out – CRACKERJACK!
But if Faber *and* Faber are named, please attack
With the cry of CRACKERJACK AND CRACKERJACK!

(But if Bloodaxe Books are spoken of, we'll expect
The reverent murmur of – *Respect......Respect......*)

To a Helpful Critic

Perhaps I wasn't writing for people like you
I can't be always working for the precious few
Maybe I was writing for a child of two
I can't write every thing I do
With one eye on the paper and the other on you

This Be the Worst

*(after hearing that some sweet innocent
thought that Philip Larkin must have written:
'They tuck you up, your mum and dad')*

They tuck you up, your mum and dad,
They read you Peter Rabbit, too.
They give you all the treats they had
And add some extra, just for you.

They were tucked up when they were small,
(Pink perfume, blue tobacco-smoke),
By those whose kiss healed any fall,
Whose laughter doubled any joke.

Man hands on happiness to man,
It deepens like a coastal shelf.
So love your parents all you can
And have some cheerful kids yourself.

from Nine Ways of Looking at Ted Hughes

Poet at Work

There he stands
a grizzly bear in a waterfall
catching the leaping salmon
in his scoopy paws

Full Moon and Little Frieda

little Frieda's life
will always be lit by that poem
and so will the life of the moon

Footwear Notes

bloody great clogs
carved out of logs
are the indoor shoes
of Ted Hughes

Not Cricket

Ted backsomersaulted to catch the meteorite left-handed,
Rubbed it thoughtfully on the green groin of his flannels
And spun it through the ribcage of the Reaper,
Whose bails caught fire
And jumped around the pitch like fire-crackers.
Said the commentator:
Yes Fred, it might have been a meteor –
Could have been a metaphor.

Rugby News

When Ted played front row forward
for Mytholmroyd Legendary RFC
his scrum strolled right through the walls
of Sellafleld and out again the other side
like a luminous lava-flow

Out of Focus

When you take a photograph of Ted
it's a job to get him all in –
like taking a snapshot of Mount Everest

Gastronomica

A large Mayakovsky
Or Ginsberg and tonic before the meal
Dry white Stevie Smith with the mousse of moose
Roast beef and Yorkshire pudding with a deep red Ted
Vintage Keats with the trifle
A glass of Baudelaire goes well with cheese
But afterwards
A bottomless goblet of Shakespeare's port
Or the blazing brandy of Blake

Fish-eye

Said the Shark at the Sub-Aquatic Angling Contest
I caught an enormous Elizabeth Bishop the other day.
That's nothing, said the Whale,
I hooked a Ted Hughes, but he got away.

Cool / Hip

cool is a pose
hip is a gift
cool is a mask
hip is perfect pitch
cool is closed twenty-two hours a day
hip is open all round the clock
cool is the suit of armour made of ice
hip strolls naked on the bay of the dock
cool pretends it doesn't go to an analyst
hip is Just William at Prince Charming's Ball
cool is the super-sarcastic panelist
hip's the green lizard on the workhouse wall
cool is a sniper on the hills
keeping going on those mean green pills
hip is a joke
as weightless as smoke
or Hamlet stalking
in his Spiderman cloak

New Movie Regulations

In all new movies
revolvers must be replaced by retrievers
punches by paunches
kicks by cooks
explosions by lotions
shots by spots.

The Terroriser draws his retriever
(in pastels)
but fails to spot the hero
who counter-attacks
with cooks and paunches
until the Terroriser
by pulling a secret lever
releases a flood of calamine lotion.

AUTOBICYCLE

All Shook Up
(Adrian Mitchell has left the building)

I catch   I fetch
As best   I can
I sit   I stay
   half-dog
   half-man

when bad rains fall
I crouch and wail

I sniff the world
and wag my tail

   half-man
   half-dog
   if a poem
should whistle

   my ears
   stick up
my haunches
   bristle

In My Two Small Fists

in that bright blue summer
I used to gather
daisies for my father
speedwell for my mother

with buttercups
and prickly heather
cowrie shells
and a seagull's feather

treasures in each fist
all squashed together
daisies for my father
speedwell for my mother

    (that's how I see it
    but I don't know
    if it really happened
    sixty years ago

    but my memories shine
    and their light seems true
    and so do the daisies
    and speedwell too)

The Mitchellesque Lineman

Walking from telegraph pole to telegraph pole
Along the sagging singing swinging wires
That's how I travel from town to town

I stand a moment on the top cross-piece
Of a creosoted if splintered pole
I look down, spit for luck on the soft verge below
I count, for luck, the small ceramic
Bee-cones, as we call them,
Which perch, like the ivory helmets
Of warriors hidden in a tree,
On the crown of every pole.

I breathe massively, taking in the deep zen of the air,
Flex my toes in their spangled satin sneakers
Then right foot on to the right of centre wire
Then give, bounce, rise, descend,
Then left foot on to the left of centre wire
Give, bounce, rise, descend
And stand there only one beat before
My right foot takes its first sure forward step
Along the curving wireway
Which leads away and over the horizon.

But the pole ahead, for now that's all I care about,
All I look at, all that exists in the universe,
The pole ahead occupies my mind and soul.
My feet feel their own way
As my fingers hold
Gently enough to sense the slightest breeze or rabbit sneeze
My peacock-feather balancing pole,
My one-blue-eyed pole which stares me on my way
As I ghost my way from pole to pole to pole.

Where am I going to yonder?
What does this journey portend?
Wherefore disturb from the wires the swallowbirds?
Where will my pilgrimage end?

As a matter of funk, for such molehill questions
I don't give a monkey's thump
You only ask because your own trainers
Are stuck two feet down in the logical mud

While I'm a cloudhead sailing through the thermals
Stately, I hope, as a Spanish galleon,
Travelling for the sake of the whirlpool excitements
Swirling around my intestines.

Come rain come shine I walk the line
From pole to pole to pole
Walking high thigh passing thigh
With the rain in my heart
And sun in my soul
And the Mitchellesque Lineman
Is still on the line
So still
The Mitchellesque Lineman
Is still on the line.

If Not, Sniff Not

'2502786 Aircraftsman Mitchell,'
Said the Group Captain, surrounded by his green glass desk,
'The day before yesterday I found you Guilty
Of losing Through Neglect
Another Airman's laundry.
I fined you and sentenced you to
Five days confined to camp.

'But yesterday the Airman in question
Returned from Sick Leave with his laundry.
So it was not lost after all.'

I risked a smirk.
The Group Captain continued:
'I will therefore rescind your fine
And scrub out your offence.
You will however continue to be confined to camp.'

I looked above his head.
On the wall – a framed copy of Kipling's fucking 'If'.

Age 65 Bus Pass

a little card
in a plastic case
bears a picture of
my shining face

and from my northwest
London base
I can ride a bus
to any place

wearing my crown
of silver hair
and having to pay
no fucking fare

Sorry Stuff

sad is the toilet on the train
with newspapers all clogged up
sad the forgotten weetabix
when all its milk is sogged up

but sadder still the daffodil
which William Wordworth squashes
wandering lonely as a clown
in his size twelve galoshes

O sorry is as sorry does
and I am super-sorry-full
the tears of years of foolish fears
O I have wept a lorryful

Student

sometimes my dog is lionlike
facing me one ear a little bit upraised,
licking her black lips and studying me
as I unscrew a bottletop, take a white pill
and slew it down with water

as if she's studying how to be a human being
she drinks in everything she's seeing

Wishing

Wish I had the head of a golden retriever
With floppy ears and a black, wet nose
Everyone on earth would have to believe a
Poet creature with features like those.

The Poet Inside

It was a loving and a gentle dog
Padded over the floor to me
She waved her tail a dozen times
And placed her chin upon my knee

A captive poet seemed to stare out
Of the deep brownness of her eyes
Longing to sing her golden songs
But all that she could speak were sighs.

Not Much of a Muchness

I think I'll go flying this afternoon
I didn't know you flew
O I can fly any time I like
But not in front of you

Lighting Candles for Boty

because I believe in light
not for god's eyes
but for the eyes of people
because I believe in
candles against the darkness
because candlelight recalls her beauty

February 12th, 1996
(for Boty's 30th birthday)

stone breaks
and the bone breaks
but the heart embraces the pain it is bearing
if only the heart could break
instead of tearing

The Unbroken Heart

the heart may alter
the heart will falter
little by little
the heart may be worn
or battered and torn
but it is not brittle

with its nine lives
the heart survives
though it is torn apart
it's last to die
with our last sigh
forgive me, says the heart

Advertising Will Eat the World

Death in his infinite mercilessness
Takes the girl in the orange dress
And sends the drug to cure the pain in the head
Two years after the patient's dead.

    Grief is such a physical thing
    the law of gravity is doubled
    whatever is almost touched falls to the floor
    everything is heavier
    especially the head
    the kneecaps and the eyeballs melt
    if anyone should sing
    grief is such a physical thing

On the Deadophone

my job as a poet
part of my job
is talking to the dead
part of my job
is listening to the dead
they tell me all sorts of stuff
on the deadophone

some of it I'm not allowed to tell you
some of it I'm ordered to tell you
but not allowed to say where it comes from

sometimes they keep waking me up
with that verr verr verr verr deadophone
sometimes I ask a really important question
and they hang up on me clunk

sometimes I get a lot of conversations at once
like gnats swarming round my head
sometimes all I get is engaged
or the sound of a snake hissing

Apart from My Day Job

In the train back from Cardigan passing
  the cow sheds
  the bull sheds
a big red shed that must have been the Dragon Shed

It was also my job
to look out of train windows
to record the fields unfolding
field after field
and the bright blue ditch
striking straight towards the hills
and the proud house carved out of white money
and a flock of grazing caravans
and a single inexplicable ten foot penguin
standing in the shadow of an old Welsh hedge

It was also my job
to record the poison yellow boiled-sweet neon streetlamps
and the grey wrinkled flanks of enormous sheds
in which giants or dragons might be secretly breeding
and the anti-matter spaces of gravel and old green tins
and the contemptuous advertisements outshining the moon

Or Something

Sometimes I think the world's my cheeseburger
Sometimes I think it's iceberg time
Sometimes I feel like a Victorian tricycle
Sometimes I feel like a robot pantomime
Sometimes I'm awash with anger or something

I wish I could change my flesh into a landscape
A useful old park where my friends could stroll
I wish I could turn my words into musicians
Playing dark blue jazz red rock n roll
So we could dance The Love or something

I'm the People's Hippo, the Geezer from the Freezer
Dumping nightmare rubbish in the Werewolf Wood.
What did you say, Miss Earthquake?
Has the Killer Caterpillar gone for good?
It's a rainy day and the forecast is rain and it's raining hate or love or something

Selfepitaphs

I Was Lucky

That's all. It was good.
Love was a planet
full of amazing creatures.

This Death is only a dark little town,
in a country, in a continent,
on a planet full of amazing creatures,
a planet called love.

Alternative Selfepitaph

I stopped living
but kept on loving

FOR THE AFRICAN CENTURY

'Being certain that not always were we the children of the abyss, we will do what we have to do to achieve our own renaissance. We trust that what we will do will better not only our own condition as a people, but will make a contribution also, however small, to the success of Africa's renaissance, towards the identification of the century ahead of us as the African Century.'

President Thabo Mbeki at his Inauguration on 12 June 1999

Here in My Skin of Many Colours

here in my skin
my redwhite skin
will, in a thousand ways,
guard me, advance me,
promote me and reward me

reassuring to some
a warning to others
till I am dead
and colour-free

I never chose it
from the flesh boutique
it looks too much like
butcher's meat

now I inspect my hands for colours
a purple-pink knuckle
violet fingernails with creamy cuticles
golden hair sprouting
from the back of the first joint of each finger
rivery blue veins
running downhill from my thumbs
light pink merging into dark pink dips
dark pink merging into light brown furrows
light brown merging into medium brown

all the tints altering
in warmth and cold
all the tints altering
with the altering light

these are my colours
till the day I die
these are my colours
till I whiten into ghostliness

Malawi Poems

The Radio Thief

They caught a man in our village
The other night
He broke a window and stole a radio

They caught him and poured petrol on him
And took out their matches –
You're going to die!

I couldn't watch
I ran away

That's what we do with thieves
We burn them
Or chop off their hands like this
Or take pins
And go pee! pee!
In both their eyes –
Now you can't see to steal!

Nowadays we all take care to keep
A litre can of petrol in our homes.

You have many thieves in England?

African Elephants

at the first sight of elephants
our boat fell silent

close to each other, touching each other,
taking note of us, warning their children

standing so calmly
dark as charcoal

it was a deep and holy silence
inhabiting all five humans

only the almost submerged hippo flotilla
hooted its derision

The Beautiful Ghosts

The fortresses of Rosebank
Shine in the sunlight
The fortresses of Rosebank
Shine in the moonlight
And there's a smell of money in the air
And there's a smell of tear-gas in the air
And there's a smell of panic in the air

And here come the ghosts
Through the high white walls
And the spiky railings
Here come the ghosts
Through the curling razor wire
And the signs saying Armed Response

Yes, here come the ghosts
Zooming on transparent motorbikes
Swooping in transparent feathered wings
Here come the ghosts
Weeping with joy
Laughing with sorrow
Here come the ghosts

Like an amazing rainfall
Upon the sunlit, moonlit
Fortresses of Rosebank
Here come the beautiful ghosts of Afrika
Scattering from their delicate hands
Ghostly black roses,
Black roses everywhere

[Rosebank, Johannesburg, February 1997]

A Song for Thabo Mbeki

Out of the enormous shadow
of the beloved tree
he walks into the ferocious light

vultures clack their cynical beaks
hyenas tingle with greed for his flesh

but the elephants raise their trunks in hope
the eyes of the mountains slowly open wide

he walks into the light
into the fierce light of work

to grow whatever can be grown
to save whatever can be saved
to heal whatever can be healed
to free whatever can be freed

he has walked by moonlight
he has walked through the mists of morning
he has walked through dirty warm rain in the cities
and icy clean rain upon the mountains

now
out of the enormous shadow
of the beloved tree
he walks into the ferocious light

[Pretoria, 16 June 1999]

A Poem for Nomtha

My name is Nomtha.
Will you write a poem about my name?

Nomtha means sunrise.
Nomtha is the rays of the sun.
Nomtha stands for hope.

The eyes of Nomtha,
So wide and dark,
Shine their light upon me
Like beautiful twin planets.

The golden fingers of the sun
Close around my heart.

Nomtha tells me a poem.
Her poem is for peace.
She longs for the wounds of Africa
To be washed and healed.

Next day I shut my eyes
And, in a Nomtha vision of hope,
I see Nomtha walking
Down the pathway
Leading to peace and justice.

I see her smiling as she bandages
The broken arm of an old woman by the path.
I see her stoop to a motherless baby
And lift it up and comfort it with songs.
I hear her telling stories to a little boy
To give his tired legs courage on the long long journey.

I see Nomtha and her friends stand on that pathway
Protecting the weak from men with whips and guns.

I see Nomtha walking down that pathway
And I see the sun of peace and justice
Blessing her with its rays
As it rises over her beloved Africa.

[Guguletu, Cape Town, 1998]

SHOWSONGS

Shake My Soul

O shake my soul with sweetness
Good guitar
Yes shake my soul with sweetness
Good guitar

I know what life is
I have held a guitar
And played it till it rang
I know what life is

I know what life is
I have held a baby
And rocked it till it sang
I know what life is

    A dance and a song
    Doesn't last very long –

O shake my soul with sweetness
    Good guitar
Yes shake my soul with sweetness
    Good guitar...

Four Windows

Living in a house with four windows
Eating in a house with four windows
Loving in a house with four windows
Sleeping in a house with four windows

Eastern window and I slide back the screen
Springtime landscape of brilliant green
Cherry blossoms a pink and white dream
Willows tickling a swivelling stream
    My window in springtime

Southern window – the pond has displayed
Water-lilies of every shade
Frogs are croaking around the blue rim
Blazing waterbirds skitter and skim
    My window in summer

        North window
        East South and West
        Which window
        Do I love best?

Western window – each autumn the same,
Forests wearing kimomos of flame,
Scarlet maples and swallows must fly
And chrysthemums perfume the sky
    My window in autumn

Northern window – a shivering sight
All the countryside covered in white
Snow keeps falling and waterways freeze
And deer are eating the bark from the trees
    My window in winter

        North window
        East South and West
        Which window
        Do I love best?

Living in a house with four windows
Four beautiful windows...

Orpheus Sings

(based on a painting by Roelant Savery
in the Fitzwilliam Museum, Cambridge).

Guitar in his hands
Leaning on an Elephant
Orpheus sings

A Wolfhound and St Bernard
At his knees

A grey Ox
Cocks his ear

Two Swans
Lift their snaking heads
Towards the music

The Geese are paddling in the shallows
Gathering peppery green weeds

A flowering Ostrich on a rock
Throws back her wings
In ecstasy

The Waterfall bounces
Silver notes

A Leopard reclining
Like a streamlined blonde

A Lion and Lioness
Roll their golden eyes

A Heron taking off
On a journey to the hidden stars

The Peacock flaunts
His starry blue
Waterfall of a tail

A million Birds
In proud mid-flight
Scattering their colours
All over the sky

A lurking Buffalo
With guilty eyes

A family of Deer
Guarding each other with their branches

Birds and Animals
Feeding   Drinking
Singing   Resting

The Trees are dancing
Stretching and swirling
And the Sky is a dance
Of speeding blue and white

It is all a dance
And at its centre
The wedding of two Horses
They have a special temple
Of grass and flowers
Among the shining rocks

The Grey Horse looks at me
The Chestnut turns away
Their flanks are touching
Silver flank against
Chestnut flank
Two Horses
So glad and close together
It can only be love

Never lose it

Guitar in his hands
Leaning on an Elephant
Orpheus sings

I lost her once
I lost her twice
I lost her once
In Paradise

Eurydice
Eurydice

I lost her once
I lost her twice
In a dark tunnel
Made of ice

Eurydice
Eurydice

I looked back
And for the second time she died
Oh grief comes in and out like the tide

Eurydice
Eurydice

Guitar in his hands
Leaning on an Elephant
Orpheus sings

The People Walking

Sometimes the people walk together
Down the streets of their own cities
With no weapons but the truth

Sometimes the soldiers and police
Turn their backs on their own officers
And walk with the people

As the people walk together
Down the streets of their own cities
With no weapons but the truth

Sometimes the people walk together
Brave and fearful and angry and joyful
With no weapons but the truth

Saint Lover's Day

There'll be love for the lovers
And for the loveless
There'll be love

The spring shall make the world swing
Till it's giddy with love
The light shall stroke the night
Till it's ready for love
The valleys shall mate with the mountains
And every lake will shake
>   There'll be love for the lovers
>   And for the loveless
>   There'll be love

Every street shall rock to the beat
Of the making of love
Every uncle and aunt and insect and plant
Will be quaking with love
Red buses shall mount on green buses
And every cop go pop
>   There'll be love for the lovers
>   And for the loveless
>   There'll be love

The trees will drop to their knees
And they'll tremble with love
The bees and the chimpanzees
Will assemble for love
Jill shall fetch a bucket of loving
And Jack shall blow his stack
>   There'll be love for the lovers
>   And for the loveless
>   There'll be love

The armies will throw down their arms
And go searching for love
The preachers will give up their psalms
And their churching for love
The employer shall sigh for the worker
And double his pay today
>   There'll be love for the lovers
>   And for the loveless
>   There'll be love

Yes there'll be love for the lovely
Who already get plenty of love
And there'll be love for the ugly
Or anyone starving for love
All the lonely shall be happy
And every bum shall overcome

There'll be love
For the lovers
And for the loveless
There'll be love

Yes there'll be love love
For the lovers
And for the loveless
There'll be love

Tissue Paper Flowers

she is a maker
of tissue paper flowers

gently she bends their petals
pink and blue and ivory
into light blossom patterns

she makes little flowers
they are no bigger than her eyes

approximately roses
approximately daffodils
but never exactly

and sometimes invented flowers
or flowers picked from her
summertime dreamfields

she makes
tissue paper flowers
and scatters them secretly
by ones or by twos
in unexpected places

on a train seat
or a briefcase
or the bonnet of a car
or the brilliant surface of a puddle

she lets drop
one or two
and they drift
towards the ground
and she is out of sight
around the corner
long before they land

paper kingcups
or buttercups
they sit and wobble
and balance and toboggan
on the small breezes
of the grimy air

she took a basket
of a thousand blossoms
to the top of a tower
in the middle of the city
and emptied them into
a passing cloud and
watched them drift
over streets and schools
and parking lots

a thousand blessings
on the city

Last Thing

First thing you notice
when you meet somebody
is male or female
Second thing you notice
is probably
black or white
Third are they old or young
Fourth are they weak or strong
Fifth are they rich
or poor as shite
high class low class
honest or faker
sexy or chilly
murderer or maker
Last thing you notice
last thing you notice
murderer or maker

from

THE SHADOW KNOWS

POEMS 2000-2004

William Blake Says:
Every Thing That Lives Is Holy

Long live the Child
Long live the Mother and Father
Long live the People

Long live this wounded Planet
Long live the good milk of the Air
Long live the spawning Rivers and the mothering Oceans
Long live the juice of the Grass
and all the determined greenery of the Globe

Long live the Elephants and the Sea Horses,
the Humming-birds and the Gorillas,
the Dogs and Cats and Field-mice –
all the surviving Animals
our innocent Sisters and Brothers

Long live the Earth, deeper than all our thinking

we have done enough killing

Long live the Man
Long live the Woman
Who use both courage and compassion
Long live their Children

THE SHADOW IN WARTIME

The Shadow Poet Laureateship

The official elegy for Princess Margaret was the final straw. There had to be an antidote: a poet who would stalk the powerful and the pretentious. The socialist magazine *Red Pepper* invited Adrian Mitchell to don the dreaded costume of The Shadow Poet Laureate and write regular poems for their columns. At a midnight ceremony in a Stoke Newington crossword den frequented by swarthy anarchist stokers, he was anointed with tomato ketchup. Then he was decked in the scarlet and red cloak, the charcoal sombrero and the Parisian blue suede shoes which are the garb of the Shadow. From his interview with intrepid Jane Shallice, we excerpt the following:

JS: *You are the people's first Shadow Poet Laureate, but you come from an honourable tradition.*

SHADOW: Yes, like Lord Byron and William Blake, both of whom wrote wonderful Shadow poetry. Byron particularly aimed his at Southey, when Southey was Poet Laureate. He wrote some marvellous stuff aimed at people like Castlereagh and mad King George; Blake wrote against kings and warriors and priests. There have always been Shadow Poet Laureates, but I'm the first to take it on as a mission.

Somebody, wearing a sort of Spanish cape and a dark hat, needs to be standing just behind the Poet Laureate, leering. To remind him that he's human and even the Royal Family are human. But I don't want to concentrate my fire on the Royals, but on the rich and powerful, those who rule and ruin this world and keep leading us into wars.

JS: *And your inspiration?*

SHADOW: For instance – I found out that Tony Blair, like all British Prime Ministers, has to write a letter, which is sealed and given to the captains of all our Trident nuclear submarines. They are only allowed to open it when England is destroyed. And they'll know that because the *Today* programme on Radio Four will not have broadcast for four days. Then they can open the envelope. So I wrote Tony Blair's Secret Note...

JS: *How did you come to write your challenge to the Poet Laureate – 'Unjubilee Poem' – which was published in the* Guardian *in February 2002?*

SHADOW: The *Guardian* had just published some sycophantic pieces about the present Laureate. I kept meeting non-poets who said that he was 'an ambassador for Poetry'. Well I don't think Poetry needs Ambassadors or any other kind of diplomat. There are career poets in every generation. You can see how many committees they are on, how many things they edit. It's important to pull the plug on them. Free the baby and the bathwater! Poets shouldn't take titles except ridiculous ones like the Shadow. And anyone can have that. When young poets complain they're not getting recognition I tell them they can be Shadow Poet Laureates too! What poets need is a democratic trades union and wages for good work. I won't be spending my time dogging Andrew Motion's footsteps. My little squib wasn't personal - it was about his work as Laureate.

JS: *May we hear it again, Shadow?*

SHADOW: If you insist.

Unjubilee Poem

Liquid sunshine gushing down
To dance and sparkle on the Crown.
I see the Laureate's work like this:
A long, thin streak of yellow piss.

Anti-Establishment Poet Is Difficult, Court Told

Totally thrilled by my appointment as Shadow Poet Laureate and the world-wide media reaction to same, I was disconcerted to be asked – before my costume was even delivered, to react to the passing of the Queen Mother. Not only was *Red Pepper* intrigued to catch my reaction – but the revolutionary *Evening Standard* wanted to reprint my reaction. (£1,000 plus VAT is my fee, *Evening Standard*).

When I was elected Poet Laureate, thirty years ago, I made two conditions for my acceptance:

1. I would appear at every Royal Wedding dressed in the costume of a Giant Banana.

2. I would be entitled to tap-dance on the coffin at every Royal Funeral.
I am still awaiting a reply. Meanwhile here is:

A Refusal to Write a Royal Elegy

When Kings and Queens decide to die
Up in a golden coach they fly
To Heaven to do Royal things
With the imperial King of Kings.

But write them elegies, you call?
They never touched my life at all.

A boy, I mourned when Roosevelt died.
For Gandhi and Martin Luther King, I cried,
Comedians died – I wept and shook
Milligan, Cooper, Morecambe, Moore and Cook.
    Weeping with grief to see them gone.
    Weeping with joy at how they shone.

    How can I write of royalty
Whose lives are meaningless to me?

Back to the Happidrome

Everybody's happy at the Happidrome
  — OLD RADIO CATCHPHRASE

But when we came round the corner out of
  Paris in the ice cream sunshine –
    There was Colombia in flames
      There was Palestine in flames
        There was Afghanistan in flames
in a backwash tidal monsoon of fire –

at what heat does the hair burn?
at what heat do newspapers burn?
at what heat does flesh burn?
at what heat do the eyeballs boil?
at what heat does the heart explode?
at what heat does the atmosphere burn?

at what heat do the people awake?

    The Army, the Navy and the Royal Marines!
With missiles and gunships and submarines!
    Lords and Commons, Presidents and Queens!

They all dance hand in hand
With the Arms Manufacturers of this land!

   All singing;
  Want to make a killing in the Congo?
    Pull my bongo!
  Want to make mass-murder in the Middle East?
    Call my beast!
Want to do some big-time fire and sword?
Pull the Armageddon Emergency Cord!
Tear the skin off the face of the human race –
    with British Aerospace
      it gives employment
    with British Aerospace
      you're laughing
    with British Aerospace!

No More War

As War eats more and more of its victims
Growing huge and strong on foreign flesh,
Quiet ladies and gentlemen in grey suits
Will ask you to learn the killing trade.

Maybe you've got no hope of work
And the Army sounds like a steady job
And you've seen Ross Kemp in *Ultimate Force*
Wasting the terrorists. Tell them: No.

As War multiplies and War and its children
Start to devour our own parents and children,
Your friendly postman will hand you an order
To leave your home and go learn to kill.

It's simpler to go when you're told to go.
Maybe you're worried what your family will say.
Maybe you're frightened by their prisons
Designed for crushing men and women. Tell them: No.

Prepare your defence. Explain to them peacefully
Why you refuse to kill or die for them.
Call your witnesses – Martin Luther King
Or Gandhi or Jesus or Buddha
Or your own loving heart.

Human Beings

(for the company of the truthful and beautiful Red Red Shoes
by Charles Way, staged by the Unicorn Theatre for Children)

look at your hands
your beautiful useful hands
you're not an ape
you're not a parrot
you're not a slow loris
or a smart missile
you're human

not british
not american
not israeli
not palestinian
you're human

not catholic
not protestant
not muslim
not hindu
you're human

we all start human
we end up human
human first
human last
we're human
or we're nothing

nothing but bombs
and poison gas
nothing but guns
and torturers
nothing but slaves
of Greed and War
if we're not human

look at your body
with its amazing systems
of nerve-wires and blood canals
think about your mind
which can think about itself
and the whole universe
look at your face

which can freeze into horror
  or melt into love
 look at all that life
  all that beauty
  you're human
they are human
 we are human
let's try to be human

  dance!

The Operation

hero executioners
forensic psychopaths
extreme venom
storm rockets
 they're all part of
The Operation

born-again dragons
Jurassic porridge
shock wheeltappers
scorpion singers
 all essential to
The Operation

and all you
grizzly crackers
colditz wannabes
boogie hungerbabes
and bungalow maniacs
 you're absolutely central to
The Operation

Roundabout

A war is born: neighbour kills neighbour,
They kill till they can kill no more.
A peace is signed, war goes into labour
And dies giving birth to another war.

Playground

dark brown eyes
scanning dusty tarmac
a boy on a swing

head down
mouth humming
a boy swinging intensely

before dusk he must go
to his grandmother's house
on the edge of the city

alone on a swing
thinking on a swing
a boy

his mother will stay home
she won't go to the shelter
people here are afraid of shelters
they remember last time

the chains of the swing
they clank they creak
the boy's head fills
with explosions

a boy on a swing

The Famous Battle

Dawn came creeping
On her soft grey paws

Dawn came creeping
On her soft grey paws

By the time the sun rose
She'd torn down the sky with her claws

SHADOW SPEECHES

The Shadow Poet Laureate moves in a mysterious way, something like a dark starfish. Occasionally it behoves him to speak rather than spout in public. Finding it hard to ad lib without swearing or soppiness, he writes down his prophetic if pathetic thoughts and reads them out. These are sometimes mistaken for poems and people even ask for copies. The rest of the pieces in this section were written for public performance.

All the Light There Is was commissioned as a New Year 2003 poem for the BBC World Service – the Shadow recorded it and the BBC broadcast it all over the planet.

When They Tell You to Go to War was spoken at a meeting about Vietnam and Iraq and also in Hyde Park at the historic rally of 15 February 2003. The Shadow was early on the bill and people had only been coming into the Park for an hour or so, but he was satisfied with an audience of around 250,000.

Work To Do was written on the brink of the 2003 invasion of Iraq and spoken in Grosvenor Square on my wife Celia's birthday. I'd been listening to a lot of speeches and some of them had seemed destructive to me. I wanted to speak up for the many pacifists in the anti-war movement.

All the Light There Is

We tossed a coin marked two thousand and three
Heads for Peace, Tails for War – which'll it be?

Came down Tails – and I heard a voice:
'Welcome to the Monster Zoo!
We're going to unlock all the cages
And save Democracy for you.

'And out will march monsters
whose work is war.
Their hearts are hot
as the planet's core.

'For power and money
they murder the poor,
then they rape each other
till war breeds war

'And the air cracks into shrapnel,
the oceans turn to lead
and the earth itself is burning
and all the light is dead.'

Yes the monsters are rattling their cages
their keepers are reaching for the keys
and some of us are cheering on the monsters,
and some of us are down on our knees

singing

    we love the light
all the light there is
  come and let's walk
into the light of peace

no more war   no more war

Yes – it was Heads for peace, and a newborn child
cuddled to its mother's breast.
Of all the visions I ever saw
this vision was the best.

  So a New Year's born –
  it gasps, it cries.
  Gather up the baby –
  gaze into its eyes

  Sing to the baby
  on the warm breast.
  Let the child drink peace,
  let the mother rest.

    singing

  we love the light
all the light there is
  love is the light
all the light there is
  peace is the light
all the light there is
  come and let's walk
into the light of peace

no more war   no more war

When They Tell You to Go to War

don't go
don't go to work
don't go to school
don't go to the movies
don't go to college
don't go to your regiment
don't go to your ship
don't go to your air base

go into the streets
take over the streets
and bring Britain to a full stop

when they tell you to go to war
don't go
don't go to war

Work to Do

I'm a pacifist.
If you're a pacifist too
You know that as soon as you say:
I'm a pacifist –
A Political Person smiles and says:
Of course I respect your position, but –

Well I say: I don't want your respect –
How about your help?
We've got work to do.
And the Political Person smiles and asks
The same stupid question time after time:
Wouldn't you have fought World War Two
To stop Hitler?
And I say: No – and here's the reason why.
Because I wouldn't have fought World War One –
So Hitler wouldn't have come to power.

Don't you understand
After all these centuries
That war gives birth to war
War gives birth to war?

That's how the murder plague grows
Unless we stop it.
Yes, we've got work to do.

Many of us feel weary.
We've been marching against the war
And talking against the war
And reading about the war
And watching the TV war
And we're tired of watching slaughter
And listening to the excuses for slaughter.

And in this time of grief
We often find ourselves on the brink of tears.
OK, let the tears flow.
Then wipe them away.
Have a party, get a good night's sleep –
And start again.
We've got work to do.

We put on the greatest demo
Ever seen in Britain.
We put on the greatest demo
Ever seen in wartime Britain.
That's a start.

But we've got to stop this war.
Stop the next war.
Stop all wars.

We find ourselves now
In the middle of World War Three –
The war which started
When nuclear bombs dropped
On Hiroshima and Nagasaki –
World War Three –
The war between the rich and the poor.
That's the task ahead of us –
To bring an end to World War Three.
To heal the wounds of the world.
To bring peace throughout the world.
We've got work to do.

We'll work with our French and German
and American and Russian and Chinese
and Pakistani and Cuban and South African
and Iraqi brothers and sisters.

We'll make the United Nations
A blessing on the world.
We'll teach our children and our grandchildren
That we have done enough killing,
That killing people is wrong.
With them, we'll examine pacifism
And ways of non-violent resistance
To cruel oppressors and benevolent oppressors.

We'll study and celebrate the lives
Of Gandhi and Martin Luther King
And their brave followers.
We'll set up Commissions of Truth and Reconciliation
All over the world – including Ireland.
We'll help to organise
The vast majority of the people of the planet
Who long for peace
And whose deepest wish
Is No More War.

And that's our work
No More War.

So, like my Jamaican comrade
Andrew Salkey used to say:
Brothers and sisters –
Keep on keeping on –
We've got work to do.

ENGLANDING

Englanding

We are the cold-eyed English
from the islands of the rain
and our cold eyes are not looking at you
so how can you say we are cold to you
when you are less than nothing at all to us
and we save the cold of our eyes
for the eyes of our cold families
on the islands of the rain

We are the cold-eyed English
and at six in the evening we raise our glasses
our glasses of luke-warm sherry
and we say cheers and here's to you
to the Manager of the Bank of Cold
and the Vicar of the Church of Cold
and the Teacher who teaches our children Cold
at the School of Coldness, which gets results
and which we can just afford
thanks to grandma's shares
in the Iceberg which sank the Titanic.

Fun in World War Two

Get your mack out
Call Uncle Jack out
To enjoy the black-out

We'll go to Piccadilly Circus
And feel up the workers
Maybe one of them will jerk us

Banned for Six Months

My Jaguar is mine and I am hers.
She's my Madonna. Say a prayer –
Orphans, widows, widowers.

I touch a switch. My wild witch purrs:
'I'll take you anyshiningwhere.'
My Jaguar is mine and I am hers.

Give her the gun and Wiltshire blurs.
Two cyclists. Wham! A hedgehog. Squash! A hare –
Orphans, widows, widowers.

Why don't they vivisect child-murderers?
Pass me the in-car vodka. Yeah.
My Jaguar is mine and I am hers.

We're off beyond speedometers
Into a ghostly fog. Who's there?
Orphans, widows, widowers.

The Court. Their family – the whimperers.
My firm fixes a driver. I don't care –
My Jaguar is mine and I am hers,
Orphans, widows, widowers.

In a Brown Paper Bag

in a brown paper bag
is a crown of gold
in the crown of gold
is a loaf of bread
in the loaf of bread
is a loaded pistol

take out the gold crown
put it on your head
order your brother
to give you the bread
it's fifty-fifty
he'll shoot you instead

To Somebody Considering Suicide

      up to you
we'd sooner you didn't
but it's up to you

      your mind
    your body
      your life
    your heart
they're all yours
and it's up to you

if you throw them all away
we'll be sorry and sad
and we'll wave goodbye
and now and then cry
but we won't throw our own lives away
we'll stick around down here
and whenever we can
we'll have a good time

      if you've got the guts
there are hundreds of other moves
you could make or try to make
instead of that one move
      you can't take back

imagine other choices
imagine those changes of
      places
      people
      jobs
missions or visions
all those other paths

but if every path leads you
   to the same brick wall
      it's up to you
      bang your head
      on the wall
   till you're dead
      or stop
take a good look at the wall

what's stuck on it?
a stupid poster advertising dread?
          tear it off
          underneath
may be graffiti by Bessie Smith
may be a phoenix by Turner

          and maybe
fingerholds and toeholds
     between the bricks
     so haul yourself up
     and climb that wall
          climb up and over
          that fucking wall

          but it's
     up to you
if you can't make it
          sorry
very sorry but we won't
carry your bones around with us
          everywhere
we've got dances to try
and other chips to fry
          before we lie
          down and let
             the wall
             fall on us

          meanwhile
whatever you choose to do
     up to you,
          love,
     up to you.

for mental patients

pull yourself together
that's what they always say
pull yourself together
throw your cares away
pull yourself together
but if they knew my heart
and how it kicks inside me
they'd say
pull yourself apart

all together now

Doctor Rat Explains

we place each subject
in a complicated maze
with high walls and bright-flickering lights

to those who work well –
pressing down the correct levers –
we give rewards

to those who prove useless –
recalcitrant, scratching themselves in corners –
we allot punishments

the rewards
are the gourmet delights of Wealth

the punishments
are the electric aches and pains of Poverty

this experiment proves
that the meaning of Money can be taught
to the majority of human beings

ARTEFACTIONS

Misery Me!

(This is a song from my stage version of *The Lion, The Witch and The Wardrobe*.
It is sung by Lucy, a young evacuee who has been sent with her brothers and sisters
to the country during the bombing of London in World War Two. There she has
discovered a wardrobe through which she can reach the magical land of Narnia.
But nobody believes her. All she can do is sing her heart out to the audience.)

When Alice came home from Wonderland
Did her family laugh and jeer?
When Crusoe sailed back from his island
Did they say: You imagined it dear?
When Dorothy flew in her ruby slippers
From the Emerald City of Oz
Did her Auntie Em say it was all a dream?
I bet they all did, because –

    Father's in the Royal Navy
    Somewhere out at sea
    I'm dreaming of submarines –
        Misery me!
    Mother would come down from London
    But she isn't free
    I'm dreaming of falling bombs –
        Misery me!

We're here in the heart of the country
And we dive in the pond by the mill
And we fish for trout in the river
And we slide down the side
Of a bumpy old hill
And I should be as happy as Larry
Playing Cowboys and Indians all day
But everyone believes I'm a liar
So I wish I could grow some wings
And fly far away

    Father's in the Royal Navy
    Somewhere out at sea
    I'm dreaming of Narnia –
        Misery me!

Mother would come down from London
But she isn't free
I'm dreaming of Narnia –
　　　　Misery me!

What Poetry Says

(a free translation from Remco Campert)

Poetry says: Yes, I'm alive.
Poetry says: No., I'm not alone.

Poetry is the day after tomorrow
Dreaming of Wednesday week
In a far country, with you, aged 89 and a half.

Poetry breathes in and out,
It puts the beat in my feet,
It makes them hesitate and hover
Over the earth which longs for them to dance on it.

Voltaire got smallpox, but he cured himself
By swigging 200 pints of lemonade
Etcetera. That's poetry, man.

And look at the ocean, look at the surf.
It breaks on the rocks.
It breaks and breaks but – it's never broken.
Up it jumps again – that's poetry

Every word that anyone writes
Is an attack on old age.
You want a safe bet?
Put your money on death.

And what is death? Only the hush in the hallway
After the last words have been spoken.

Death, death, death –
It's an emotion.
It moves.

Blake on His Childhood Visions

The first time I saw God
Was when I was four years old.
He put his head in the window
And set me a-screaming.

When I was about eight
I was walking on Peckham Rye
When I looked up into a tree
And it was full of angels –
Their bright wings
Bespangling every bough like stars.
I ran home to tell my parents.
Mother had to stop my father beating me for lying.

Everyone has the gift of seeing visions, yes.
But they lose it, because they don't work at it.

King Lear's Fool Waves Goodbye

here I go
holding on to sanity
in one hand
like a bottle of green and stagnant
mineral water

here I go
holding on to nonsense
in the other hand
like a mobile phone
made of marzipan

I take a swig of pond:
Hello, I'm on the surface
of some sort of planet
or peanut

holding on
brothers and sisters
holding on

A Sense of Complicity: *Advertising Supplement*

William Sieghart likes poetry. He sponsors poetry competitions which help some poets, even if many of us don't much like poetry beauty contests.

But the day after May Day this year, William sent me 'a rare poetry commission opportunity. A leading advertising agency would like to use poetry in a forthcoming advertising campaign for one of its clients. As a result, I am helping them commission poems from poets.' Each poet will be paid £200. Up to £3,000 will be paid to authors of the 24 poems used in TV and radio adverts.

What sort of poems? Well, the adverts are aimed at the 45-60 age group. 'They are adverts, so although very different from normal commercial break fodder the poetry needs to be relatively upbeat, conversational, witty and thought-provoking. The main criterion is that the poems should give a sense of complicity and should make the listener feel understood.' And so on.

Why does this matter a damn? Because poetry is one of the few places in our civilisation where you can expect to be told the truth. And advertising is (very well paid) prostitution. So I wrote to William:

Advertising Will Eat the World

art is the desperate search
for truth and beauty
a matter of life and death

advertising is the cynical hunt
for maximum profit
a matter of lies for money

poetry makes love with the language
advertising rapes the language

music dances with children and gives them wings
advertising steals from children and artlsts
art is the opposite of advertising

poetry just ran to me
she is weeping on my shoulder
It hurts her to be in the same poem as advertising
'Get rid of them,' she whispers to me,
'Send those fucking advertisers away.'

yours sincerely,
Adrian Mitchell, Shadow Poet Laureate

PS: I hope no poets collaborate with your mistaken scheme.

NOTE: I also enclosed the following two advertising poems, but William never replied to me, so I published the lot in *Red Pepper*. William still doesn't write.

Rest in Peace, Andy Warhol. Enjoy.

Elvis and Jackie Onassis
Marilyn and Mao-tse Tung –
They all looked alike to you

You sucked out their veins
Now all that remains
Is a series of lifeless adverts for you

Shallow as a shiny puddle
You were proud of your shallowness.

You started as an advertising man.
You ended as an advertising man.
And you sold your product – Selfishness.

Relax, Andy, you weren't the first.
And you certainly weren't the worst.
Necrophilia got much sillier –
Step forward Damien Hirst.

Pioneers, O Pioneers!

Guns before Butter!
Strength through joy!
    Knock-out slogans.

SS lightning bolts!
Swastika armbands!
    Stunning logos.

Hitler and Goebbels!
    Brilliant admen.

The Café Kafka

A curving corridor
of vanilla pillars
and pistachio plasterwork.
It's an edible café,
the Café Kafka.

Lampglobes bulge
and overflow
with splashing light.
Even the draughts which flow
along the diamond-patterned floor
are warm in the Café Kafka.

Outside the Café Kafka
the third snow of winter
is slinking through Helsinki
and my charcoal fedora sits proudly
on the black marble table-top.

Only six hours ago,
when I met her
in her magical studio,
her first words were:
'What a beautiful hat!'
Who said that about my hat?
The mother of the Moomins,
Tove Jansson.

AUTOMAGIC

Memoirs

let ghosts imagine
   being alive
I well remember
   being dead

Her Life
(another for my mother)

She didn't know the value of money –
it filtered in her purse and flooded out.

She didn't know the value of the body –
something she shrugged about.

She didn't know the value of the love
which she transmitted ceaselessly.

She tried to hoist the wounded world on her frail shoulders –
It seemed a possibility.

Disguise

Every morning after I shampoo my fur
I climb into my humanskin costume and
Put on my human mask and human clothes.

Then I go out into the human city
And catch a human bus to work.

As I sit at my computer
Summoning up images of the financial world
None of my colleagues knows
That inside my human hand gloves
Are the brown and burly
Sharp and curly
Paws of a grizzly bear.

Yes, I am a bear in a cunning disguise,
Only passing as human
Trying not to yield to temptation
As I lumber past
The sticky buns in the baker's shop
The honeycombs in the health shop

I am married to a human woman who knows my secret
We have a human daughter
Who is rather furry and has deep golden eyes
And gentle paws
We call her Bruinhilda

I took Bruinhilda to a circus once
But there was a performing bear
Riding a unicycle, juggling with flames
Dancing to an accordion

I sat tight
Though she might have been my mother
I sat tight
While the inside of my human mask
Filled up with the tears of a bear

Sorry

Sure, I worked as a slave to Time
And knew his bullwhip's vicious touch
But didn't know who punished me
Or why my shoulders hurt so much

He rode me like a motorbike
On some mad ride through towns in flames.
My mind and body tensed with overwork
Till I could hardly say my children's names

And, maddened by his rhythmic lash,
Sometimes struck out at those I met
And hurt the innocent and weak –
I am still scarred by that regret.

Thanks to My Dog in an Hour of Pain

weariness
blankness in my bones
tears like molten lead shoulders down my throat
a dead white pebble
in the left side of my chest an empty fur glove where my heart
should be sitting
the clock strikes and won't stop striking
striking the time of grief
weariness
blankness in the bone

don't tell me I'm wrong I know I'm wrong
My Adam's apple like a knotted up wrongness
I should be dancing in muddy boots
but I find myself addressing this Deathbed Congress

and I say:
melodies carved down to the bone
fears like a stock exchange movie in a foreign language
I power-steer my pony down the off-side of a canyon
me and my dog have come to clean up this anguish

oh the dust bites and keeps on biting won't stop biting

                    but
        sweet dog in the moon
        sweet dog in the snow
        sweet dog in the wheat
        sweet dog in my sweat
        in my mind in my heart
        and in my arms
        sweet dog how you save my life

for you see how bleak I am
        how blank I am
you view my collapse with love and no surprise
dear goldenface and deep down toffee eyes

Pour Soul

My body was a pleasant house
bit of a responsibility
what with a leaky roof frozen pipes
that burglary a touch of dry rot
and the legendary subsidence
but it mildly pleased me
as I strolled from room to room
or curled up on the window-seat
to watch the ebb and flow of the street

But one night I dreamed the dream of death
and woke up in the ashes of my house
a homeless soul
two dark eyes
a towelling dressing gown
and two blue feet
that's what I felt like
a soul without a home

The cold street wind ruffled my mind
and loneliness ran through my veins
I floated to my wife's house and rang the doorbell
but my fingers were made of mist

and the button wouldn't press
when I knocked the door with all my might
my knuckles produced only a flimsy hiss
and when I breathed on the window
the glass did not even reflect my face

Of course I tried other houses –
my children, my best friends –
houses bursting with voices
and lights and lives and music
and food and animals –
but I couldn't make myself heard
poor soul
couldn't make myself heard

Finally, my spirit exhausted,
I lay down on the air
and let myself lie loose
and nothing happened for quite a time
quite a long white time full of nothing until
I felt myself drifting down the street
and out of the town past the farthest houses
into a dimmish countryside
and swerving round the side of a bare hill
and into a deep forest

As I floated among the trees
I began to sing the song of a poor soul
and I could see that song fluttering in front of me
like a vermilion humming bird
and so I followed my songbird through the woods

I was surrounded by green
by a thousand shades of green
and gradually I found my song was joined
by other voices
so I smiled and looked up
and in the branches I saw perching
so many singing souls

And as I travelled from tree to tree
visiting the singing souls I found
that many of them were old friends of mine
and sometimes stayed holding each other's hands
to sing our hearts out for a time

And yet I always travelled on
and finally, in a grove of silver birches,
found my lost daughter
and my mother and my father

So here I perch
happily in the silver birches
singing with those I love our songs of love

Take your time, but when you're ready
come and join me in the silver birches.

Not Fleeing But Flying

I don't run away
But turn and stare
Into death's empty
Headlight glare

A take-off run
My wings unfold
Heartbeat wingbeat soaring
Up into the gold

Now if they ask you
Was I fleeing?
If they ask you
Was I crying?
If they ask you
Was I falling?
Tell em I was laughing
Tell em I was flying
Tell em I was sailing
Tell em I'm gone

IN THE OUTLANDS

The Ballad of the Familiar Stranger

Well the sun was whiskey-yeller
And the tumbleweed was still
And the stubble sprouted blue upon his jaw
As the charismatic gringo
Fixed me with his eyes and said:
I ain't never going to Dogwood any more

I was ten days out of Pecos
When my Chevvy hit a bull
Bust a windscreen lost a hubcap bent a door
What a man receives a man retrieves
So I pushed it back to town
But I'm never going to Dogwood any more

Well she stood thar like a cactus
And I trembled like a clown
While a steel guitar played *Speed Me to the Shore*
When you've found a hat that fits you
Then you might as well go home
But I'm never going to Dogwood any more

Now when I smell buckwheat pancakes
Or I hear some fancy dude
Imitating Donald Duck my heart feels sore
For the something in between us
Was too big for both of them
And I'm never going to Dogwood any more.

So pass the Chivas Regal
And the Penthouse for July
If I slide right down this wall I'll find the floor
I got teardrops on my moustache
Armadillos in my jeans
And I'm never going to Dogwood any more

There's a kid in Sacramento
With a phone book on his head
There's a vulture with a big toe in its claw
There's a story-telling stranger
In the alcoholics ward

And he's never going to Dogwood
No he's never going to Dogwood
They won't let him into Dogwood any more

(This song should be punctuated by the whistle of a lonesome train in the distance.
Should an encore be called for, the audience deserve the following)

There's a Mayor in Zalamea
There's a Mill upon the Floss
There is punishment and crime and peace and war
Well they say that Michael Jackson
Is the Shadow Peter Pan
And I'm never going to Dogwood any more

Every Day Is Mothering Sunday to Me

The sea is mother to the shore
The scalp is mother to the hair
The bread is mother to the butter
The table is mother to the chair
The town is mother to the country
The zoo is mother to the bear

Come down to the Mother Market
Millions of Mothers are on view
Their smiles shine down the mile-long aisles
And there on a shelf is the perfect Mother for you

Oh seek her and take her by her motherly hand
She steps into your silvery shopping cart
Pay at the till the amount on her label
And wheel her out of the Mother Mart

But should you be still dissatisfied
Fill in our Mother-Cover-Guarantee
And you'll be shipped another Mother
From the Mother Factory.

Rosaura's Song

Dreamed I was the lover
Of a beautiful thief
But when I woke up
I was a shipwreck on a reef.
Dreamed that I was happy
Or so it seemed to seem.
My lover smiled
Like a clown in a dream.

A clown in a dream
A clown in a dream
I had a dream
We were clowns in a dream.

Dreamed I was a husband
Dreamed I was a wife
But when I woke up
I wanted vengeance with a knife.
Dreamed I was the knife
And blood began to stream
But when I woke up
I was a clown in a dream.

A clown in a dream
Failing upside down
And when I woke up
I was a dream in a clown.

(from Calderon's *Life's a Dream*)

The Knife-thrower's Slender Daughter

The Knife-thrower's slender daughter
Sent me a letter one day
Meet me just above the forest
Daddy's going to be away
All day
Daddy's going to be away

I climbed up the path to the forest
And – sitting astride a log –
I saw the Knife-thrower feeding
Egg and bacon to his one-eyed dog
I did
Egg and bacon to his one-eyed dog

The first three knives he threw at me
I dodged his every shot
Then his one-eyed dog ran past me
And retrieved the bloody lot
He did
Retrieved the bloody lot

Well I started throwing bits of brick and stone
Cos the blades fell around me like rain
But they bounced off the Knife-thrower's helmet
And he started in to throw again
Damn him
And the dog retrieved the knives again

I seemed to see him in close-up
Intense and stony-eyed
And the rocks I chucked didn't reach him
He was further up the mountainside
With the dog
Further up the mountain side

Well the Knife-thrower's slender daughter
Looked down to the valley road
And she saw a blue and white cop car
Sitting there like a toad
So she took a little hatchet from her hip
She gave it a swing
And she gave it a flip
And the hatchet flew like a meteorite
And smashed into the cop car's revolving light

The cops switched on their siren
And I heard their engine roar
And zooming up from the valley
Came the forces of the Law
With pistols
Came the forces of the Law

They locked up the Knife-thrower
For six months and a day
With his daughter and his one-eyed dog
I made my getaway
You know
And here's all I want to say

Now I don't blame the Knife-thrower or his dog
For protecting his daughter from me
And if you saw Knife-thrower's slender daughter
You sureashell wouldn't blame me
Oh no
You sureashell wouldn't blame me.

Philosophical Agriculture

The Cow of Friedrich Nietzsche
was a recalcitrant creature
who kicked Rainer Maria Rilke
whenever he tried to milk her

ON BOARD THE FRIENDSHIP

For Dick and Dixie Peaslee

my friends and I
are trees in a wood
we glory in autumn's
goldenhood

on our branches sing
the owl and the lark
and the small deer trot
through the mist for our bark

and the river below
runs silvery-grey
with barges to carry
the timber away

and that voyage to the ocean
seems happy and good
to me and my friends
as we dance in our wood

How William Blake Dies a Good Death

(for John McGrath)

It was a summer evening.
The window was wide open.
I was sixty-nine
And I'd been ill for months.
I was sitting propped up in our bed and drawing.

I said: Stay Kate, keep just as you are,
I will draw you
For you have ever been an angel to me.
I drew her lovely face.

Then I put down my pencil and said:
Kate, I am a changing man.
At night I often rose and wrote down my thoughts,
Whether it rained or snowed or shone,
And you arose and sat beside me
And held my left hand as I wrote my poems.
This can be no longer.

And then I made up a song
And sang it, quietly, into Kate's ear.
And then another song
And then another.

And Kate said: I like your songs.
So I said: They are not mine,
My beloved, they are not mine.

I took one last breath of the summer air
And let it go
And my life flew out of the window
And upwards, singing joyfully.

For Miranda and Tom

(two babies who did not live long)

a handful of days
a handful of daisies
floating down a piano-playing river

o life is so little
far too little
but love flies on for ever

A Song for Maeve

I love to watch rivers
and the way they go
young rivers tumble
old rivers flow

I love to watch friends
when they're letting go –
the tumbling laughter
and the story flow

and the words sweet Maeve uses
with such gaiety
go tumbling and flowing
to join the great sea

Seventy More Years

(for Gordon Snell on his birthday)

I was fifteen, and shaking.
I'd been asked to write the House Play
And I'd said yes and now I was terrified.
I couldn't do it alone, so I sought you out
Because I'd heard you'd written a dozen plays
For your own puppet theatre.

You were fifteen too.
As I spoke to you for the first time
You looked at me as if I were
An intriguing painting, by Breughel maybe,
Listened to my invitation
And smiled Yes.
What had I taken on?
In the gym and at rugby you were agile as an ape,
But I could tolerate some sportiness.
The prefects had you down as Trouble,
With a deadly line in Dumb Insolence
And a reputation as the eloquent School Atheist.
Well, that was fine with me,
Speaking as a close friend of the School Communist
And a loose troupe of jazz fanatics.

We walked and talked and sat down and laughed
As we plotted our blockbuster for the Drama Competition.
Half an hour long said the rules, and we knew that
To impress our toffee-tough audience of teenage boys
The play better have a lot about Death.

And so we wrote *A Friend of Ours* –
In which Death himself, an old man in a wheelchair
Wearing Matron's black and scarlet cloak,
Invites a job-lot of odd guests to his country house.
A Sailor, a Scientist, a Poet (me) and –
You as Miss Marguerite Hyde – described as a Traveller.
Death accuses Miss Hyde of nameless crimes
And she replies with this interior monologue:
'I've met the danger of death before,
But it's always been a danger I could fight –
In the East one can fight the terrors of the jungle but this...
I never reckoned with having to fight Death 'in person'.

To think that old man has the power to end anyone's life,
Anyone's at all – to end mine.
To think HE is Death – It almost seems absurd –
But it's not funny.
How can I fight Death?...

Did we win the play competitions
By ten lengths and a carrot!
We always won.
You and I took turns to win the Poetry Competition
And the best parts in the School Shakespeare production.
When I played justice Shallow, you were Doll Tearsheet.
When you played a dazzling Hamlet,
I was your grumpy Uncle Claudius.

Only once failure seemed to loom. Instead of a tragedy
We entered a farce for the Play Competition –
The Third Ham – a parody of the Harry Lime movie
With my Trevor Howard, your Orson Welles.
But the censorship committee banned our entry
For blasphemy and obscenity.
We glared at them and exited,
Sat down and wrote another tragedy – *Dead End*.

Its first stage direction reads:
'David Hayes is seated, alone and rather dishevelled.'
(No wonder, he has been shot at by the police
And is dying of his wounds in a warehouse).
His opening blank verse monologue was spoken by me,
But written, I would claim, mainly by Gordon.

'Cobwebs cast stealthy shadows in the soft dust
The weary bales loom dark against the warehouse wall
The black rain caresses the blank indifferent bricks...
I cannot see the steps that led to this dead end
I do not understand.
Bewildered, bewildered, there are mists about my eyes,
And I am dying without knowing the reason.
This bullet in my stomach is my life's result,
The culmination of the sequence of my acts,
A sequence I must try to follow...
How did it all begin?...
How did it all begin?...'

Did we win the Competition?
Does the Pope shit in the woods?

383

Pausing only to re-cycle *The Third Ham*
As a cowboy epic called *Cow-Cow Bogey*
In which we played the Front and Back halves
Of the mooing, Charleston–dancing heroine,
We founded the Symbolic Society
Which improvised weird and subversive plays
On the verandah of the cricket pavilion
To an audience of moonlit grass.

And together we sat in the great secret attic
Up above the Farmer Hall,
Discussing Love and War and Thurber and Duke Ellington
Seated in enormous wooden Shakespeare thrones
Puffing at our Park Drives
And laughing ourselves into a kind of
Heaven of understanding.

Together we cycled across Wiltshire
To a weekend school on the poetry of John Donne
Whom we'd never heard of
Then J.B. Leishmann burst into the lecture room
With a bicycle and Mickey Mouse hair
And began to read aloud to us
But after two lines threw down the book
And carried on by heart:

'Go and catch a falling star,
Get with child a mandrake root,
Tell me where all past years are
Or who cleft the devil's foot.

Teach me to hear mermaids singing,
Or to keep off envy's stinging,
And find
What wind
Serves to advance an honest mind.'

And we glanced at each other,
Realising that Donne was of our gang,
And, cycling back to school,
Chanted the words of Donne,
Laughing with love
For his daft and dangerous language.

Called up to do National Stupidity in the RAF
We squarebashed side by side
Trying to keep each other sane
In that insane little world of blanco, bootpolish
And being broke and bullied –
Always you were my ideal friend.

When you were promoted to be an Acting Corporal –
It seemed, at first, a betrayal –
Had Snell joined the Establishment?
But no, within weeks you had been shorn of your chevrons,
Demoted back to my humble level
For bureaucratic sabotage.

On leave, tramping over Lakeland
We rewrote its literary history
In a musical movie called *The Road to Keswick*
Starring Bing Crosby as Wordsworth,
Bob Hope as Coleridge,
Dorothy Lamour as Dorothy Wordsworth
And Louis Armstrong as the Leech Gatherer
And endless fantasy melodramas
Most of them building to a Rabelaisian climax
Involving all the Windsor-Mountbattens.

You went to Balliol, I went to Christ Church.
At Oxford, our adventure playground.
Every night we were walking on the rooftops
Or using your room as a basketball court
For a balloon version of the game
Played with a beer in one hand.
We acted, we wrote poems and stories,
We founded the Universal Monster Club
Which turned up at movies like
The Creature from the Black Lagoon
To cheer the monster and hiss the awful actors...
We have heard the chimes at midnight, Master Gordon...
But you actually worked and won a good degree
And landed up in the BBC
And there were Bush House sessions
And Twite and Dromgoole
And Moira and Annie
And Bruce and O'Toole
And high above the streets of Earls Court
The laughter circus of your flat in Hogarth Road.

We found ourselves the only inhabitants
Of a caravan site on the Gower Peninsula
In the depths of a Bible-black winter
Trying to write a sitcom about
A troupe of nutty actors in a theatre on a pier
But continually breaking away from work
For trips to the cliffside pub
Or our own madly competitive
Two–man Olympic Games
With events like Sand Dune Jumping Downwards,
Tossing the Boulder and
The Walking Backwards Into the Sea Race.
After each event we stood on the caravan steps,
The loser on the lower step,
For the presentation of gold and silver medals
Fashioned from Barley Wine bottle top wrappers,
To sing the winner's National Anthem...

And it was all very wild and wonderful
But there was something the matter with the weather
Something the matter with the light –
The work was fine
And the fun and the friendship were fine
But love arrived and threw her arms around you sometimes,
Stayed awhile,
Then, painfully, left.

That's not enough love for a man
When the greatest among his many talents
Is a huge gift for loving others.
Love is tough stuff, and it was tough of love to be so mean
To the most generous man in the world.

But the world turned
And the weather changed to summertime
And the monochrome streets
Were suddenly bright
With all the colours sunshine paints on London,
With all the music sunshine plays on Dublin.
And you sailed away, for a year and a day,
In a beautiful pea-green sieve
And magic-carpeted round the globe –
What a runcible way to live!
And you sat in a tree-top side by side
By the light of the Chablis sun,
Writing green and blossoming poems
And stories for everyone.

Maeve and Gordon,
Gordon and Maeve,
Two names which sit together
Like two loving cats in an armchair.
Beauty meeting beauty,
It was so clear, so happy,
So unconditionally
For ever.

Maeve and Gordon
Gordon and Maeve,
Your deep joy shines
All around you
Warming the hearts
Of your numberless friends,
Warming us all
With your deep joy.

For ever
For ever
Flowing like a river –
Your love and your deep joy.

SEVENTY MORE YEARS!

to all our friends

August
blue seas for ever
a spicy breeze
bears us towards an ancient island

the harbour opens its arms to us
in an embrace
of boats with clinking masts
brown children leaping over ropes
donkeys fishermen dogs
women with baby bundles
shadow cats
and the sun
shining down upon a maze
of whitewashed alleys
leading up towards
bright domes and shining towers
and beyond all these
the dark hills of enchantment

we have come home
to the island which we've been creating
for so many years
with our buckets and spades

and here we all stand
with salt spray in our eyes
makers of dreamcakes and mudpies

from

TELL ME LIES

POEMS 2005-2008

RIVERS RUN THROUGH IT
or *Waterworking*

West End Blues
(a river trip)

West End Blues was recorded by Louis Armstrong and his Hot Five
in 1928. Louis played cornet, Fred Robinson was on trombone,
Johnny Dodds played clarinet and Earl Hines was the pianist.
These verses follow, more or less, their improvisations that day.
But their subject is not the responsibility of Louis and the Hot Five.
It was inspired by a holiday at Tom and Sally Vernon's house in the
Cévennes in 2007, when my wife Celia and I spent several happy weeks
in the river Hérault at the bottom of their garden with our Golden
Retriever, Daisy the Dog of Peace.

CORNET

Louis Armstrong
picked up the sun
and blew it
with all of the gold
in his wonderful thunderful heart

then he blew a little tighter
till the sun was double brighter
playing a song together
said we belong together
      shine
saying that soon you'll be mine

Come along
come along to the river
let's go on down
The rivers a real wonderway
birds and fishes
let's go on down
and sit together there
on the sweet riverbed
let's go on down
to that sweet riverbed
we'll lie till dawn
in the cool clear water
and name all the stars in the sky

TROMBONE

Long way
to walk
I'm tired
maybe I won't find my way to
that old river
But I want to go down
Yes I want to go meet you
I'll be coming
someday I'll join you
at the water way down there

CLARINET

waterbird
swooping low
dragonflies
all aglow

butterflies
    fluttering
little fish
    flickering

river's my home
river's my home
        yes
river's my home

SCAT SINGING BY SATCHMO

sunny skies
breezy and blue
and April air
for me an' you

the tall trees are swaying
they dance with the stream
        little clouds drifting
            free as a dream

    river's my home
    river's my home
            yes
    river's my home

PIANO

pebbles rolling underneath our toes
eddies running round in spirals
down where the boulders form a dam

come and take my hand
come and walk along the dam
and we'll dive
in the swimming hole
while all the dogs stand staring
at you and me
down on the riverbank
they wag their tails at us
laughing in the swimming hole

CORNET

Here we are...

now we're river walking
down the river
river walking
through the country
splashing down the river
to a little boat
a small green boat

Let's climb aboard
and sail away
right out to sea

PIANO

on board
set sail
and out
to sea
yes

CORNET

Now we'll have our dinner
and then go to bed.

Five Walks

I was asked to write a poem to the beautiful music of Chet Baker's
Sad Walk by the magazine *Sirena*. First I wrote a poem called *Sad Walk*,
about a morning when I walked my dog a few hours after hearing the news
of the death of my adopted daughter and the world seemed cold and grey.

I wrote it so that the words fit some of Chet Baker's solos, but not
exactly. But then I thought that the music of *Sad Walk* isn't simply sad.
It has a beauty to fit any mood. So I wrote a cheerful poem on a similar
pattern and called it *Glad Walk*. Then a child's bad dream poem called
Bad Walk. Then, remembering my father at the seaside – *Dad Walk*.
And finally, since nonsense makes sense to me, *Mad Walk*.

Sad Walk

down a dark purple
    tarmac path
        under a sky
full of ashes and smoke

    broken-down trees
        pale yellow moon
near the edge of the world
        on the edge

now the heart is grey
    even grass is grey
and the city traffic
keeps screaming and screaming
    where have you gone?

    down a dark purple
        tarmac path...

Glad Walk

walk up the silver
   tower stairs
   into a sky
of a zillion stars

zebras may graze
   friendly giraffes
take their ease in the light
   of the moon

as my eyes delight
   in the singing grass
and the flying foxes
   are diving and soaring
I take your hand

walk up the silver
   tower stairs...

Bad Walk

over the high wall's
   razor wire
plunge to a moat
   where the crocodiles lurk

stumble through thorns
   into the swamp
till you feel yourself sink
    into dark

    as you gasp your last
  you are grasped and raised
    back into the air by
  the hand of an ogre
who laughs and throws you

    over the high wall's
     razor wire...

Dad Walk

lie by a rockpool
watch the green
    hair of seaweed
and the flickering fish

    climb up a rock
        big as a house
you can almost see France
        from the top

    we will dam the stream
    running down the beach
    till we've formed a salt lake
    so deep we'll swim and then
        flood mum's deckchair

        lie by a rockpool
    watch the green...

Mad Walk

roundabout backwards
    songs of cheese
        chanted through teeth
of potatohead spooks

    accelerate
    past logic bog
pay the beggars of time
    with an owl

    safari me out
for the glue's in flower
and the nightmare police
are all kens and barbies
    marching in flames

roundabout backwards
    songs of cheese...

CITY SONGS
or *Don't Mutter in the Gutter*

The Baby on the Pavement

People keep telling me about Human Nature
and how vile it is.
I have made up this story for them:

There is a naked baby
lying on the pavement.

No, the naked baby
is lying on a blanket
on the pavement.
(I find I can't leave it there
without a blanket,
even in a story.)

Watch the first human being
who comes walking down the pavement.

Does he step over the baby and walk on?
Does he kick the baby and walk on?

He picks up the baby,
wraps it in the blanket
and tries to find somebody
to help him look after the baby.

Isn't that your Human Nature?

More Friends of Mine

One friend refused a title
One took a bad black pill
One friend wept her heart out
Another one forged his will

I send my wildest wishes
To each and every friend
I'll keep washing up the dishes
As my train rolls round the bend

I could have been with you much more
But work stole all my time
And I hurt many I am sure
By neglect, that shoddy crime.

I drank a bottle of Dylan
A powerful Celtic blend
It brought out my hero and villain
And it rolled me round the bend

Some friends they say *Take Care* to me
I answer *Take a Chance*
They say *Revolutions always fail*
I ask *What happened to France?*

Buy yourself a seat in the House of Pretence
Find the number in the Yellow Pages
Rent Arthur's Round Table for your Conference
Welcome to the Middle Ages

We're going to have another Old Etonian
As her majesty's PM
While New Labour melts into a pool
Of ineffectual intellectual phlegm

The Dirty Smokers

Beyond the golden portals of the Otis lifts
Beyond the atrium's marbleised floors
Beyond stolid Security
Beyond languid Reception
You stand in huddles, out of doors

You are the Dirty Smokers, free again,
The designated smoke-break has begun.
You guard your cigarettes against the rain
And puff blue clouds that half-obscure the sun.

You must stand fifteen feet away
From your home base's portico,
Your fingers blue, your faces grey,
You concentrate on that tip's cheery glow.

Oh silent outlaws from high offices
Filled with a plastic disinfectant smell
I tell you, once upon a tumour
I struggled up and out of Dirty Smoker Hell.

So here I stand, the re-born, pristine one
Who misses all the Dirty Smoker fun.

Live It Like Your Last Day

Dig what can be dug

In the tunnel from Kennedy
the ceiling of metal or plastic
or plasticised metal or metalled plastic
reflects the red tail lights
of a hundred moving automobiles

like a river of red light
I told my Albanian cabdriver
who never noticed it before

I said that's my job
noticing stuff like that –
I'm a poet

An upside down
river of red light,
he said laughing.

Now you're doing it,
I said.

THE REALLY GOOD OLD DAYS
or *The Underbelly of History*

About the Child Murderer Marie Farrar
by BERTOLT BRECHT

1

Marie Farrar, aged sixteen, born in April.
No birthmarks, bent by rickets, orphaned.
Apparently of good behaviour till
She killed a baby – this is how it happened.
She claims that, in the second month of pregnancy,
She went to a woman in a basement room
Who gave her two injections to abort it.
Which, she says, hurt – but the child stayed in the womb.
    But you, please don't be angry or upset.
    We all need all the help that we can get.

2

Well, anyway, she says, she paid.
She laced her corset very tight,
Drank schnapps with pepper, but that only made
Her vomit half the night.
Her belly was now visibly swollen.
When she washed up, she was in agony.
She was, she says, a young girl and still growing.
She prayed to Mary, very hopefully.
    And you, please don't be angry or upset.
    We all need all the help that we can get.

3

Her prayers turned out to be, it seems, useless.
It was a lot to ask. She put on weight.
At early mass her head was full of dizziness.
She knelt at the altar covered in cold sweat.
But still she kept her condition secret
Till, later on, birth took her by surprise.
She was so unattractive that
Nobody thought temptation could arise.
    And you, please don't be angry or upset.
    We all need all the help that we can get.

4

On the day itself, she says, just about dawn
She was scrubbing the stairs, when suddenly
Great nails clawed at her guts. She is torn.
But still, she keeps the secret of her pregnancy.
All day long, as she's hanging out the washing,
She thinks and thinks – then all at once she knows
She should be delivered. Her heart is heavy.
She finishes work late. Then up the stairs she goes.
    But you, please don't be angry or upset.
    We all need all the help that we can get.

5

As she lay down, they called her downstairs. Right away.
She must sweep up the newly-fallen snow.
That took until eleven. It was a long day.
She had no time to give birth till night. And so
She brought forth, so she says, a son.
This son was like all others that are born.
But she was not like other mothers – though
I find that I can't think of her with scorn.
    And you, please don't be angry or upset.
    We all need all the help that we can get.

6

So now I'd like to go on telling
The story of what happened to this son,
(She wants, she says, not to hide anything),
So what I am and what you are is clear to everyone.
She'd just climbed into bed, when she felt sick.
She was all alone. She wanted to shout.
She didn't know what was going to happen
But managed to stop herself crying out.
    And you, please don't be angry or upset.
    We all need all the help that we can get.

7

Her room was cold as ice, so she,
With her last strength, crawled to the lavatory
And there, she doesn't know when exactly,
Gave birth to a son without ceremony
Just before morning. She was, she says,
All muddled up, she did not know
If her freezing hands could hold on to the child
Because the servants' toilet was adrift with snow.
    And you, please don't feel angry or upset.
    We all need all the help that we can get.

8

Between her room and the lavatory.
(Nothing happened till this point, she insists),
The child started crying unbearably, so she
Beat it, blindly, without stopping, with both fists,
And went on beating it till it was quiet, she says.
And then she took it into bed
And kept it with her all through the night
And hid it, the next morning, in a shed.
But you, please don't be angry or upset.
We all need all the help that we can get.

9

Marie Farrar, aged sixteen, born in April,
Died in the Meissen jail.
This guilty single mother will
Show that all creatures of the earth are frail.
You who give birth in clean and comfortable beds
And call your pregnancy a blessed state,
Do not condemn the wretched and the weak –
Their sins are heavy, but their suffering is great.
And so, please don't be angry or upset.
We all need all the help that we can get.

version by Adrian Mitchell
literal translation by Karen Leeder

The Plays What I Wrote by Shakespeare

My name's William Shakespeare
   best poet in Britain
   these are the plays
   what I have written

I've mainly tried to use this system –
In the order I wrote them down to list 'em
With rhymes to help you learn their monickers –
One of the first was *Titus Andronicus.*
(That was full of wild and gory terrors).
I nicks *The Comedy of the Errors*
From a Plautus play about mixed-up twins;
The audience likes it so I begins
A piece about lovers double-crossed
Pessimistically named *Love's Labours Lost.*
A historical chronicle next I picksth
The *First, Second* and *Third* parts of *Henry the Sixth.*
I use all the wickedest tales I've heard
To celebrate villainous *Richard the Third.*
Then I have a hit with *The Taming of the Shrew*
About men and women and the nonsense they do.

Most people remember *Two Gentlemen of Verona*
For Crab the dog and Launce his owner.
My history of England rolls on and on
With one of my least popular plays – *King John.*
But I quickly recover with my biggest hit yet –
Ever-loving *Romeo and Juliet.*
Time for more Histories, my Director reckoned
So I nippily scribbles down *Richard the Second*
But tops it with *Henry Four Parts One and Two*
Which introduces Falstaff and his Krazy Krew.
Then lovers and fairies form the magical theme
Of my favourite *A Midsummer Night's Dream.*

A flashback tale, *The Merry Wives of Windsor*,
Brings good old Falstaff back agin, sir.
Then the uncomfortable *Merchant of Venice*
With Christian justice versus Jewish menace.
War make it feel great to be alive
Is my main message in *Henry the Five.*
Next comical sex-war sets the groundlings buzzing –
Beatrix and Benedick – *Much Ado About Nuzzing.*

Each new play is staged – they wouldn't dare spike it
After my hit comedy – *As You Like It*.
And I makes another romantic kill
With *Twelfth Night or What You Will*.
Then I tackle that famous geezer
London's favourite Roman *Julius Caesar*.
For good luck I wear a magical amulet
While I'm writing my masterpiece *Hamulet*.

Love will find a way, in a nutshell,
That's your *All's Well That Ends Well*.
Most of my lovers have ended up blesseder
Than the ill-fated *Troilus and Cressida*.
There's ethical mayhem and illegal pleasure
In the moral maze of my *Measure for Measure*.
A human fiend, Iago, torments a fellow
Of simple nobility named *Othello*.
But the greatest of my lines you'll hear
In the heart-shaking *Tragedy of King Lear*.
While insane ambition and sudden death
Rule the bleak Scotland of *Macbeth*.

Honest *Timon of Athens* comes to the belief
That every man is a born thief.
Mad, passionate love etcetera
Are practised by *Antony and Cleopetera*.
The People are two-faced as the god Janus –
But they are denounced by *Coriolanus*.
Less easy to understand than these
Is the rambling fairy tale of *Pericles*
And I'd just been given a vat of good wine
Before starting work on *Cymbeline*.

True love may suffer, but cannot fail
Is the mixed moral of *The Winter's Tale*.
My last play of all can't be called great
A mixed-up pageant – *Henry Eight*.
But I'll end by naming one of my best –
Magical-lyrical – *The Tempest*.

And if anyone asks who composed this ritual
it was done, without shame, by Adrian Mitual
   who loves William Shakespeare
      best poet in Britain
    and these are the plays
      what he has written.

ENJOY THE LIGHT
Love, friendship and sheep

Enjoy the Light

In my dream, all the wisest people in the world had come together at an observatory on a hill to decide if the stars were trying to communicate with us, or whether they were meaningless. After some years of trying to decode celestial movements, they were about to give up when some excited children pulled them outside and pointed up to the night sky, where the stars were spelling out, in enormous shining star-letters, the words:

ENJOY THE LIGHT.

I woke up with those words branded on my memory. It seemed like very good advice and I have tried to follow it.

Death Is Smaller Than I Thought

My Mother and Father died some years ago
I loved them very much.
When they died my love for them
Did not vanish or fade away.
It stayed just about the same,
Only a sadder colour.
And I can feel their love for me,
Same as it ever was.

Nowadays, in good times or bad,
I sometimes ask my Mother and Father
To walk beside me or to sit with me
So we can talk together
Or be silent.

They always come to me.
I talk to them and listen to them
And think I hear them talk to me.
It's very simple –
Nothing to do with spiritualism
Or religion or mumbo jumbo.

It is imaginary.
It is real.
It is love.

Our Mother

blue eyes, silver hair...
so close, all we see is a
lovely blur of her

her eyes were
April the 24th blue
as she weeded the borders
she knelt on the moss

Our Father

his face was gracefully
carved from oak
you heard Scotland
when he spoke

his silence was
deep as a well
he had served four years
in the trenches of Hell

Early Daze

I was born on the Moon
On a sunlit night
it was Saint Diablo's Day
My Egg cracked apart
with a happy heart
I dived into the Milky Way

I was found in that bath
by my Father and Mother
A Unicorn and a Dove
They took me to their home
In an ice-cream Dome
And all they ever taught me was to do with Love
And everything they taught me was to do with Love

Beattie as Smike

(at Gospel Oak School on 14 July 1978,
her last performance in her last term)

    small   determined
she pushes an invisible heavy trunk
  all the way across the floor
 has to bend her backbone right down
to get her shoulders square behind the trunk
  and gather her body for the long heave
she pushes two more invisible heavy trunks
  all the way across the floor

those trunks are in the wrong place stupid
        push them all back

down on all fours she concentrates
    her weight and her muscles
        into her hands
then she gathers her body for the long shove
    one by one pushes all three
heavy invisible trunks back into place.

there's a lazy character annoying her
she pushes an invisible trunk in his way
    he trips   heavily   over it

Beattie/Smike walks to the front of the stage
    the long curtains close behind her
        she takes her stand
    she holds her right forearm
      with her left hand
  which is not a random gesture
    but shows how cold she feels
she focuses on the clock at the back of the hall
    behind the Noah's Ark audience
        and begins to sing

         her low notes are rocks
         her high notes are jewels
      her low notes are the eyes of goats
her high notes are the eyes of humming-birds
      strongly she stands there
   and strongly her voice walks among us
        blessing us

   she stands so strong in love
parents, teachers, her sister and friends
     giving her strength

and suddenly singing behind her singing,
   the choir state most clearly
     that they love her

       so strong
    so strong in love
     so strong

(and when everybody cheers
she breaks out of character
    and smiles)

Edward Lear's Imagination

Oh you shove your sadness down the Funnel
Push your terror through the Grinder
Take all those years of ugly tears
And fling them in the Binder

There'll be thrashing and smashing
Crashing and bashing
And ferocious jets of steam
But then the great Engine
Will stop its avenging
And melt into a melodious dream

As out steps the Pobble who has no Toes.
The courageous Jumblie Crew
And the Dong, the Dong with the Luminous Nose
And the Owl and the Pussycat too
    Bless you Mr Lear
And the Owl and the Pussycat too –

A Visit to Ivor

The seventh floor of the Royal Free.
In the television room
the screen was blank and silent.
Ivor sat facing two of his favourite friends –
Maggie and Joyce –
both of them sweet and strong
with the sort of smiles
make a man feel like living.

Ivor's eyes seemed empty
as he turned his face to me.
But the more I talked
the more I knew he remembered me.
I saw that sparkle.

He flipped over the bright pages
of the Jack B. Yeats catalogue I'd brought him
and smiled at the little illuminated Blake book.

Ivor said: What are you doing?
I said: Writing for children mostly.
do you remember when we did a TV show
and you brought some kids with you, Ivor?
You marched them round the studio
shouting their poems
and told them:
Speak up or I'll bite your heads off.
Ivor said: I don't remember biting their heads off.

I said I was sorry
I never took up his offer
of teaching me how to play blues piano.
Ivor said: It's not too late,
you can play.

He raised his left hand and brought it down on his left knee
gently over and over.
Then he introduced his right hand
playing his right thigh in another rhythm,
and all the time, over the two silent beats,
Ivor was talking about playing the piano,
how the two hands walk together but differently.

Then, with a strong gesture of his right hand,
he marked a line down the middle of his brow
all the way down to his thighs, saying:
And this is where the humanity enters the music.

It was a beautiful speech,
softly and soulfully spoken
and we leaned forward to catch his words
but often they were interrupted
by shouting or a wild cry from a nearby ward.
Each time, Ivor, who was in love with silence,
flinched from the sharp noises
scratching his brain,
then recovered and regained his lovely speech
about the beauty of piano playing.

Joyce and Maggie said that on another visit
they danced with Ivor,
and would he like to dance?
Would you like me to dance for you? he asked.
We all said Yes like children.

Ivor stood up, walked to the far corner of the room.
Waited.
He was making an entrance.
He backed against the corner, then stepped forth.
He stood, head bowed,
being nothing but a Beckett puppet.
One hand was lifted halfway, then dropped.
The other lifted halfway, dropped.
He took two ancient steps,
but then, at the moment when I felt like sobbing, somehow,
a bounce entered his feet –
at the moment when I felt like sobbing –
and his hands were on his hips –
he was flouncing along, swaying along,
throwing wicked glances over his shoulder,
eyes sparkling like glitterballs.
The bleak Television Room
became a Galactic Music Hall
for Ivor the Entertainer.

He bowed his head to our
love and laughter and applause.
He asked us to stand up. We did so.
He moved towards the door.

On the way he paused to pat his two new books –
'Blake' he said, and 'Yeats'
as if he were patting two favourite dogs.
We said: Goodbye, Ivor.

Goodbye, Ivor.
We do love you.

July 2006

With Love for Mike Westbrook

on his 70th birthday

Performing my poems in a breezeblock arts centre Cape Town shanty town
I was shouting on the offbeat of the drummers next door and the red sun was
        diving down

Well an old guy sat on a wooden school desk and he had this killer guffaw
So I aimed my poems straight at him and he puffed and shouted for more

So I let him have a tonguetwister lyric with an old Chuck Berry beat
And he opened his mouth to show me three good teeth and he stomped with
        his blue suede feet

It was right at the height of the poem and I was pushing it I suppose
But my top set of false teeth popped out of my mouth and nearly bopped him
        on the nose

But I caught them just before they hit and I stuck them back in my gob
And I got a grip on the poem again and went on to finish the job

And of all the poetry gigs I've done that one is the brightest pearl
And Mike I dedicate it to you – for you are the Duke of Earl.

2 April 2006

Sheepishly
(written in the week after the deaths of three of my friends –
Tilly Laycock, John La Rose and Ivor Cutler)

between the fields of waking
and the fields of dreaming

so many of those old
   limestone walls
      have crumbled down

gaps in the walls

waking   walking
in the wake of the waves of my dreams

waking walking
in the dawn as it dawns upon me

I am no Tyger
I am no Lamb
At seventy-three
I am a senior sheep

high up on the dales by day
down flat in the swamps at night
daydreaming moondreaming
shadowdancing
in a Samuel Palmer countryside

but don't imagine
I'm not working bloody hard
for the New Jerusalem

I'm growing visionary sweater-wool
to keep the children warm
as I stand here
gaping at the gaps

visionary wool
which will be woven
into tapestries and coverlets
and scarves and mittens
of that great country-city of peace

my wool is often wild
multi-coloured and exciting
but sometimes softer
creamy and comforting

much of my work is done
by mountain waterfalls
head low munching heather
ears brushing the bracken
and a sniff of ice in the highland air

and some of my work is done
on the rich green banks
of casual muddy southern rivers

it's not all the same to me
but I'm all the same to them

these meadows I survive in
frosty or fiery
celandine or olive tree

I'm happy to meander
from one to the other
tasting so many different weathers
growing so many different dreams of wool

gaping at the gaps

This evening I'm watching that famous field
Anfield on the television
hoping that Liverpool will score
and Arsenal despair

from the Kop I trundle out
with my good dog to our dark garden
where I help her with my chanting
to squat and piddle

out of the garden
up the rocky stairs
towards the stone stars
and into bed
where a few wings of a book
fly me on to

a meadow of dreams
where any animal may enter
now the old limestone walls
have crumbled away

nowadays nowadays I meander
from dreamfield to wakefield
from amazement to grumpiness
from vision to radio
from stupidity to genius

but I keep on keeping on
I keep on keeping on
growing my wool
growing my wool of many colours

thank you

A WALK ON THE WEIRD SIDE

or *Better Out Than In*

This Morning's Dream

(21 June 2006)

I was prepared for a public lecture by being hypnotised in a dentist's chair by a man in a white coat whom I suddenly realised was Jools Holland.

I was very tense but suddenly went all loose. I opened my eyes to see Jools and a nurse with dark curly hair both laughing uproariously

'What's so funny?', I asked.

The nurse said: 'Well, we just moved all of the bad things out of your head and put in good things from mine.'

So here they are:

Wongo the Wonder Dog

(theme song for a new TV series)

Wongo the Wonder Dog
Smarter than the average cat
She can steal a bone
Eat a parking cone
And shit in your favourite hat
Wongo the Wonder Dog
Is definitely man's best friend
She can scramble an egg
While she's shagging your leg
She's the living end

Wongo the Wonder Dog
　Ah Wow!!

Ghosts on the Line

darling, we're ber-ake-ing up itseeems
could be your phone, maybibby mine
listen – I'll ring you in my dreams –
     ghosts on the line

make booze, not cars, the robots cry,
down the mass production belt pours blue wine
I'm too fucked-up to reason why –
     ghosts on the line

hang all your dirty laundry in a gallery
throw your clean clothes into the Serpentine
let plasticated corpses earn your salary –
     ghosts on the line

the London Underground regrets to say
this train's been stopped by a huge porcupine
who's singing *Yip-Eye-Addy-Eye-Ay-Eye-Ay* –
     ghosts on the line

the artist draws his love through tears
which drop and blotch that soft outline
he hasn't seen the woman for ten years –
     ghosts on the line

after I'm dead, I'll visit you each spring
as long as you consider you're still mine
later you may still hear me whispering –
     ghosts on the line

TELL ME LIES
or *Truth-Ache in the Anglo-American Empire*

At the Crossroads

I built the best of England
With my brain and with my hands.
Liberty Equality Fraternity –
That's where I took my stand,
And the people called me Old Labour
The brave heart of this land

I walked out of the smoky streets
To enjoy some country air,
But when I came to the crossroads,
I saw a weird sight there –
A man in a silver business suit
Swivelling in a black leather chair

He jumped right up and shook my hand
And giggled with mysterious glee.
Then he stared and said: 'Old Labour,
I can tell your destiny.
I'm the Great Political Entrepreneur –
Would you like to do a deal with me?'

Well, the style of his smile and the size of his eyes
Made him look like a shopping mall.
I told him straight: 'I'm a socialist,
I support fair shares for all.
He said: 'Capitalism *means* fair shares,
Provided that you play ball.'

I said: 'I can think of something
Capitalism can't arrange
And that's the common ownership
Of the means of production, distribution and exchange.
And war makes so much more profit
That the idea of peace is strange.

'I was born for peace and justice
For every race and nationality
I'm for people, not for profit,

I want to see the children free
With no more than twelve kids in a class
Revelling in liberty.'

'But let's not talk about the people,'
The sophisticated stranger said.
'You must have targets of your own –
Let's talk about you instead.'
And my brain was enthralled by his silver voice
Though my heart was filled with dread.

'I know you have a heart,' said the shining voice
'And I know you have an excellent mind.
Why not become an Entrepreneur –
Leave those people of yours behind?
You shall live in mansions and grand hotels
And be constantly wined and dined.

'You shall have your own island and bodyguard
And your own show on TV,
And a heated pool and a gymnasium
And become a powerful Celebrity.'
'I think I could fancy that,' I said,
But what's the cost going to be?'

Well, I knew. But I signed – in my own life-blood.
He extracted my soul with care
And placed it in his credit card case
And gave me his black leather chair
Then he laughed and said: 'You are New Labour now.'
I said: 'Thank you, Mr Blair.'

Tigers and Monkeys

(for the Campaign Against the Arms Trade)

A tiger, trying to hunt a herd of deer
is followed through the woods
by hooting monkeys in the trees,
        who warn the deer:
    There's a killer coming –
Long live the monkeys!

The Doorbell

I was in bed, the silvery light of dawn
blessing our quiet suburban street,
when the window darkened,
and the doorbell rang.

Pushed my face deep in the pillow.
but the doorbell kept ringing
and there was another sound,
like the crying of a siren,
so I slopped downstairs
unbolted, unlocked, unchained
and opened the front door.

There, on the doorstep, stood the War.
It filled my front garden,
filled the entire street
and blotted out the sky.
It was human and monstrous,
shapeless, enormous,
with torn and poisoned skin which bled
streams of yellow, red and black.

The War had many millions of heads
both dead and half-alive,
some moaning, some screaming,
some whispering,
in every language known on earth,
goodbye, my love.

The War had many millions of eyes
and all wept tears of molten steel.
Then the War spoke to me
in a voice of bombs and gunfire:
I am your War.
Can I come in?

Peacetime Haiku

Try one hundred years
Without any wars at all —
    Let's see if it works!

Dust And Ashes

The Cedars of Lebanon have been stripped of their bark,
cut down to the sap, hacked down to the roots.
Now they are ashes floating over blackened villages.

Israel has locked herself in the bathroom
and is slowly cutting her own throat.

England is hunting down insurgents in Iraq
and terrorists in London,
While selling weapons to anyone who wants to kill.

The USA arms the world at an enormous profit
under the trading name of Shock and Awe.
Washington is the new Rome
whose rulers plan the domination of the world.

What if the weird Barbarians resist?
Bomb them to dust and ashes.
Before we're through
the whole world of Aliens
will become a desert.

Yes the buildings, the cedars, the animals
and the people will be one dust storm,
a nuclear dust storm swirling round the world..

And when all the men and women and children are dead
in Dubai, Chicago, Beijing, Sydney, Rio de Janeiro and Paris –
when they are all dead
and all the animals
and all the trees
and all the birds
and all the insects –
their ashes will fly in their hot agony
and descend upon the waters,
and the poison ashes will murder the oceans
and all life will be wiped out –
    goodbye, my love.

The Question

a favourite pond on Hampstead Heath.
a village in Lebanon, after an air raid.

> peace or global suicide?
> you decide.

watching over the pond, a wise heron.
in the village, a crushed house.

> peace or global suicide?
> you decide.

the heron takes flight as three dogs splash into the pond.
in the ruins of the house, a rescue party.

> peace or global suicide?
> you decide.

three dogs gallop out of the pond.
one of the rescue party shouts, Come here!

> peace or global suicide?
> you decide.

the dogs shake themselves and all the children laugh.
like a midwife, the rescuer draws a baby out of a heap of dust.

> peace or global suicide?
> you decide.

children and dogs scamper over the Heath.
the baby is covered with cement dust.

> peace or global suicide?
> you decide.

Is it all right to Kill People?

I was watching the war
with my Mum and my Dad.
   I said: is it all right to kill people?

Dad said: *If you're a soldier in a war*
it's OK to kill enemy soldiers
otherwise they'll kill you.

Is that the only time it's right to kill?

Well if a burglar broke in
and held a knife to Mum's throat —
it would be OK to kill him

How would I kill him?

Well, if you had a gun
you could shoot him.

I might hit Mum.

You could edge round from behind her
and shoot the burglar.

Can I have a gun?

No.

Then what am I supposed to do about Mum?

You'd better sneak out and phone 999.

Is it OK to kill a maths teacher?

Only if he's going to kill you.

I think my maths teacher
is trying to kill me
very gradually with maths.

Why do enemy soldiers want to kill us?

Because they've been taught
we want to kill them.
So they want to kill us first.

So are you teaching me
they want to kill me
so I'll want to kill them first?

Listen, son.
You're not the kind who ever learns
to clean and load and fire a gun.

What kind am I, Dad?

You're the kind who asks questions.
You're the kind who gets killed.

Peace and Pancakes

(A song, with music by Andrew Dickson, from the epic play, The Fear Brigade,
first performed at the Global Village, near Maidstone, Kent, on 7 August 2006 to
5000 international young people. The play was commissioned by the Woodcraft Folk.)

the old world began
with a big bang
a big bang, a big bang

the new world begins
with a big song
a big song, a big song

it's got a strong beat
like your heartbeat
so use your two feet
to stomp out the beat

of a big song
of pancakes and peace
of a big song
everybody sing along

everybody loves pancakes
and everybody loves peace
you can find pancakes all round the world
north south west and east

dosas for breakfast in India
with spicy veg in the middle
Canadian maple syrup

on buckwheat cakes hot off the griddle
long live peace and pancakes!

the Greeks make pancakes with semolina
Russians make their blinis with yeast
red-hot quesidillas in Mexico City
yes pancakes turn any meal into a feast
long live peace and pancakes!

in Beijing they fill pancakes
with plum sauce and roast duck
every Shrove Tuesday in England
my pancake always gets stuck
        bad luck!
long live peace and pancakes!

the Koreans call their pancakes pa'chon
and cook 'em with sesame seeds
the Romans serve cannelloni
pancakes are the banquet everyone needs
long live peace and pancakes!

South Africa's banana chapatis
Brittany's crêpes suzettes
every woman and man from Chile to Japan
they're eating all they can get

everybody loves pancakes
and everybody loves peace
you can find pancakes all round the world
north south west and east

long live the planet earth
long live the animals
long live the birds and fishes
long live the forests and the oceans

long live the man
long live the woman
who use both courage and compassion
long live their children

long live peace
long live peace
long live peace and pancakes

To Whom It May Concern Remix

Come all ye –
   wartbrain psychics
with asteroid sidekicks
    prostate agents
    and plastic Cajuns

   royal doggerellas
cluster bombsellers
 alternative surgeons
   torturesport virgins

heavy vivisectionists
columnists, Golumnists,
priests of the beast
who are secretly policed
by highranker bankers
playing pranks with tankers

ghost advisers
death advertisers
vampire preachers
sucked-dry teachers
beheaded dead bodies
of blank-hearted squaddies

billionaire beauticians
fishing for positions
from poison politicians
with obliteration missions –
I'm alone, I'm afraid
And I need your aid
   can't you see – can't you see – can't you see?

I was run over by the truth one day
Ever since the accident I've walked this way
    So stick my legs in plaster
    Tell me lies about Vietnam

Heard the alarm clock screaming with pain
Couldn't find myself, so I went back to sleep again
    So fill my ears with silver
    Stick my legs in plaster
    Tell me lies about Vietnam

Every time I shut my eyes, all I see is flames
I made a marble phone-book, and I carved all the names
    So coat my eyes with butter
    Fill my ears with silver
  Stick my legs in plaster
    Tell me lies about Vietnam

I smell something burning, hope it's just my brains
They're only dropping peppermints and daisy-chains
    So stuff my nose with garlic
    Coat my eyes with butter
    Fill my ears with silver
  Stick my legs in plaster
    Tell me lies about Vietnam

Where were you at the time of the crime?
Down by the Cenotaph, drinking slime
    So chain my tongue with whisky
    Stuff my nose with garlic
    Coat my eyes with butter
    Fill my ears with silver
  Stick my legs in plaster
    Tell me lies about Vietnam

You put your bombers in, you put your conscience out
You take the human being, and you twist it all about
    So scrub my skin with women
    So chain my tongue with whisky
    Stuff my nose with garlic
    Coat my eyes with butter
    Fill my ears with silver
  Stick my legs in plaster
    Tell me lies about –
Iraq
Burma
Afghanistan
BAE Systems
Israel
Iran

Tell me lies Mr Bush
Tell me lies Mr Blairbrowncameron

Tell me lies about Vietnam

MY LITERARY CAREER SO FAR

peace

My Literary Career So Far

As I prowled through Parentheses
I met an Robin and a Owl
My Grammarboots they thrilled like bees
My Vowelhat did gladly growl

Tis my delight each Friedegg Night
To chomp a Verbal Sandwich
Scots Consonants light up my Pants
And marinade my Heart in Language

Alphabet Soup was all my joy!
From Dreadfast up to Winnertime
I swam, a naked Pushkinboy
Up wodka vaterfalls of rhyme

And reached the summit of Blue Howl
To find a shining Suit of Words
And joined an Robin and a Owl
In good Duke Ellington's Band of Birds

December 18, 2008

Merry Crambo and a Hippy New Year
        with love from

Adrian Mitchell, The Shadow Poet Laureate

(I can't write letters and it's hard to phone yer as I recover from two
months' in Pneumonia so take this new riff with a glass of good wine
and drink to Peace in 2009)

[*Adrian Mitchell died on 20 December 2008*]

ADRIAN MITCHELL: SELECTED BIBLIOGRAPHY

POETRY

Fantasy Pamphlet No.24 (Fantasy Press, 1955)
Poems (Jonathan Cape, 1964)
Out Loud (Cape Goliard, 1968; Writers and Readers' Publishing Cooperative, 1976)
Ride the Nightmare (Jonathan Cape, 1971)
The Apeman Cometh (Jonathan Cape, 1975)
For Beauty Douglas: Collected Poems 1953-1979 (Allison & Busby, 1982)
On the Beach at Cambridge (Allison & Busby, 1984)
Love Songs of World War Three (Allison & Busby, 1989)
Greatest Hits: His 40 Golden Greats (Bloodaxe Books, 1991).
Blue Coffee: Poems 1985-1996 (Bloodaxe Books, 1996).
Heart on the Left: Poems 1953-1984 (Bloodaxe Books, 1997).
All Shook Up: Poems 1997-2000 (Bloodaxe Books, 2000).
The Shadow Knows: Poems 2000-2004 (Bloodaxe Books, 2004).
Tell Me Lies: Poems 2005-2008 (Bloodaxe Books, 2009).
Come On Everybody: Poems 1953-2008 (Bloodaxe Books, 2012).

POETRY FOR CHILDREN

Nothingmas Day (Allison & Busby, 1984)
Strawberry Drums, ed. (Anthology, Macdonald, 1989)
All My Own Stuff (Simon and Schuster, 1991).
The Thirteen Secrets of Poetry (Macdonald, 1993).
The Orchard Book of Poems ed. (Orchard, 1995).
Balloon Lagoon (Orchard Books, 1997).
Dancing in the Street, ed. (Orchard Books, 1999).
Zoo of Dreams (Orchard Books, 2001).
A Poem a Day, ed. (Orchard Books, 2001).
Daft as a Doughnut (Orchard Books, 2004).
Umpteen Pockets: Collected Poems for Children (Orchard, 2009).
Shapeshifters: Tales from Ovid's Metamorphoses (Frances Lincoln, 2009).

PLAYS & THEATRE

Marat-Sade (Marion Boyars, 1965).
U.S. (Calder Boyars, 1968).
Tyger (Jonathan Cape, 1971).
Man Friday and Mind Your Head (Methuen, 1974).
You Must Believe All This (Methuen, 1981).
Gogol: The Government Inspector (Methuen, 1985).
Animal Farm Lyrics (Methuen Young Dramatists, 1985).
The Pied Piper (Oberon Books, 1988).
Lope de Vega: Fuente Ovejuna and Lost in a Mirror (Absolute Classics, Oberon, 1988).
Calderon: The Mayor of Zalamea and two other plays (Absolute Classics, Oberon, 1990).

Plays with Songs: Tyger Two, Man Friday, Satie Day/Night and In the Unlikely Event of an Emergency (Oberon Books, 1996).
The Siege (Oberon Books, 1996).
The Snow Queen (Oberon Books, 1997).
The Lion, the Witch and the Wardrobe (Oberon Books, 1998).
The Mammoth Sails Tonight! (Oberon Books, 1999).
Alice in Wonderland and Through the Looking Glass (Oberon Books, 2001).
Two Beatrix Potter Plays: Jemima Puddleduck and Her Friends and Peter Rabbit and His Friends (Oberon Books, 2004).
Just Adrian (Oberon Books, 2011).
Pushkin's Boris Godunov (Oberon Books, 2012).

CHILDREN'S STORIES
The Ugly Duckling (Dorling Kindersley, 1994).
The Steadfast Tin Soldier (Dorling Kindersley, 1996).
Maudie and the Green Children (Tradewind, 1996).
Nobody Rides The Unicorn (Transworld, 1999).
My Cat Mrs Christmas (Orion, 1999).
The Adventures of Robin Hood and Marian (Orchard Books, 2004).

RECORDINGS
The Dogfather: double CD (57 Productions, 2000).
Adrian Mitchell reading from his poems (The Poetry Archive, 2003).

Many out of print Adrian Mitchell titles are available from Ripping Yarns Bookshop, 335 Archway Road, London N6 4EJ, EMAIL yarns@rippingyarns.co.uk